THE PEOPLE WHO STAYED

The People Who Stayed

SOUTHEASTERN INDIAN WRITING AFTER REMOVAL

Edited by
Geary Hobson, Janet McAdams, and Kathryn Walkiewicz

University of Oklahoma Press : Norman

Library of Congress Cataloging-in-Publication Data
The people who stayed : southeastern Indian writing after removal
/ edited by Geary Hobson, Janet McAdams, and Kathryn
Walkiewicz.
    p. cm.
ISBN 978-0-8061-4136-7 (pbk. : alk. paper)
1. Indians of North America—Southern States—Literary
collections. 2. American literature—Indian authors. I. Hobson,
Geary. II. McAdams, Janet, 1957– III. Walkiewicz, Kathryn, 1981–
    PS508.I5P465 2010
    810.8'0897075—dc22
    2010010318

The paper in this book meets the guidelines for permanence and
durability of the Committee on Production Guidelines for Book
Longevity of the Council on Library Resources, Inc. ∞

Contents

Contemporary Writers

IV. Arkansas, Louisiana, and East Texas

Acknowledgments

The editors wish to extend a genuinely felt *wado/mado* to the following individuals and institutions who proved to be extremely helpful in the compilation of this anthology:

Mrs. Frela O. Beck and Mrs. Mary O. Melquist of Cherokee, North Carolina

Ms. Joyce Dugan, former chief of the Eastern Band of Cherokee Indians, Cherokee, North Carolina

Dr. Barbara R. Duncan, Museum of the Cherokee Indian in Cherokee, North Carolina

Ms. Patricia Q. Foster, Tribal Historian, Tunica-Biloxi Tribe of Louisiana

Ms. Lana Grant, Native Writers' Circle of the Americas, the Sam Noble Museum of Natural History, and the Sac and Fox Tribal Library, Norman, Oklahoma

Dr. Meredith K. James, Eastern Connecticut State University, Willimantic, Connecticut

Ms. Nancy Laub, Oklahoma Historical Society, Oklahoma City, Oklahoma

Dr. Daniel F. Littlefield, Jr., American Native Press Archives and the University of Arkansas at Little Rock

MariJo Moore, poet, novelist, and editor, Candler, North Carolina

Dr. Donald B. Smith, University of Calgary, Calgary, Alberta

Alexander Taylor, Publisher, Curbstone Press, Willimantic, Connecticut

Keith and Heloise Wilson, Las Cruces, New Mexico

The Robert P. Hubbard Fund, Kenyon College, and the student interns supported by the fund, Jeremy Hawkins and Brendan Sullivan

And to the many other writers from, or with roots in, the indigenous South who we were unable to include in our book, because of insufficient knowledge on our part of the fine work they've been doing, or because we simply didn't have room for every piece of writing, we mention their literature in the book's introduction and here extend to them a warm handshake of friendship for the work they've being doing all along.

Many poems, essays, and works of fiction in *The People Who Stayed* have previously appeared in publications, and, as noted in this volume, we gratefully acknowledge permission to reprint them.

Introduction

The South Seldom Seen

In 1912, Walter Ashby Plecker, an M.D., became registrar of the Virginia Bureau of Vital Statistics. A committed racialist, Plecker spent the next thirty-four years reclassifying Indian and mixed-blood Virginians. Dr. Plecker's obsession with racial purity is legendary.[1] Instrumental in passing Virginia's 1924 Racial Purity Act, Plecker "intimidated midwives, wrote threatening pamphlets, editorialized in newspapers, and trained an entire generation of county clerks and health service workers in his methods."[2] While his hasty designations of Virginia citizens as either white or black (but never Indian) based strictly on their skin tone may seem odd—absurd even, given our present-day understanding of the complexities of race, ethnicity, and culture—the extent of Plecker's influence was astonishing. Through the "paper genocide" decisions, which he believed his office entitled him to make, he is estimated to have changed hundreds of Indians into white or black people simply by the use of his pen. Plecker hated Indians, and he believed strongly that all vestiges of Indianness must be eradicated through such measures as he practiced, mainly because he felt that governments, both state and federal, should get on with their agendas without consideration of the appearance and visible means of livelihood of their "paper victims." Thus, genocide by administrative or clerical fiat occurred through these and other such methods used by government officials and, later, sometimes, by anthropologists and linguists as well. How many more Pleckers were there? And how does the case of Plecker point to the cruel history of Native disappearance from the American Southeast?[3] What other agents and agencies of disappearance still exist in the Southeast, and are still at work denying identity and sovereignty to indigenous peoples and their descendents?

Even while clerical erasing and vanishing was being conducted, many other Southeastern Indian people found solace and escape in certain nearby communities of whites and blacks. Miscegenation, whether through marriage or not, was much more widespread and prevalent throughout the centuries than historians and cultural anthropologists have generally acknowledged. At the same time, local and family histories and legends have sometimes—but not always—insisted upon Indian heritage in their own often partial, but complex, stories.

This anthology seeks to tell some of these stories—the stories of the people who stayed. The forces of disappearance have been, and remain, strong. Yet Indian people of the South resist, survive, persist. Through song, story, picture, declaration, and declamation, they use language and art to claim—and reclaim—their identities and homelands, to say: "We are still here."

"We Are Still Here"

Anthropologists and archaeologists continue to revise the dates for the time when aboriginal people first became fixtures of (not "on," but "of") the lands that are now the southeastern United States. It is generally agreed these days that Paleo-Indians were in the region from about 20,000 B.C. on, becoming successively Archaic, the Woodland, and the Mississippian mound-building people, always with seemingly little change in lifestyle. To modern-day Indians, however, all the foregoing peoples are progenitors.

For hundreds of years, perhaps even millennia, Muskhogean-speaking peoples were of the land that today is called Florida, Georgia, Alabama, Mississippi, eastern Louisiana, southern Tennessee, and western South Carolina. It was and is a vast domain of hardwood forests, swamps, rivers and creeks and bayous, rolling hills adjunctive to the long Appalachian mountain chain, astonishing savannas, and wonderfully fertile bottomland soils. The people there were of numerous nations and tribes, of subtribes and breakaway bands on the way to evolving into yet other tribes, even confederacies of nations and tribes, all holding in common their variant Muskhogean speech, religious practices, and even more adhesively, held by their blood relations determined through matrilineal clanship, all the essential elements that comprised a Muskhogean. Timucua, Coosa, Yemassee, Muscogee, Choctaw, Chickasaw, Chakchiuma, Natchez, Calusa, Miccosuki, Alabama, Hitchiti, Hilibi—and several score others, numbering in all, say, around the year 1650, approximately one-hundred tribes. Modern-day map place names, such as Muskogee, Tulsa, Eufaula, Okmulgee, Wewoka, Tombigbee, Tuscaloosa, Houma, and Pascagoula attest to their once greater presence.

Northward of the Muskhogeans, Algonquian-speaking tribes inhabited what is now North Carolina, Kentucky, western West Virginia, Virginia, Maryland, and Delaware. These represented the southeastern branch of a very large grouping of people, since their kinsmen from other tribes held sway over virtually all the remaining eastern states, eastern and central Canada, and the northern Great Plains, with enclaves even in California. Many of the modern-day states and provinces of the United States and eastern Canada reflect this Algonquian presence in names such as Potomac, Rappahannock, Powhatan, Piscataway, Ohio, Connecticut, Massachusetts, Michigan, Illinois, Mississippi, Ontario, Quebec, Manitoba, Ottawa, and scores of other place names.

For many hundreds of years, quite literally, that was the way it was—until invaders came. Around 1000 A.D., perhaps a little later, Iroquoians, a totally different language grouping, swept southeastward from the Great Lakes region and, like a stout hickory wedge pounding its way into a cottonwood log, they impelled themselves V-ward into New York, Pennsylvania, and Ohio. Their forerunning enclaves drove even further southward into the Virginias and the Carolinas, spilling over into the two areas that came to be called by words of their foreign tongues—Kentucky and Tennessee. These southern Iroquoians—Cherokees, Tuscaroras, Meherrins, and a dozen others—came to stay in and near the mountains that the Algonquian-speaking peoples then named for them—the Alleghenies.

And right behind these south-going Iroquoians came their close relatives, the Siouans. They moved in much smaller enclaves and were much more inclined toward amalgamating themselves to both the lifeways of their more numerous Iroquoian kinsmen and to the people whom they recognized as having been there "forever," the Algonquians and Muskhogeans. Always, in the South's prehistory, as well as in its written history, Southern Siouan tribes, such as the Biloxi, Ofo, Quapaw, Cheraw, Catawba, PeeDee, Monacan, Saponi, and Oc-caneechi groups, have been small in numbers, then and now.

Muskhogeans and Algonquians have in common their origin accounts of ancestors coming up out of the earth, emerging onto the good land where they found themselves new and dazed and wet from inner earth, where, as they faced the Sun, ever holy, they dried themselves out and became This World people. Later-arriving Siouans and Iroquoians recount stories of how the earliest of their people came out of the sky, descending earthward in small groups, gently drifting downward like cottonwood fluff until they settled in the foliage of holy trees, like, for example, red oaks for the Quapaws. There they abided for how long—a week, a year, a millennium?—until they finally drifted downward to touch the earth and become people of This World.

Yet older stories maintain that all four groupings—sky-born Iroquoians and Siouans and earth-born Algonquians and Muskhogeans—were all at one former time the same people, and modern-day archaeology seems to bear this out. Give or take the countless millennia of Paleo-Indian, Archaic, Woodland, and Mississippian eras, they are all from the same ancestral source, so that a story of going downward to create oneself is likely only another variant of climbing upward, given the nature of the circling world inhabited by them all.

Following the cataclysmic invasion by Europeans in the sixteenth century, modern tribalism developed when new diseases, warfare with steel and on horseback, and slave-catching raids, prompted the survivors to abandon their former lifestyles of settling in large towns and cities, and instead adhere to smaller clan-oriented units. By 1700, the modern form of Southeastern Indian tribalism was fairly universally established. The Muscogee, or Creek, Confederacy was a great union of approximately sixty tribes, with each tribe made up of several villages. The Cherokees had recently assimilated several smaller neighboring groups of people into their union, and its seven clan network, permeating throughout the more than forty towns of their nation, was by then strongly established. The Choctaws, solid in their three districts with numerous villages in each, were in place, and their brothers, the Chickasaws, were steadfastly settled due north of them.

The ensuing century brought continued chaos as the European powers— England, France, and Spain—played one tribe off against another. And a look at eighteenth century events in the region reveals a catalog of almost continual warfare, in which Indian people found themselves less in control of the world they had always known. By the 1780s, so many whites had moved into southern Georgia and Alabama that scores of Creek towns began relocating southward, their inhabitants becoming in effect *siminolas* (runaways). Soon a new tribal designation emerged and Florida became their homeland. These Indians, amalgamating with the remnant non-Creek Muskhogean tribes in the region, and, in some instances, with runaway black slaves from American plantations, became the Seminole tribe.

A vast influx of white settlers in the newly acquired lands, numerous land-devouring treaties, and the disappearance of forests and prime agricultural lands, presaged a new world coming. Between 1803, the time of the Louisiana Purchase, and 1830, the United States made twenty-three treaties with the five major tribes—nine with the Cherokees, six with the Creeks, four with the Choctaws, three with the Chickasaws, and one with the Seminoles—all, without equivocation, for the purpose of attaining more Indian real estate.[4] Even the "great democrat," Thomas Jefferson, foresaw that some of the lands within the Louisiana Purchase, west of the Mississippi and far away from Americans in the new states, would have to become an Indian territory, which he believed would be sufficiently far enough away from the lands that Americans felt they must have. Yet, scarcely a generation later, in the second quarter of the nineteenth century, further cataclysm in the form of the federally mandated Indian removals became governmental policy under another great "man of the people," President Andrew Jackson.

On May 28, 1830, the United States Senate, following an intense and bitter debate, passed the Indian Removal Bill, thereby setting the stage for the upheaval to come. For the previous three decades, the young American republic had been steadily whittling away at Indian-held lands east of the Mississippi River through the enactment of numerous treaties with the Indian tribes. For the purpose of clarity, the term "treaty," in those early empire-building days, simply meant "land acquisition" to the average white American. Rarely was there serious reflection on the part of white Americans about the sovereignty of tribal nations, and there was even less consideration that land, in all aspects of its being, might mean something different than merely another form of monetary coinage. To most Indian people, then as now, the term "treaty" meant theft of their homeland. For Indian people in the South, in particular, it also meant exile to lands west of the Mississippi River.

Exile came immediately, after the Indian Removal Bill became law, followed by removal treaties with the tribes. The five large tribes—Cherokee, Chickasaw, Choctaw, Creek, and Seminole—and certainly the numerous smaller ones in the region, had already been greatly reduced in population and land base through wars, land-grabbing, diseases, and assimilation. These smaller tribes, in part, were (and in some cases still are) Alabama, Apalachee, Assateague, Attakapa, Avoyel, Biloxi, Caddo, Catawba, Chakchiuma, Cheraw, Chickahominy, Chitimacha, Coharie, Conoy, Coree, Gingaskin, Grigra, Haliwa, Hattaras, Houma, Koasati (Coushatta), Koroa, Mattaponi, Meherrin, Miccosuki, Monacan, Nansemond, Nanticoke, Natchez, Ofo, Pamunkey, PeeDee, Piscataway, Powhatan, Quapaw, Rappahannock, Saponi, Tunica, Tuscarora, Waccamaw, Wassamasaw, Yemassee, and Yuchi. Some tribes were amalgamated with the larger tribes by the time of removal, forfeiting to varying degrees their original sovereignty (such as the Ofo, Grigra, Koroa, and Avoyel people within the Tunica-Biloxis), or, in some cases, remaining staunchly individual within such amalgamations (such as the Miccosukis, among the Seminoles in Florida, and the Natchez among the Cherokees). However, most tribes remaining in the East continued as distinct Indian communities, separate from larger Indian groups through varying degrees of acculturation and accommodation to the outer white and black societies around them, while still maintaining to the present day their specific identities as Haliwa, Tuscarora, or Monacan. Even though many contemporary scholars too frequently contend that, for the most part, these are no longer viable tribal entities, the people who identify themselves as such affirm the opposite view. The above list of tribes still represents only a small portion of all the Indian peoples who were in the Southeast when the first major group of Europeans, De Soto's Spanish freebooters, invaded the region in the mid-sixteenth century. The first thirty pages of John R. Swanton's 1946 volume, *The Indians of the Southeastern United States,* and especially the accompanying maps delineating tribal domain and population distribution at the time, reveal many times the number of actual sovereignties located in the Southeast than are to be found there today.[5]

President Jackson hoped that every Indian in the Southeast would be removed and the land vacated by them, so that a new era of occupation would open for his fellow white southerners, and although his administration tried to accomplish this removal in totality, it failed as it actually fell short of its intention. The land, certainly, was no longer legally in Indian hands, but there were "some Indians" still around. It is likely that for every eight removed Indians relocated to Indian Territory, perhaps one or two of his or her fellow tribal members found some means to remain in their homeland. Now, more than one-hundred and seventy years after the Removal era, what strikes one as amazing is not only a contemplation of how systematically devastating the removals were for the people who were its victims, but also an awareness of the surprising degree to which many Indians were actually able to persist in remaining behind. It is the supremely human efforts of those thus affected, the methods and means by which these people—whether a surviving son or daughter, a family, or in some cases even an entire small community—survived in the land, and how they still do, that provides the basis of a genuine Southeastern Indian presence, now as well as yesterday.

"Indians are everywhere," the Acoma Pueblo poet Simon Ortiz says in a poem published in the early 1970s, a statement that reflects his eye-opening experiences as he drove through the American South in the 1960s. In "Travels in the South," the poet tells of visiting Alabama-Coushatta people in rural Texas, of stopping by to visit some Indians in the Texas state prison at Huntsville, of spending some time with Chief Calvin W. McGhee of the Poarch Band Creeks of Southern Alabama, and of encountering Indians in such cities as Dallas and Atlanta. Remarkable in several ways, Ortiz's statement is particularly important in its acknowledgment and celebration of the continuing presence of Indian people in the southeastern United States. Indians *are* everywhere, and in the American South, all popular misconceptions to the contrary, they are there in surprisingly large numbers and in virtually every part of the region.[6]

Despite their quite visible presence in many western states, American Indian people have been regarded as a "vanishing race" for almost two centuries in the popular American mind. However, it is from the Southeast that they are generally assumed to be even more "vanished" than anywhere else. In a region long defined by racial conflict usually couched in strictly white and black terms, Indians rarely come into consideration as a distinct people at all, much less as an often-problematic third race in biracial states. A very real "rhetoric of disappearance" is in force with regard to Indian people in the South, and it has been for decades. It is a collective mindset that has, at almost every turn since the 1830s, sought to "disappear" a people whose homeland was taken from them.

Every state in the Southeast has Indians who are federally recognized (North Carolina, South Carolina, Mississippi, Alabama, Louisiana, and Florida), or who have state recognition (Alabama, Virginia, North Carolina, Louisiana, Texas, and Florida), or tribes and communities yet to be recognized by either federal or state governments (who are found in all the aforementioned states, as well as Maryland, Virginia, Delaware, Tennessee, Georgia, and Arkansas). In addition to the people within these three categories, there are yet thousands more who claim an Indian identity and live in urban areas, away from the traditional land-based communities. As of January 1, 2003, there were approximately eighty Indian tribal groups in all the southern states (with enclaves of some of these groups in states such as New Jersey, New York, Ohio, Indiana, California, and Oregon). Some tribes are state-recognized and others are non-recognized, with an overall population of Indian people numbering approximately 370,000. There are also many people who still hesitate to proclaim Indian identity, and who continue to be classified as white, black, or "other" on census returns.[7] Of these various groups, there are at least thirty Cherokee, eight Muscogee (Creek), and four Choctaw "tribes" represented in the accounting, along with Catawba, Seminole, Pamunkey, and dozens more.

The "Rhetoric of Disappearance"

Despite the reality of Indian survivance in the South, the popular notion of the "Vanished Indian" appears as prevalent as ever. Although a pan-American phenomenon, it is probably much more pervasive in the South than anywhere else, with the possible exception of New England, where Pilgrims and Puritans did their best to make the country habitable for only their own kind. Despite the southern backdrop for one of America's most cherished myths—the so-called "Princess" Pocahontas and her fictionalized rescue of Captain John Smith—Americans, as a rule, believe that there are no more Indians in the region, and what is more, that there haven't been any there for decades.[8]

While it has become commonplace to regard stories of Cherokee grandmothers and great-grandmothers with suspicion (and sometimes even ridicule), given that the Cherokees were, and still are, the largest tribal group in and from the American South, the Cherokees are indeed likely the tribe of origination for many modern-day white or black claimants to Southeastern Indian heritage. Furthermore, "Cherokee" often functions as a catch-all designation, since an individual asserting such ties might in actuality be descended from one of the many tribes that comprise the Muscogee, or Creek, tribe, or may be from the Natchez or any of the many other smaller groups—Chakchiuma, Houma, PeeDee, Timucua, Waccamaw, Yemassee, Yuchi, etc.—that merged into larger groups. Many families throughout the South have cherished the passed-down stories of Cherokee grandmothers, at first revealing their ancestry with great fear and reluctance, and nowadays with pride and openness.

Indeed, the great extent to which many families in the South, both white and black, are of mixed races is much more prevalent than the various legal authorities have been comfortable in freely acknowledging. Federal census reports since 1970 reveal that most black people currently living in the South and who trace their roots at least three generations in the region have some degree of Indian blood. Among white people, the percentage of Indian blood is smaller, although in certain rural areas it is higher. This, then, is often the crux of the matter for most people in and from the South who have attempted to reconstruct their identities based on more informed examinations of their family heritages. Marginalized for generations, many Indian-blooded people were "remade" into either white or black, depending on surrounding circumstances and the particular kinds of dominant white institutions with which they had to contend. Half-educated census takers, county officials eager to reduce the number of possible future claimants to newly acquired Indian land and of possible monetary remunerations to Indians, and state officials zealously charged with protecting the purity of the white race (like Plecker) as they beheld the dark-skinned person in front of them—all played their part.[9]

Many Indians, some reluctantly and others eagerly, were absorbed into either a white community or a black one, again depending on circumstances, often with virtually nothing that they could do about it. The author of a recent article, describing the contemporary trend of Indian-blooded people "proclaiming" themselves to whatever extent and degree as "Indians," labels the phenomenon "the Southeast Syndrome." The author, whose dislike of such people reclaiming their Indian heritages is quite apparent, fails to take into consideration the extent to which American cultural dominance has discriminated against marginalized people, and especially against those who claim affiliation with cultural matters the dominant society considers vanished, or at least in the process of vanishing. Thus, even after several centuries, cultural and racial "disappearing" still goes on.[10]

The tremendous degree of assimilation of Indians into neighboring white and black communities can also be seen in the claims of some much more "visible" modern-day Americans to Native ancestry, such as Burt Reynolds (Cherokee, from Florida) and Loretta Lynn and her sister Crystal Gayle, coming out of the Kentucky hills, with claims of Cherokee blood. The same is true for Johnny Cash (Cherokee, from Arkansas), Elvis Presley (Choctaw and Cherokee, from Mississippi), Johnny Depp (Cherokee, from Kentucky), James Earl Jones (Cherokee, from Mississippi), Rita Coolidge (Cherokee, from Tennessee), Wayne Newton (Powhatan, from Virginia), Heather Locklear (Lumbee, from North Carolina), Ava Gardner (Tuscarora, from North Carolina), Willie Nelson (Cherokee, from Texas)—all from the entertainment world. Edith Bolling (Mrs. Woodrow) Wilson (Powhatan, from Virginia), Cornelia Turnipseed (Mrs. George) Wallace (Creek and Cherokee, from Alabama), and Senator John Randolph (Powhatan, from Virginia)—from the political arena —claim Indian ancestry, as do Alice Walker (Cherokee, from Georgia), Ishmael Reed (Cherokee, from Tennessee), Lewis Green (Cherokee, from North Carolina), Win Blevins (Cherokee, from Arkansas), and Charles Plymell (Cherokee, from Kansas) from the literary world. Even former President Bill Clinton is said to have a remote Cherokee ancestor.[11]

"Slightly Off-Colored People": Indians in Southern Literature

Americans are more familiar with Southeastern Indians in their literature— in actually all of their popular culture—than they probably realize. Acclimated to the popular Plains-type imagery, of warbonneted Sioux warriors on horseback and Ricardo Montalban lookalikes, this stereotype of Indian presence bespeaks only a tiny portion of true Indian identity and culture. Yet it is the model by which all other Indians are judged, and usually found wanting. A great portion of American literature abounds with images of the Indians of the Plains, the Iroquois and Algonquians beside the presence of Pilgrims and Puritans in the Northeast, and Apaches from the southwestern desert. With Disney's recent full-length movie cartoon *Pocahontas,* which focuses (however mendaciously) on a historical figure from the Powhatan Confederacy of tribes in Virginia and Maryland in the early seventeenth century, Southern Indians have once again been a focal point of America's interest in things Indian, albeit in perhaps an even more incredibly romanticized and totally untruthful rendition of the people's actual lifeways and history than previously portrayed.

Long before this latest incarnation of the putative princess, however, South-ern Indians occupied a rather large place in American writing. From the prevaricating John Smith onwards—with first a brief acknowledgement of the prior contributions of the earlier Biedma, Gentleman of Elvas, Cabeza de Vaca, Joutel, Charlevoix, and Le Page du Pratz writing in Spanish and French —to the eighteenth century's Beverly, Archer, Adair, Timberlake, William Byrd, Bartram, and Jefferson, all of whom are among the progenitors of American literature, Southeastern Indians were depicted variously and exten-sively. William Gilmore Simms, the southern version of popular "Indian ex-plainer" James Fenimore Cooper, depicted Noble Savages and Red Devils in *The Yemassee,* thus replicating the "passing of a people" theme and fictional format established in the popular American mind almost as successfully as Cooper had done. Later fiction writers, such as Johnson Jones Hooper, in *The Adventures of Captain Simon Suggs,* and Mary N. Murfree, in her historical romance, *The Story of Old Fort Loudon,* presented semirealistic descriptions of Creeks and Cherokees, respectively, in conflict with frontier whites. Davy Crockett's *Autobiography* and George Washington Harris's Sut Lovingood sto-ries provided amusing, and sometimes unexpected, slices of realism in their literary treatment of Indian people in the South.

During the same period in which Crockett and Harris lived near and wrote about Indian people in the 1830s, Washington Irving discovered Indians on his return to America after a seventeen-year stay in Europe. While he might be criticized for his rather stylized portrayals of such actual Indian people of the day as the Quapaw Pierre Beatte in *A Tour on the Prairies* and the Seminole Eneah Emarthla in "The Warrior Chief," such works are nonetheless notewor-thy in the degree to which an accomplished craftsman took pains to create Indians as people instead of types. Indians, however, remained peripheral in the work of Mark Twain and George Washington Cable, the major southern authors in the generation following the Civil War. While Cable usually de-picted his occasional Choctaw sympathetically, Twain, in contrast, seemed to have had nothing positive to say about Indians at all, always hopelessly ster-eotyping them in his works, as, for example, the nearly subhuman Injun Joe of *Tom Sawyer.* In the first half of the twentieth century, an immense flood of historical romances by such authors as Murfree (although she strove to tran-scend stereotyping), James Boyd, Welbourn Kelley, Harry Caudill, Janice Holt Giles, and Caroline Gordon were common literary fare up to the last genera-tion. Their fictional renditions of the eighteenth-century border wars, with white pioneers and long hunters pitted against Cherokee, Creek, and Shawnee warriors, who give way to white expansion only after much hard-fought and bloody warfare so that Tennessee, Kentucky, and Alabama can be made into cotton and tobacco country, are always presented, of course, from the settlers' point of view.

In William Faulkner's work, most notably *Go Down, Moses* and the short stories "Lo," "Red Leaves," and "Mountain Victory," Chickasaws in Mississippi are given relatively realistic treatment, although at times his descriptions are somewhat deficient in verisimilitude to actual Chickasaw customs. Faulkner is great as a writer for so many characters and situations, but rarely have he and his work been much examined with regard to the "tripartite intercultural" relationships (white-black-Indian) existing in the world of his fictional Yoknaphatawpha County. No American writer before Faulkner, and few since, has engaged the incredibly complex interworkings of certain modern-day southerners, who are often the genetic mixing of two of the races and sometimes all three, as in the character Sam Fathers of *Go Down, Moses.* Such interplay of Indian, black, and white ancestry is a subject that is examined with close scrutiny by such Southeastern Native writers as Jack D. Forbes, Ron Welburn, Honorée Fanonne Jeffers, Jennifer Lisa Vest, and Dale Marie Taylor.

While miscegenation is a subject that most polite white southerners generally choose to remain quiet about, it is yet a fact. Mixed-bloodedness is there, as it has always been. Even a very minor character in *Gone With the Wind,* the house servant Dilcey, a slave at Tara, the O'Hara family's plantation, is depicted as displaying more of an Indian appearance and bearing than that of a black, though for it what it is worth, she is no less a slave and is legally black. It is disappointing that Margaret Mitchell did not venture further into the complexities of such a character, but her recognition of the phenomenon at least underscores the prevalence in the South of such disenfranchised people, all products of the hundreds of Indians forced into black slavery and the thousands of blacks who fled slavery for the relative freedom in Indian societies.[12]

Following Faulkner, the rare contemporary serious southern writer, when he or she chooses to examine any portion of the region pertaining to Indian cultures and peoples, often acquits himself or herself quite well. Guy Owen's *Journey for Joedel* is a highly effective and sensitive treatment of a Lumbee family during the Depression, and a generation later, Josephine Humphreys's *Nowhere Else on Earth* depicts Lumbees during the Civil War era. William Styron's short story, "Shadrach," features an impoverished Mattaponi family in rural Virginia, living in the shadows of white opulence in the land "where they have always been," during the same time period as Owen's novel. Whites with Indian blood regularly appear in southern literature.[13] The Boatright family in Dorothy Allison's *Bastard Out of Carolina* has remote Cherokee ancestry. Although as Uncle Earle is prompted to say, "whether our great-granddaddy was or wasn't (a Cherokee), it don't really make a titty's worth of difference," thus underscoring the usual realistic manner in which most such people must negotiate their identities and lives.[14]

Pocahontas continues to resurface in the American popular psyche. Not only as the highly popular cartoon character in the Disney movie, but also in popular romantic novels. In Susan Donnell's *Pocahontas,* a recent popular work of fiction, the Indian "princess" is brought forth in all the glory reflected in centuries of white fantasizing. Donnell rehashes the same tired plot of Pocahontas-as-heroine and the savior (several times) of the Jamestown colony, as well as the eternally true lover of Captain Smith—claims that have all been shown by literary scholars and historians to be fabrications. Donnell also reveals, in a biographical note at the end of the book, that she is a direct descendant of the Virginia Indian princess. In her treatment of the Powhatan Indian people, however, she never misses a chance to stress Pocahontas's superiority over other Powhatans because of her fantasy nobility (though, quite simply, Southern Indians did not have concepts of kings, queens, and princesses). It is apparent that Donnell is much more enamored with staking a claim to would-be nobility, however spurious, than to any degree of empathy and fellowship with the Powhatan people of the seventeenth century from whom she is in effect claiming descent. One must wonder about the nature and extent of her relationship with and regard for contemporary Powhatans.[15]

Actually, Donnell's *Pocahontas* is typical of the many slovenly researched and ineptly written renditions of the "princess," since virtually every retelling of the Pocahontas story rehashes the same tiresome romantic claptrap. Donnell's book is noteworthy only because of the author's obsession with would-be royalty. In actuality, Pocahontas was singled out by the Jamestown colony as desperately needed proof that the colony there was succeeding in its relationship with the Indians. At first held prisoner by the Jamestown colonists, until it was learned that she was Powhatan's daughter, Pocahontas was then Christianized and quickly allied in marriage with John Rolfe in a "state-arranged" marriage. Through these measures, the colony sought to guarantee further financial backing from wealthy benefactors by exhibiting her back in England as the preeminent "success story" of their colonial undertaking. In England, Pocahontas became a symbol for European triumph and an exotic banner for the standard bearers of white racial superiority and posturing. She, or rather "it"—since there has never been very much of a real person behind the Eurocentric presentation of her, but only the convenient symbol—represents the enduring fascination that white Americans (and the British) have for their ideas regarding one particular Southeastern Indian woman whose personality, presence, and spirit should at last be reclaimed by her people.[16]

Southeastern Indian Writing Today

Until recent times, the literature of Southeastern Indian people has been primarily the orally transmitted knowledge of storytellers and medicine makers who told things to white recorders. At the apex of the Vanishing American era, in the last two decades of the nineteenth century and the first decade of the twentieth century, ethnologists made valiant efforts to record the stories of Indian elders. James Mooney and Frans M. Olbrechts gathered stories from Cherokee people; John M. Swanton went among Creek and other Muskhogean-speaking tribes; J. W. Dorsey collected materials from the Quapaws and other Siouan-speaking tribes; Albert S. Gatschet worked among western Gulf Coast peoples, such as the Atakapa, Houma, and Chitimacha tribes; and Frank Speck drew from the Cherokees and certain Algonquian-speaking tribes. These are the major scholars who came into the Southeast during this crucial period of the Indian peoples' cultures. Some of the native informants achieved a degree of renown because of their work with these ethnologists—Ayuinini (Swimmer), John Ax, and Will West Long among the Cherokees; Jackson Langley of the Koasati (Coushatta) tribe; Creek Sam and Watt Sam of the Natchez people, and others. Their stories, preserved for posterity, are for the most part in the volumes of the annual bulletins of the Bureau of American Ethnology and the Smithsonian Institute. Still earlier, in the third decade of the eighteenth century, William Byrd II remarked on Saponi stories related to him by his guide, a Saponi man named Bearskin, while Byrd served as the commissioner of a boundary survey party along the borders of the colonies of Virginia and North Carolina.

Shortly after the beginning of the twentieth century, writings by Indian people who remained in the Southeast were brought before the public. Various letters and articles were published in government-sponsored schools, such as Carlisle and Hampton. A sampling of these, included in the present volume, demonstrate the desires of young writers who sought to explain some of the verities of their tribal cultures to the outer world. Often the result of school writing assignments, the works nonetheless reveal each young person's views as an Indian and as a student and gave him or her the opportunity to relate legends and customs.[17] How the buzzard came to have a bald head; a retold version of the life and personality of Virginia Dare, the "first white child born in America," as American history books maintain; and a report on the contemporary (1909) Catawba Nation are among the topics discussed in the articles. The writers thus emerge as Native American authors. The fact that there is fancifulness in some historical matters, such as the Virginia Dare episode, is to be expected. Indian students of the era, not at all unlike those in many high schools today, had all too often been fed the watered-down and highly romanticized versions of their tribal histories, and it is evident in some of their writings.

Many Southeastern Indian writers who emerged on the literary scene with the beginning of the so-called Indian literary renaissance, starting in the late 1960s and early 1970s (and, arguably, still flourishing), began their careers as writers by publishing their works in the numerous small press journals that proliferated during the period. William Jay Smith, Norman H. Russell, besmilr brigham, Gladys Cardiff, John Woodrow Presley, Ralph Salisbury, Ron Welburn, Geary Hobson, Jack D. Forbes, Jimmie Durham, and Adolph F. Dial all published in these journals during this period, while they were also often involved in establishing other such magazines. At the beginning of the next decade, Moses Jumper, Jr., Jean Starr, Louis Owens, and Marilou Awiakta joined in with their contributions to small press journals, and all soon published their first books. University presses, at the same time, issued books by Forbes, Owens, and Hobson, and such venues continue to be strong sustainers of Indian writing to the present day, while filling much of the vacuum left when many small presses folded after federal and state assistance to the arts dried up in the 1980s. Tribally supported presses, most notably the Choctaw Heritage Press and the Seminole Tribe Press, helped out a great deal during this period by providing support for tribal members-as-writers such as Moses Jumper, Jr., Betty Mae Jumper, Rose Powhatan, Kenneth York, Thallis Lewis, and, toward the end of the decade, Karenne Wood and Roger Emile Stouff.

The 1990s saw the greatest proliferation of Southeastern Indian writing and publishing, including, in addition to the aforementioned writers, poets such as Kennette Harrison, MariJo Moore, Allison Adelle Hedge Coke, Janet McAdams, Dawn Karima Pettigrew, and Deidra Suwanee Dees, and others. Storytellers, such as Betty Mae Jumper, Gregg Howard, Lynn King Lossiah, Kathi Smith Littlejohn, and Freeman Owle, began expanding their talents and honing their skills in modern-day perpetuations of the older oral traditions. Several of the writers of the past three decades have published novels—Louis Owens, Jack D. Forbes, Dawn Karima Pettigrew, Geary Hobson, and MariJo Moore. Some—particularly Delano Cummings, Betty Mae Jumper, and Allison Adelle Hedge Coke—have published book-length personal memoirs, or autobiographies. Of the writers featured in *The People Who Stayed*, many have been involved in community and tribal affairs, and their writings often reveal it. These include Betty Mae Jumper, Moses Jumper, Jr., Earl J. Barbry, Sr., Edythe S. Hobson, Karenne Wood, Will Moreau Goins, Teresa Morris, Loretta Leach, Redbird James, Roger Emile Stouff, and Larry Richard.[18]

Small presses, amenable to Indian concerns, have nonetheless, since the hard times of the late 1980s, evolved in the 1990s. Various Indian Publishing, rENEGADE pLANET pRESS, John Blair, and Phoenix Publishing, all originating in the South, have provided a much-welcomed haven for Indian authors, several of whom are represented in *The People Who Stayed.* Coming from a region of the nation where there are not supposed to be any Indians anymore, much less Indian writers, several writers who are represented in the present work have won the Native Writers' Circle of the Americas First Book Award for Poetry and for Prose—Janet McAdams, Chip Livingston, Karenne Wood, Edythe Simpson Hobson, and Kimberly G. Roppolo—an award that is one of the major literary awards for Native writers to be founded and continually maintained in Indian Country throughout the United States and Canada. Janet McAdams and Allison Adelle Hedge Coke have won the American Book Award for their writing as well.

Over the past two decades, numerous anthologies of Indian writings have been issued from the larger mainstream presses, university, and small presses —all as part of the current Native American literary renaissance steadily in vogue since the early 1970s. Very few, however, have had what might be defined as a "Southeastern focus." *The People Who Stayed*, while being entirely a Southeastern Indian anthology, is not, however, the first to explore the region. There are several notable precursors. In 1995, Daniel F. Littlefield, Jr., and James W. Parins published *Native American Writing in the Southeast: An Anthology, 1875–1935.* The title, however, is a misnomer, since only four, or possibly five, of the twenty-eight contributors were born in the Southeast prior to the Removal period of the 1830s and 1840s. All of the remaining writers were born in Indian Territory (later Oklahoma). Furthermore, all twenty-eight contributors identified with the western removed tribes and not with their kinsmen east of the Mississippi River, since they all lived their lives in Indian Territory. Excellent as it is, *Native American Writing in the Southeast* is not then, specifically, a Southeastern Indian anthology, but it is the most important literary link between the Removal era and the modern period.[19]

Barbara R. Duncan's *Living Stories of the Cherokee* (1998) contains recorded stories by seven contemporary Cherokee storytellers from the Cherokee Reservation in North Carolina. It is extremely well balanced, admirably edited, and aesthetically assembled and is overall a work that showcases outstanding talent in the verbal sphere. MariJo Moore's *Feeding the Ancient Fires: A Collection of*

Writings by North Carolina American Indians (1999) and Will Moreau Goins's
*The People Speak: A Collection of Writings by South Carolina Native Americans
in Poetry, Prose, Essays, and Interviews* (2002) are specifically targeted to the two
states mentioned in the titles and not to the entire Southeast as a whole. Yet
both works are highly informative and are works of which Carolina Indians, on
both sides of the line separating the two states, can be proud.

In *The People Who Stayed*, we have attempted as editors to manifest the
qualities of each of our preceding colleagues, while extending and widening
their approaches as we strive to present the broadest range of writings by
Southeastern Indian people. This anthology includes not only a diverse representation of genres—from poetry to web page posts—but also a broad range of
acculturation and lived Native experiences. The writers here engage the local
and the global. They work in contemporary mixed modes, such as lyric poetry
or postmodern drama. They tell traditional stories. They tell contemporary
stories. You may visit the mountains of Virginia here, the Everglades of Florida, the Delta swamps of Arkansas, or the gritty small tobacco towns of North
Carolina. You may hear a story about Wounded Knee, or how Turtle's shell
became cracked. You may even see Rabbit strolling through these pages.[20]

Notes

1. Helen C. Rountree, "The Indians of Virginia: A Third Race in a Biracial State,"
in *Southeastern Indians since the Removal Era*, ed. Walter L. Williams (Athens: The
University of Georgia Press, 1979), 40–45; also, Rountree, *Pocahontas's People: The
Powhatan Indians of Virginia through Four Centuries* (Norman: University of Oklahoma Press, 1990), 219–37.

2. Jack D. Forbes offers a thorough examination of similar legislative and administrative atrocities in other southeastern states in *Black Africans and Native Americans* (London, UK: Basil Blackwell, 1990).

3. See Rose Powhatan's "Surviving Document Genocide" (included in this collection) for a unique Virginia Indian response to Plecker and his pernicious impact on
her people.

4. Grant Foreman, *Indian Removal: The Emigration of the Five Civilized Tribes of
Indians* (Norman: University of Oklahoma Press, 1932), 19. Foreman places the
number of government-sponsored removed Indians at sixty thousand. Subsequent
historians have boosted the number of removed people upward since then.

5. John R. Swanton, *The Indians of the Southeastern United States*, Bureau of
American Ethnology, Bulletin 137 (Washington, D.C.: Smithsonian Institute, 1946),
1–39.

6. Simon J. Ortiz, *Woven Stone* (Tucson: University of Arizona Press, 1992), 72.
Ortiz errs in his use of Chief McGhee's name in the poem, rendering it as "Alvin
McGee." See J. Anthony Paredes, "Back from Disappearance: The Alabama Creek
Indian Community," in *Southeastern Indians since the Removal Era*, 130.

7. Established and maintained by Professor Troy Johnson, California State University at Long Beach.

8. The Mexican Indian woman Malinche, (or Doña Marina), the benefactress of Cortés during his conquest of the Aztecs, and the two Timucuan women, who rescued Juan Ortiz from execution following his capture during the Narváez Expedition in Florida, provide sixteenth century and Spanish prototypes for the "helpful Indian woman," who set the stage for Pocahontas's "creation" by the English a century later.

9. Jack D. Forbes's *Black Africans and Native Americans: Color, Race, and Caste in the Evolution of Red-Black Peoples* (London, UK: Basil Blackwell, 1988) offers a superlative examination of several centuries of the dynamics of European racialism, in which mixed-blood individuals were almost always forced into "arbitrary categories which tend(ed) to render their ethnic heritage simple rather than complex" (p. 271).

10. William W. Quinn, Jr., "The Southeast Syndrome: Notes on Indian Descendant Recruitment Organizations and Their Perceptions of Native American Culture," in *American Indian Quarterly* 14, no. 2 (Spring 1990): 147–54.

11. Jack D. Forbes, an authority on jazz in addition to his preeminence as a historian, adds to this list in *Black Africans and Native Americans*, mentioning "Adelaide Hall, Willie the Lion Smith, Paul Robeson, Josephine Baker, Bunk Johnson, Lena Horne, Pops Foster, George Lewis, Pearl Bailey, Leadbelly, Tina Turner, and others (all of whom) have made specific reference to Native American ancestry" in biographies and autobiographies (p. 190).

12. Margaret Mitchell, *Gone With the Wind* (New York: The Macmillan Company, 1936; reprint New York: Avon Books, 1973), 65.

13. It is disappointing that an otherwise excellent anthology such as the recent *The South in Perspective: An Anthology of Southern Literature*, edited by Edward Francisco, Robert Vaughn, and Linda Francisco (New York: Prentice-Hall, 2001), virtually ignores Southeastern Indians, both in terms of writings about them and a consideration of them within the context of how southern society evolved, and certainly by its exclusion of writers of Southeastern Indian background. While the collection is a commendable array of southern authors from the Colonial era to the present-day, Southeastern Indians are almost entirely erased from the equation. The "perspective" of the editors not only fails to allow for a single author of Native background or ancestry but also excludes much of anything else suggestive of Indian expression. With the exception of two of James Mooney's century-old renditions of some Cherokee incantations, there is little else, other than an antiquated apologist essay in defense of the Pocahontas myth written by a turn-of-the-century racial purist and historian–literary critic. As a saving grace, however, and quite notably so, Styron's "Shadrach," is included.

14. Dorothy Allison, *Bastard Out of Carolina* (New York: Dutton), 27.

15. Susan Donnell isn't too dissimilar from several other writers of Southeastern Indian ancestry who have sought in varying ways to renegotiate identities for themselves. The "Princess," or Nobility, Syndrome, as it is often derisively labeled by most non-Native people and many Southeastern Indian people themselves, is rather quite

commonplace. The urge of someone "not entirely white" to remake him or herself in what they perceive as an oppressive environment in much of the "White South" is obviously the prime impetus for doing so. Still, the need for reclaiming one's people's lost heritage, regardless of the degree of justification for doing so or of how the actual goal is to be accomplished, is undeniably important. The examples among writers, in fact, are numerous. Rita Ann Sentz, growing up in extremely impoverished circumstances in a mixed-blood family and community in North Carolina, remade herself into Princess Pale Moon and then exploited the new identity in her work in evangelical Christian causes before she wrote her auto-biography. Natachee Scott Momaday, from a mixed-blood family in Kentucky, not legally Indian, recast herself in her teens as Little Moon and left home to attend Haskell Indian School in the early 1930s, and she later became a highly respected BIA teacher and author of children's books. Forrest Carter, from Oxford, Alabama, and inclined toward a stance of political/social/racial ultraconservatism and Negro-baiting, suddenly reemerged as a highly traditional Cherokee from the mountains of North Carolina, an "identity" he rounded out in an extremely popular "auto-biography," *The Education of Little Tree*, written at the same time he was writing Western novels such as (*Gone to Texas*) *The Outlaw Josey Wales* and *Look for Me on the Mountain (Cry Geronimo!)*. Diane Fisher, self-reinvented as Dhyani Ywahoo, claims to be "of the twenty-seventh generation" of her Cherokee family's line of medicine-makers and culture-keepers, while remaining irritatingly coy in her book, *Voices of the Ancestors*, about revealing exactly where she and her family are from. In a very un-Cherokee way, she lives and practices her "Cherokee medicine teachings" in upstate Vermont, which she maintains is now "sacred Cherokee ground."

However, the most dramatic of these refashionings is that of Sylvester Long [Long Lance/Chief Buffalo Child Long Lance], who spent his boyhood in North Carolina in the 1890s and early 1900s (see the contributor's note on him in this volume), and his evolution from his mixed Indian-black-white background, loosely defined as Croatan (pre-Lumbee). Long's evolution from his actual origins as Croatan (Lumbee) to Cherokee to Blackfoot (Blood, or Kainai, band) to "Hollywood Indian," is nothing short of astonishing. Donald B. Smith's biography, *Long Lance: The Glorious Impostor* (Red Deer, Alb.: Red Deer Press, 1999), is a superb study of the man's complex life and circumstances.

When a Navajo man once asked one of the editors of the present book why it was that so many "Southern Indians" changed themselves from "white, or 'near that,' 'off-colored,' or 'what-have-you,' to Indian," the editor responded much like Quentin Compson does in William Faulkner's *Absalom, Absalom!* When asked why he "hates the South," Quentin responds with a harsh vehement denial that actually underscores his shocked insight of his ambivalent feelings of love and hate toward the region: "I don't. I don't hate it! I don't hate it!" The editor's reply, which he imagined needed no amplification, went something like: "You just have to know the South. There's no place like it anywhere." With the region's grim history of an often highly constrictive, proto-Calvinistic social structuring, is it any wonder then that a young Asa Earl (pre-Forrest) Carter would first try to be the "whitest of whites" and then a "super Indian"? Sometimes, through such protective coloration, the super self-conscious "off-white" eagerly embraces the anonymity of a lynch mob and, indeed, is often the loudest of all the yapping dogs circling the hanging tree. Or, they may opt for super-Indianness—of either the popular pan-Indian version—like Natachee Scott, Rita Ann Sentz, and Sylvester Long—or a totally tribal representation of that person's tribal background, the "more Cherokee (or Creek, or Choctaw) than thou" figure, again like Forrest Carter and certainly Dhyani Ywahoo.

16. Rose Powhatan's "Surviving Document Genocide" marks an excellent beginning toward this end.

17. Ginny Carney's doctoral dissertation, "A Testament to Tenacity: Cultural Persistence in the Letters and Speeches of Eastern Band Cherokee Women," recently published, under the name of Virginia Moore Carney, as *Eastern Band Cherokee Women: Cultural Persistence in Their Letters and Speeches,* examines this "era of scarcity" (ca. 1880s–1950s) of Native American expression in the region.

18. We are purposely omitting the writings of Indian people who are descended from Southeastern tribes that were removed to Indian Territory and whose orientation is essentially from "Oklahoma" rather than the southeastern United States. It needs to be mentioned, however, that there have been and are many talented writers who represent the "removed" tribes in Oklahoma. Some of these writers are John Rollin Ridge (Cherokee), DeWitt Clinton Duncan (Cherokee), Alexander L. Posey (Creek), Will Rogers (Cherokee), John M. Oskison (Cherokee), Lynn Riggs (Cherokee), Louis Littlecoon Oliver (Yuchi-Creek), ["William Harjo"] Thomas E. Moore (Creek), Glenn J. Twist (Cherokee-Creek), Raven Hail (Cherokee), Carroll Arnett [Gogisgi] (Cherokee), Eula Doonkeen (Seminole), Charles G. Ballard (Quapaw-Cherokee), Jim Barnes (Choctaw), Robert J. Perry (Chickasaw), Robert J. Conley (Cherokee), Diane Glancy (Cherokee), Wilma Mankiller (Cherokee), Linda Hogan (Chickasaw), Roxy Gordon (Choctaw), Donald L. Birchfield (Choctaw-Chickasaw), Phillip Carroll Morgan (Choctaw-Chickasaw), Judy Lee Oliva (Chickasaw), LeAnne Howe (Choctaw), Joy Harjo (Creek), Sara Sue Hoklotubbe (Cherokee), Devon A. Mihesuah (Choctaw), Joe Dale Tate Nevaquaya (Yuchi-Comanche), Craig S. Womack (Creek-Cherokee), Daniel Heath Justice (Cherokee), Julie Gibson (Cherokee-Creek), and Julie Moss (Cherokee).

19. It might, on the surface, seem ironic, if not contradictory, that many of the writers featured in *The People Who Stayed* are presently residing outside the Southeast. However, given the dynamics of modern-day Indian life within the United States, this is probably the rule rather than the exception. Federal censuses since 1980 have revealed that approximately one-half of all American Indians nationwide reside away from their traditional communities and reservations, and, quite particularly, many such people are to be found in urban areas. Why should Southeastern Indian people be regarded any differently? The contemporary Cherokee (Oklahoma) poet Carroll Arnett [Gogisgi] states in a poem: "Indian people were not/meant to live in/cities, and none do./Some reside there/but none live there." This particular distinction does more than merely underscore the "living" aspect of their connection with regard to the lands, always sacred in ways that few non-Indian people have understood, that they were forced away from physically, but certainly not psychically and spiritually.

20. Always, whenever an anthology is brought forth as accomplished fact, queries are addressed to the editors and publisher and to the public at large about "why so-and-so" was left out. Undoubtedly, our anthology can be arraigned on similar charges, despite our attempt to be as generally representational, if not as exhaustive, as possible with regard to large Indian tribal areas and virtually almost every state in the region. Early on, we made the aforementioned decisions not to include work by writers of Southeastern Indian background who do not write about that background, but rather instead write of Indians in other areas, particularly the Plains and the Southwest, "where all the Indians are supposed to be." Yet we acknowledge many other writers who we wish we could have found room for, but, because of the constraints of space and other similar considerations, had to be left out: Mississippi Choctaws such as Thallis Lewis, Roseann Tubby, and Kenneth York; Lumbees Lew Barton, Barbara Brayboy-Locklear, Malinda Maynor, Joseph Oxendine, Linda Oxendine, Helen Maynor Schierbeck, David K. Wilkins, and Robert A. Williams, Jr.; Cherokees Davey Arch, Lloyd Arneach, Robert Bushyhead, Mary Gloyne Byler, Edna Chekelelee, Meredith K. James, Barbara K. Robins, Marie Junaluska, Tony (Mack) McClure, William Meyer, B. J. Nash, Richard Paugh, Lee Piper (Ugidali), and Montana Hopkins Walking Bull; Creeks Donald Ryburn and Paula Brush; Powhatan Phoebe Ferris; Houmas Bruce Duthu and T. Mayheart Dardar; also, folks of multiple tribal origin, Gerald Wilkinson (Cherokee-Catawba), E. K. (Kim) Caldwell (Cherokee-Creek-Shawnee), and Denise Low (Cherokee-Delaware). These are a few of the many that, by mentioning them, if not including work by them in the book, we hope to honor.

I

Virginia, Maryland, and Delaware

Rose Powhatan

Rose Powhatan (Pamunkey) is an enrolled member of the Pamunkey Tribe of Virginia. A teacher for more than thirty years in the Washington, D.C. area, she is also a prominent artist who has had many shows of her work throughout the United States and England. She holds a B.F.A. and an M.A. (cum laude) from Howard University and has done graduate work in history, humanities, and education administration at several other universities. Powhatan serves on numerous boards, including the Maryland Commission on Indian Affairs, the American Association of Museums, the National Museum of the American Indian, the John F. Kennedy Center for the Performing Arts, and the American Indian Society of Washington, D.C. She has published articles in journals and newspapers, such as *The Sun* (Baltimore), *Kent Today* (Gravesend, Danford, England), *The London Times*, and *The Washington Post,* and recently served as a cultural consultant on the movie, *The New World.*

Surviving Document Genocide

[Document genocide (n. dok'yə mənt' jen'ə sīd'), n. 1. the deliberate extermination of a race of people through changing information about them in an official paper.]

Here I am, at 3:30 A.M., the day before the deadline for submitting this story, and the very morning of the first family reunion of my father's family that's not a funeral. (Although I'm an enrolled member of the Pamunkey Indian Nation of King William County, Virginia, through my mother, my father's family is one of two families historically documented as "Indian" indigenous to Fairfax County.) I still can't decide what to write about in relation to what it's like to be officially recognized as an Indian outside the indigenous community, thanks to a cartoon movie about my ancestors. Oh, excuse me. You, too? Okay. I'm an enrolled member of the Pamunkey Indian Nation. Never heard of us before? Yes, you have. Pocahontas was Pamunkey, and her father, Powhatan, is buried in a mound on our reservation in King William County. That's right. Now you know who we are. You just forgot for a moment. I'm not surprised. After all, I'm living in a country with the curious distinction that your tribe can be changed and you can be erased from the Book of Life when you change your address. Move off the reservation and you cease to be

Indian. You're dead. You never existed. You become a member of the "Walking Dead Extinct Indian Nation." That's the reality of trying to be a survivor of "document genocide."

Document genocide regulates your relationship to others with whom you interact on a daily basis. It's not easy to be upbeat about your tribal identity when most people around you constantly remind you that you are not supposed to exist. Even well-intentioned librarians are smug in their knowing responses to my requests for information about Indians indigenous to my tribe's ancestral home region. They tell me that my ancestors became extinct through contact with European and African germs. When I identify myself as an enrolled Pamunkey Indian, they act sanctimonious and try to correct me. They tell me I must be a Cherokee or a Blackfoot. I'm told that I'm extinct, since all Indians indigenous to the Washington, D.C., Maryland, and northern Virginia region became extinct "hundreds of years ago." "Government Indians" who have come to Washington to work at the Bureau of Indian Affairs and other federal agencies play the same game with me. Why, they even form social clubs and perpetuate information about the people in the "official" organization mission statements. Supposedly, the main reason for starting such organizations is because, in their view, "there were no Indians in the region"—despite the fact that many members of one such organization have repeatedly been shown hospitality by Virginia tribes, invited to enjoy the amenities of the reservations (the Pamunkey and Mattaponi reservations, the two oldest in the United States.)

New Indian arrivals in my home area constantly inform me that "back on the rez" they have been told that there are no Indians east of the Mississippi River. In response, I frequently reply to their ignorance by informing that, on the contrary, there are still many here, and some are descendants of warriors who fought long and hard battles against the invasion of our homeland. I encourage these Western Indians to return home and thank God that, because of us Eastern Indians, their ancestors were given extra time to enjoy their culture before the onslaught of a European ethnocentrism that believed in destroying all vestiges of indigenous culture whenever and wherever they found it. Southeastern indigenous people paid a very high price for the misfortune of being the first to live in close proximity to the first permanent English settlement in America. While the English did indeed come here for better opportunities than existed for them back in the old country, you might say that they actually bore a close resemblance to a later group often found in the region, those known as "Carpetbaggers."

Growing up under document genocide requires constant vigilance if you intend to be a survivor. Residing in the Washington, D.C., and suburban Fairfax County, Virginia, area makes you painfully aware of the insidiousness of document genocide. Whenever you fill out forms requiring you to identify a racial or ethnic designation, you are challenged by the intake personnel. Since I'm a "carded" Indian, I show them my official tribal identification. Other Indians who lack the same papers generally have their identities changed, after having endured a condescending lecture on how they should be proud to be a member of the race to which the clerk's "eyeball test" has thus relegated them. I have also had the personal experience of having had my race changed without my knowledge. I've found out about it later on when I've gone back to get copies of a particular official document. The Washington, D.C., Vital Statistics Office once informed me that I would have to retain the services of an attorney if I wanted to correct the misinformation appearing on my records.

Oh, I'm a pro when it comes to administering, as well as taking the "eyeball test." I have been teaching school in Washington since February of 1973. Every year, homeroom teachers are asked to fill out an official ethnic designation "head count" form to identify the races of the students in their classrooms. Teachers are instructed to survey the class, and then, by casually glancing at the students, write down on the form how they "fit" in the various racial classifications. One year, I asked students to raise their hands if they knew they had a family history of descendants from indigenous American ancestors. Most of the students raised their hands in affirmation of having Indian ancestors. I wasn't surprised. When I was appointed by the secretary of the interior to the nine-member Underground Railroad Network to Freedom Nation Committee, I engaged in in-depth research on African displacement in the American South. The committee's findings revealed that since the overwhelming majority of Africans brought to America were male, and since so many male Indians had been killed in conflict with invading colonists or made into slaves and absorbed into African slave groups, it generally holds that most African Americans claiming Indian ancestry will cite a particular Indian woman in their lineage to show their claim to Indian heritage. European Americans like to refer to this country as the "New World." More appropriately, it should be called the "Widowed World." Countless Indians are "hiding out" or "passing" in African and European American communities, due in great part to the eternal shame of the legacy of slavery. To add to this travesty is the recent trend of calling legally and tribally enrolled Indian people "black Indians" instead of their more correct tribal names. Misguided authors in search of a quick buck or some instant public attention perpetuate this racist misnomer.

"Where are you from, honey?" is the question I have been asked my entire life. It is a question that is never asked of me by indigenous people. Nonindigenous Americans have made me conscious that I don't "fit in," no matter where I go. Most people assume I am a Latina or I've recently arrived from the subcontinent of India. Hispanic people speak to me in Spanish and grow angry or impatient with me when I respond to them in English. Continental Indians are accepting of me when I am by myself, but frown when they see me with my Taino Jamaican husband. I'm not surprised at both groups' reactions to me. It's a commonly held joke in the Indian community that Latino people are really Indian cousins from the South, coming up North to help us repopulate the United States of America with Indian people. As for mistaken Hindu Indian identity, one can always remember that Christopher Columbus made the same mistake when he landed in the Caribbean and encountered the Taino (one of several Arawak tribes) and Carib people. We have all been called Indians ever since that fateful encounter.

In the school year of 1994–1995, when I was on a Fulbright Teacher Exchange Fellowship to the United Kingdom, a colleague from Spain told me that I was called an "India," whereas someone from India was called an "Indu." It would seem as though the Spanish are still confused about who we are. I found that the Brits and Africans in the UK also had the same problem in recognizing my true identity. After each of the three times I had been mugged in London, the police reported the incidents as "Paki-bashings," a term used to designate crimes perpetuated against Southeast Asians.

My most memorable and positive experience during my Fulbright year was due mainly to my ancestral cousin, Pocahontas. Oh, I know what you're thinking—"Here we go, back to the Disney cartoon story." No, it's not at all related to make-believe. After the last time I had been assaulted in London, I decided to go to Gravesend, Kent, where Pocahontas is buried in the St. George's Church of England sanctuary. I wanted to lay some flowers at the foot of the statue erected to her memory (the statue is a twin to the one erected at the original site of Jamestown, Virginia), and pray, since she was the closest link to home that I had in England. I had initially planned to go to Gravesend on March 21, 1995, which would have coincided with the anniversary of her death date in 1617. There was a mix-up at the railroad station, and I wasn't able to complete my journey. As a result, I was a day late arriving in Gravesend. However, March 22nd was a more personally significant day for me since it is the day, in 1622, that Opechancanough (brother of Powhatan, the father of Pocahontas, and his successor—because of his place in the matrilineal line of descent—as head of the Powhatan Confederacy, following Powhatan's death in 1618) launched his war against English imperialists in Virginia.

When I arrived at St. George's, the church just happened to be open for a special service, although it was usually closed on that day of the week. I went inside and identified myself to the pastor, the Reverend David Willey. He seemed genuinely glad to meet me. He told me about a special teacher at the church named Di Coleman, who was currently writing a play in honor of the 400th anniversary of Pocahontas's birth. He said that she would welcome my help with the production and that the children of the church's school would benefit from my working with them. I called the school and received permission from Head Teacher Jean Bannister to give a lecture at the school and to work with the Resolution Theater Group, directed and sponsored by Di Coleman. I assisted Ms. Coleman as cultural consultant, set designer, and costume designer, and it was truly a godsend experience.

The experience, however, stands out in stark contrast with that of my initial dealings with the Disney Corporation when they began their work on *Pocahontas*. Soon after I had agreed to work with them as an advisor, when I insisted the true story of Pocahontas should be told and not the fantasy it became, I was dismissed. Disney eventually hired one of my cousins to work on the movie. She later pretended not to know that Disney would deviate from actual historical fact in order to fabricate the love story between Pocahontas and John Smith. The movie was universally panned by well-informed members of the indigenous community when it was released. My cousin benefited from her collaboration with Disney by being able to charge higher fees for appearances as an entertainer.

My affiliation with the staff and students at St. George's and Di Coleman remains one of the highlights of my life. There I was, thousands of miles from home, being accorded respect and recognition that I had never experienced in my homeland. At the end of the historic performance of the Pocahontas commemorative production (which was also performed at other locations in England before it went on to the International Folk Festival in Scotland), I marveled at how far I had come to receive such respect for who I was, instead of the ridicule that is commonplace in the United States. I thanked Head Teacher Jean Bannister and the people of Gravesend for extending hospitality to me in the same spirit of humanity that they held for my ancestral cousin Pocahontas. I felt as though I was partially repaying their kindness to her through the work I was engaged in with their children. I was fortunate that document genocide against me and my people did not extend to the town of Gravesend. The Virginia Indian presence is a viable part of the ongoing, living history of the town. Our history is shared by them as a legitimate source of cultural tourism and a source of pride in themselves.

Where do I go from here? As an educator and curriculum writer, I lecture and write about the history and cultural retentions of my people. I'm an active member of the "powwow circuit," and I set up exhibits and displays, which celebrate the cultural possessions of my people. I serve on numerous historic, educational, and cultural boards, where I can have a direct impact on information and participatory events that are made available to both regional and national audiences. I'm both a Washington Teachers' Union building representative and a member of the Local School Restructuring Team, given the mandate to improve education for young people at the grassroots level. As a practicing professional artist, my culturally based artwork is exhibited through numerous venues and is, at present, touring the country in a show commemorating seven decades of American art. I'm the founder/director of the Powhatan Museum and the Center for Indigenous Culture in Washington, which is affiliated with the City Museum of Washington. I'm the mother of three sons, all of whom are dedicated to do all they can to help eradicate document genocide that is directed towards indigenous Americans in courtrooms, schoolrooms, living rooms, and film-screening rooms in this country. My never-ending battle continues, but I am determined that my people and I will survive document genocide.

Karenne Wood

Karenne Wood (Monacan) won the Native Writers' Circle of the Americas First Book Award for Poetry in 2000. Her winning manuscript, *Markings on Earth*, was published by the University of Arizona Press the following year. She is currently enrolled in the graduate program in cultural anthropology at the University of Virginia. Formerly an instructor in English at George Mason University and at other institutions, Wood is presently serving as the chair of the Virginia Council on Indians; at the same time, she is the tribal secretary of the Monacan Nation, a position she has held since 1990. She resides in Charlottesville, Virginia.

Blue Mountains

Bury me up there in the high blue mountains
and I promise that I will return to teach the wind
how to make poetry from tossed about and restless leaves.

—*Lorna Goodison*

Beyond Charlottesville, mountains lift ridges toward
clouds, cropped where towers or ski slopes are rising.
The land undulates
                 in paintspots of redbud, azalea, columbine,
dogwood apple blossom, then pine and cedar, surprising
chartreuse of new hay that, come autumn, will sit
spiral-rolled in the fields, steam wavering upward
as though it could breathe—
                 past white-fenced
pastures in Albemarle, each claimed by someone
the ground will eventually own.
                 Sometimes, enveloped in fog,
we become almost spirit, lifted away—we think
this is like wanting to die—and wrench ourselves back
to breathe our way hard into Amherst, home country.

Drive down, up Father Judge Road, where Bear Mountain
leans from Tobacco Row, a row of blue mountains we never

abandoned and lavender mist that swathes High Peak
the way old women's shawls wrap around their knees.

Now a thin glint of light flashes, tears of one or another
who still weeps for us and the ever-loving earth. The mountains
speak in our voices:
>   *this too will pass,*
this, and this. We, who remain, also will pass
into their realm,

>   restless as leaves, to shine
beneath feet of contemporary Pilgrims, tearing
at surfaces, skittering across the earth's face.

We have nothing to teach the wind nuzzling itself
across the land, its poetry beyond mortal language.
Bury us in the blue mountains, our bodies
the earth they have always been.
>   We will grow
into trees and animals, turn soil back to elk's grass
and ask to return as an elemental brightness
that gleams with the furious love.

Directions, I–VII

I.

East is a genesis, *house made of*
dawn, where streaked clouds in
lavender, red, orange brush the
world's edge, where the dance
circle begins. Doors of domed
wigwams face morning. From
pipestone, tobacco smoke wafts
as striated light washes rivers
with green. Deep in the forest,
fiddleheads unfold. Green of new
leaf: the bright glossy hair rises
through red clay, lighting the world.

II.

South is the summer's white heat
without shade. Yellowing grasses
bend with wind's breath as bulrushes

lean over bodies of lovers, clothes
peeled like fruit skins, the limp
sleeves of August forgotten.
Hydrangeas blossom in blues,
whites, beyond tongues of tiger
lily's flames. Among bee balm,
hummingbirds hover. Every
live thing grows, sinking roots
deeper into the black rock.

III.

West is a space of thought, sparse
land with cliffs brushed magenta
and gold. Leaves slowly turn
to sunset hues as women gather
chokeberries, the elder men
crafting gourd rattles, singing
thin clouds into lightning for
corn. We, who cannot stay here
forever, read the cliff's face
where our ancestors wrote to us,
pictures in ochre. Beyond a vast
darkness, they wait for us.

IV.

North is the country of reflected light.
Shadows like wolves: the curved fang
takes moose by its haunches, spatters
scarlet fire onto ice. Footprints
recede into tundra. Aurora borealis—
a dance with spirits—new snow
piled on boughs, ribs gnawed with
scrimshawed grooves. Death groans
startle horizons, grow still. Bones
trace edges of ptarmigan, caribou.
White-out: a porcelain bear waits
Beside the world's ice-crusted rim.

V.

Sky is the casing of our breath,
suspending stars. The azimuth's

violet arc sends snow, gently,
and hurtles bright flashes like war
cries through darkness. Lightning
bugs zigzag above us, tiny
phosphorescent lamps. Celestial
palette: turquoise, cerulean, cobalt,
azure. Among its luminaries,
the sun walks the world's edge.
A brilliant moon rises while bats
leave caverns for air, another home.

VI.

What to say about the earth, whose
love lives like bright knives within us?
Like us, it is alchemy: chromium,
zinc, magnesium, copper. Like us,
a fire swirls within. Disordered,
too, the balance skewed. The
stones, the trees, the waters speak,
And if we are dust, as earth is,
let it receive us into the embrace
we barely left, memory remembered,
green as young bones: O, let the
next world look just like this one.

VII.

This is a prayer, its palms
already curved around our dust.
Lovers sing out from grasses they
become, sing to us: Here. Now.
This ground. These mountains,
skirted in mist. This hallowed
distance between worlds, where
sage, sweetgrass, and cedar burn,
the smoke intertwined with your
hair. We who have loved you
grow as dark roots beneath your
toes. We touch you. Here. Now.

Jack D. Forbes

Jack D. Forbes (Powhatan-Delaware) is a major Native American writer—historian, political scientist, social commentator, philosopher, essayist, novelist, short story writer, and poet—whose numerous books, approximately forty in number, have been in the vanguard of Native American Studies internationally for four decades. Forbes was born in Bahia de los Alamitos (Long Beach), California, in 1934. He has spent most of his life on the West Coast, but he maintains strong familial and cultural connections with Virginia tribal and other East Coast Indian communities and prefers to designate his tribal background as Powhatan (Renape) and Delaware (Lenape), with an admixture of Saponi and Cherokee. He was a founder of the Dekanawida-Quetzalcoatl (most often designated as D-Q) University in the 1960s, located within the University of California system at Davis. Among his nonfiction titles are *Apache, Navaho, and Spaniard* (1960), *The Indian in America's Past* (1964), *The Education of the Culturally Different* (1969), *Aztecas del Norte: The Chicanos of Aztlan* (1973), *Tribes and Masses* (1978), *American Words: An Introduction to those Native Words Used in English in the United States and Canada* (1979), *Atlas of Native History* (1981), *Native American Higher Education: The Struggle for the Creation of D-Q University* (1985), *Black Africans and Native Americans: Color, Race, and Caste in the Evolution of Red-Black Peoples* (1988), and *Columbus and Other Cannibals* (1992). Three poetry chapbooks, *Naming Our Land, Reclaiming Our Land* (1992), *El-Lay Riots: Memorias de Ya-Town and Home Boy Poems* (1992), *What is Time?* (1997), a novel, *Red Blood* (1997), and a collection of short stories, *Only Approved Indians* (1995), constitute the body of his published creative works. In 1997, Forbes received the Before Columbus Foundation's American Book Award for Lifetime Achievement, and in 1999 he was named Writer of the Year by the Wordcraft Circle of Native Writers and Storytellers. In 2009, he received the Lifetime Achievement Award from the Native Writers' Circle of the Americas. Forbes lives in Davis, California. His website is: http://cougar.ucdavis.edu/nas/faculty/forbes/personal/forbes.html.

The Dream of Injun Joe:
A Page from the Alcatraz Seminars

Dear Reader: I was indeed fortunate to be alive in 1969–1970 and to be able to join the throngs of Native Americans visiting or living on Alcatraz Island in those exciting days. For those of you too young to remember,

I will provide only this background: for several years that sad rock in the Bay of San Francisco, long the locale of a notorious prison, was liberated from its forlorn destiny by Indians from many tribes. For a brief time, then, the Isla de los Alcatraces knew a different existence, one filled with the sounds of drumming, singing, laughter, and angry but proud speeches.

I remember very distinctly my impressions: the blueness of the bay dotted with little boats of every description making their way to the miniature island; the happy faces of the native people, long black hair tied back with red headbands; the putt-putting of ancient motors in old boats whose seaworthiness was open to doubt; and the fog banks courteously holding themselves out to sea, allowing the sun to have a few hours of dominion.

One thing that especially struck me was how the U.S. government had spent great sums of money to build and maintain a massive prison on the island, only to be ultimately—and inevitably defeated by the intrepid and natural liberators of salt and water, fog and wind.

And I thought to myself, "Thus it will be! All the might and wealth of the United States cannot prevent its ultimate decay." It seemed as if natural law had led the Indians to Alcatraz, to begin a process of rebirth amid the visible signs of rusting cell doors and decaying barred windows.

"We must become like the salt and the waters of the earth. We must slowly, but certainly, rust away this prison erected all around us."

But enough of my personal feelings! What I want to recount, dear reader, is the nature of the intellectual life that developed on the island in those days, and, more especially, I wish now to recount, as faithfully as I can from my extensive notes, the precise content of one of the now legendary Alcatraz seminars.

The colloquium commenced when a Cherokee scholar named Marshall (I can't recall whether this was his first or last name) asked and then answered a rhetorical question: "How can we describe the character of the whites who came over here from Europe, especially the negative traits that caused so much trouble?

"What is it that dominates their character?

"It isn't just materialism, nor is it just greed—what makes many white people so strange and so dangerous is a restless dissatisfaction that is constant, never satisfied. They are crazy for wealth, voracious. They will go to any lengths, go to any place, use any means, to get what they want.

"In less than a century they have consumed most of the United States' oil and gas reserves, reserves that took millions of years to accumulate.

"They have wiped out forests, destroyed grasslands, turned deserts into dust bowls, and seriously diminished almost every other natural resource. What are their characteristics? Igana-noks-salgi. Those who are greedy for land, the old Creek Indians called them. They are always gobbling up land, taking it from Indians, Mexicans, or less successful white people.

"They are always looking for gold, for uranium, for oil, for more profits, for new real estate deals, for better-paying jobs, for a new place to live.

"In truth, it is not wealth that they want; it is always *more wealth* or *new* wealth.

"It is not so much *having* something but *getting* something that drives them. If they already have, they want to get more—always more." He paused for a moment, staring up at the high prison ceiling with its bare patches where plaster and paint had fallen away.

"They are crazy—driven, restless, dissatisfied—but it is *to get* that they are crazy. Of course, many are crazy to spend, to display, to show off, but this need for consumption only serves to make the *getting* all the more important.

"They are crazy with the *getting* of wealth, the *getting* of land, the *getting* of gold, the *getting* of a new car, the *getting* of a chance to spend the way the Hollywood stars spend or the way the oil-rich Texas millionaires spend.

"Since they are Getting-Crazy People, they seldom enjoy merely *having*. This is the root of their restless character. This is why they plunder Lake Tahoe, the Sierra Nevada foothills, the Arizona desert, the Colorado Rockies, and so on. They want to *get* a place at the beach, or on the lake, or in the desert. They don't care that one of the consequences of their getting such a place will be the destruction of that very place.

"It is not the having but the getting! After the place bores them or is destroyed, they can *get* some other place. So what else is new?

"Maybe this is also why some of them chase after religious cults in such a relentless, frenetic, capitalistic way. They have a need not to *have* a spiritual life but to *get* some kind of experience. Many will try dozens of techniques, cults, and formulas, different brands to be consumed and tossed aside."

He paused and someone asked him, "What do we do with them?" Many people smiled or laughed to themselves.

"What do you do with them? For one thing, it's no good to set up a communist society. The Getting-Crazy People will shrewdly figure out that they can still wheel and deal. Sure, they will join the party! They will work their way up to leadership positions and become a new ruling class, getting new cars, new apartments, country estates, privileges of all kinds, just as in Russia. Or some will become scientists or technicians and join the technical-bureaucratic new rich.

"What can you do with them? They create a world of pornography, dancing naked girls, selling sex as a commodity, motels with piped-in X-rated movies, waterbeds, and vibrators, prostitution, Las Vegas, Reno, Tijuana, Gay Paree. Get some sex! Buy it! Sell it! Soon every house (maybe offices, too, and subway stations) will have robot crawl-in sex machines right next to the washer and dryer or the soft-drink dispensers. Psychologists will endorse the machines (it will protect young women, diminish sexual aggression)."

Discussion then ensued on this point for a while, but soon shifted back to an anthropology of white people. Marshall had a great many stimulating thoughts, not surprising for an Indian who had studied at the Sorbonne and had written plays in Cherokee.

"Right now, the Alcatraz Nation is negotiating with white bureaucrats and a political appointee of the vice president. What do you know about any of them? What do I know? What kind of people are they? It is highly likely that they are a part of, or at least work for, the Getting-Crazy culture I spoke of before.

"I'm not just talking about studying gun-carrying KKKers, or Nazis, or white vigilante groups. I'm not just talking about studying holy rollers or rattlesnake handlers. I'm talking about studying the Kissingers, Bundys, Rostows, Nixons, Erlichmans, and Johnsons, in short, the ruling class of leadership in this society."

That particular gathering also included an Iroquois young man who, although completely traditional in appearance, had traveled widely and was always setting forth deep thoughts. He rose and began speaking:

"Let's get back to the question of what can be done with white people. We may not have the power to *do* anything, but I have learned a lot about the study of Europeans by just dealing with the question.

"I'll tell you what. Let me describe an Indian and his ideas, or maybe I should say fantasies. Since my name is Joe, I'll call him Injun Joe. They could be my own daydreams, but I'll just say that they belong to Injun Joe, since I know they are shared by other fantasizers among us.

"Now this Injun Joe often daydreamed. Sometimes he would go back in time, in the spaceship of his mind, to the days of the Osceola, one hundred thirty years ago, when the Seminoles and their black allies were fighting for the simple right to have homeland. The Seminoles, Miccosukees, and their allies were great fighters, but Joe knew that there were too few Indians to defeat the whites in Florida. The available manpower could never be sufficient both to wage offensive warfare and to defend liberated zones. Joe's strategy was therefore to organize a large assault force that would trap and cut to pieces the major enemy units without, however, holding any territory. It would remain a mobile force, striking at will, disarming whites everywhere, but not setting up any garrisons. Its major purpose, after eliminating U.S. units in Florida, was to strike deep into Georgia, toward the Guale coast, in order to free and arm thousands of slaves.

"Joe was able to recruit several thousand Creeks, mixed-bloods, and freed slaves to join his main force. Rapidly this unit was supplemented by armed slave armies organized in Georgia. In this manner the white settlers in Florida, cut off from the North and mostly disarmed, were forced to flee to fortified positions. It was now they who were on the defensive; while the liberation armies were free to probe into Alabama and central Georgia.

"The U.S. government was caught off guard by the loss of its invading units in Florida, and this provided the liberation forces with the chance to move tens of thousands of freed slaves into Florida.

"Gradually, armed liberation units, using captured artillery pieces, were able to capture all of the invaders' positions in Florida (which is now called the Republic of Bimini). To the north, meanwhile, the slave population was rebelling throughout Georgia and Alabama, with guerilla units spreading also into South Carolina.

"In the meantime, Joe had set up an effective system of sending news bulletins to newspapers in Boston, New York, and Philadelphia. By this means it became clearly established in peoples' minds that the war was nothing more or less than a struggle between slave-owner imperialism, on the one hand, and freedom and justice, on the other. Would New England and the North support a war to crush the Indians and the other nonwhite people in order to advance the interests of the slave-owning classes?

"Joe knew that it didn't matter. The freedom fighters could get some help from New England, but the problem still remained that the slavocracy ran the federal government and that tens of thousands of whites from Kentucky, Tennessee, North Carolina, and so on would enroll in the militia in order to crush the hated red and brown and black niggers (and in order to get a chance at bounty land).

"The Bimini strategy was to remove all Indian and other nonwhite women and children of color from South Carolina, northern Georgia, and Alabama and send them either to Bimini itself or to safe regions in Guale and along the Appalachee River. Northern Georgia and Alabama were to serve as a no-man's-land buffer zone where whites were disarmed but otherwise left alone (most fled north) and where slavery ceased to exist.

"Another element in the Bimini strategy was to send out spies to locate places where the white governments were assembling militia units or stockpiling arms. These areas were then hit by mobile assault forces before the state troops were prepared or organized. A similar strategy was followed as regards the organizing of U.S. regular forces.

"The Bimini intelligence system was quite good. It had to be, since the freedom forces were the weaker party and their success hinged entirely upon preventing any large army from being fully organized.

"Gradually, as the ex-slaves and free Indians became more experienced and confident, and as thousands were armed with liberated weapons, it became possible to launch major rapid assaults into the tidewater of southside Virginia, North Carolina, and other areas where the slaves outnumbered more than half of the population. Guerrilla units were organized in many areas as the war zone expanded.

"Anyway, this was one of Joe's dreams. This one, like most of them, came up against some hard realities. What do you do with white people when you defeat them militarily? Joe was not about to adopt the white value system of enslavement and genocide. Still, many of the whites would be just as aggressive and villainous after conquest as before. They would scheme and plot and try to find ways to recover their lost empire. They were experienced at politics and knew how to organize. Few could be trusted.

"Joe hit on one plan: to divide up the rich planters' estates among poor and landless whites as well as among the ex-slaves. But would that really work? Would the poor whites appreciate having small farms of their own, or would they listen to the slave owners' propaganda of white racial superiority and unity?

"And, of course, another problem was, would the U.S. government *ever* agree to allow Indians and nonwhites to be free and independent? Could the USA ever tolerate a brown victory, or would it keep recruiting new white armies, one after another, to try to crush the injuns and niggers (even if this meant a war of genocidal intensity and ever-expanding character)?

"Joe realized that by the 1830s and 1840s it was too late for a real Indian victory. The whites were just too numerous. White families had ten or twelve children every generation, the women being little more than walking (working) incubators. Indian families usually had three or four children, and many died because of always being pressed against the wall of constant white aggression. The slave birthrate was higher than that of the Indian, but it, too, was being overwhelmed by the constant flood of European immigrants. In any case, the slaves were usually terrorized systemically and prevented from learning about things essential for effective rebellions.

"Joe's dreams often focused on earlier times, before the U.S. war for independence, for example, or he would shift the locale to Mexico. Sometimes Joe's great Indian alliance system was able to defeat the white colonial settlers, free the slaves, and establish a benign federal democracy (patterned after the Iroquois League). But the problem still remained—what to do with white people?

"If you had five hundred thousand, or a million, or two million whites under your control, how could you change their culture so that they would stop trying to get more wealth all the time? And they reproduced so fast that if you didn't watch out, they would be flooding into Indian regions by sheer numbers.

"Indian people traditionally are brought up to live in a democracy. They don't need big government, prisons, police, zoning commissions, investigative bodies, or things like that. They have small families and raise their children to be polite and observant, worship the Creator, and respect each other. So you can have a very loose confederacy insofar as Indians are concerned.

"But what can you do with a million (or more) restless, aggressive, materialistic, scheming, proliferating white people who like to break laws, don't respect other people, and consider themselves to be New Israelites, God's chosen people, destined to get whatever they want?

"That's a real dilemma, isn't it? Now, old Injun Joe realized that that was why the USA was not, and probably could never be, a democracy. Indians can live in freedom. Whites have to be controlled, or they will exploit each other. So every white state has to have a big government. If it doesn't, factory owners will enslave their workers, manufacturers will cheat (or poison) their customers, land speculators will get control of all the good land, railroads will charge whatever the traffic will bear, and the earth, water, and air will be raped, scraped, looted, and polluted.

"Of course, white people also have had big governments to help control slaves and to even invent (or at least okay) the idea that free Indians and Africans can be captured or bought and kept in chains forever from that day forth.

"So what do you do with them? Nobody knows. That's what the problem with U.S. politics is today, right now. The president doesn't know; he's one of them!

"So, anyway, what is Injun Joe going to do with white people in his dreams, in his fantasies? He's got them defeated, let's say, but how can he change them enough so that they can live in a democracy? Joe toyed with the idea of establishing Indian garrisons to control the whites and a totally Indian-run colonial administration to supervise them. But that idea bothered him. That's just what whites do to Indians.

"The bad thing about it, Joe thought, is that if native people had to have standing armies, police, and colonial officials to control the whites, they would have to change their own way of life to do so. What happened to the Mongols, the Manchus, the Turks, the Arabs, the Macedonians, the Greeks, the Romans? Injun Joe had studied history enough to know that ultimately empires enslave the victors as much as the defeated. He could not imagine a Black Elk, or a Tecumseh, or a Sitting Bull, or a Geronimo sitting around giving orders to white people, watching them, becoming fat and lazy off of other peoples' work. Indians were free, because they let others be free. Many white people were slaves to their own systems of exploitation. Sure, he thought, the rulers can have all the luxuries they want, but that only whets their appetites; they can have any slave woman they want, but that only corrupts their own natural sexuality, makes it into some kind of rape, the birth of sex as pornography.

"No, Indians must win, *but they cannot rule*, because to rule is to become a slave to the evil passions that come with secular power. The white people must be free, but how?

"Injun Joe's dreams led him to the conclusion that the only means available was to divide up the land in the liberated areas in such a way that every rural family, white, mixed, or black, had at least a forty-acre farm. These farms would be given out in such a manner that most areas would have blacks and browns mixed in with whites. Of course, the whites would outnumber the nonwhites about three to one overall, but during a transition period the former slave owners and other exploitative classes would be prohibited from holding office. Schools and colleges would favor nonwhite enrollment, and no whites could bear arms.

"Joe fantasized that immigration from Haiti, Mexico, and other nonwhite areas might gradually help increase the brownness of the race mixture, and cultural borrowing might blunt the hard edges of the European character. The result might be something like a Brazil or a Puerto Rico, a land full of mixed people but, and this was the big one, without the political oppression resulting from the uninterrupted economic and political power of white elites and the uninterrupted poverty and ignorance of the brown masses.

"Utopia, you say? A land of mixed-bloods in North America guided toward democracy by wise native guardians. Could it ever be? Could it ever have been?

"But Joe's dreams were not too far-fetched. Right there in Oklahoma, before 1890, it was happening in the Muscogee Creek Republic, and it happened in the Seminole Republic as well. Indians, blacks, whites, red-blacks, mulattoes, half-breeds, you name it, living together, intermarrying, sharing life, getting along, until the sacred treaties were broken and the white ruling class decided that brown people had no right to self-government anywhere in the territory of Yankee-Dixi-Doo. Paradise was plundered and terror replaced tolerance.

"What do you do with the Getting-Crazy People? If only they would leave you alone, or maybe they could find another planet (with lots of gold) and go there.

"In Joe's dreams there was always a place for good people of all races. He realized, in fantasy as in real life, that the majority of white people were not bad, that they were also victims. He tried in his dreams to fantasize ways that Indians could somehow communicate with these silent white people.

"He never found a way."

For a long time there was nothing but silence in the seminar. All of the people just sat there looking inward, vibrations of Injun Joe filling the room.

Marshall broke the silence: "Do Indians have dreams? You bet we do! How else could we have survived all these years?

"The white people have never known of our dreams, our fantasies. They think Indians just sit, staring into space, from the top of a mesa somewhere.

"Our dreams belong to us. Now the time has come to share them with each other and to see what we can do with them."

Ron Welburn

Ron Welburn (Cherokee-Assateague/Gingaskin) lives in Amherst, Massachusetts, where he is a professor of English and the director of Native American Studies at the University of Massachusetts-Amherst. For his book of essays, *Roanoke and Wampum: Topics in Native American Heritage and Literatures* (2001), he was a cowinner of the Wordcraft Circle Writer of the Year 2002 Award for Creative Prose (nonfiction category). He is the author of several volumes of poetry, including *Peripheries: Selected Poems, 1966–1968* (1972), *Brownup: Selected Poems* (1977), *The Look in the Night Sky* (1978), *Heartland: Selected Poems* (1981), *Council Decisions* (1990), and *Coming Through Smoke and the Dreaming* (2000). He also writes music reviews of jazz recordings for such periodicals as *Jazz Times* and *Down Beat*. Welburn was born April 30, 1943, in Berwyn, Pennsylvania, an area known historically as a stopping place for many mixed-blood southern Indian-blacks moving northward from their Delmarva Peninsula homelands after dispossession. He holds a doctorate in American Studies from New York University.

For a "Home" Girl

Without malice, I say
we have little of common origin.
What people do you mean
when you speak of unity?
Back in Chester county
some old families know little of "soul food" but tended
their beans and corn.

Several turtle and turkey people,
wild potato and wolf folks there
a generation ago lived close
to the horse.
We picked squash, not cotton,
south of West Chester.

Still, the benefit of tribes
escaped so many of us; take my
grandmother who only knows
that her parents and theirs are red;
take mother's father, continuing his
father's songs into a Cherokee wife.
Some of us always lived here
or followed deer who sought refuge
in this place between two rivers.
"Colored" became best for
the Drapers, the Bowers, Cooks and Swans,
the Grays and Tyres and the Wallses
and the Welburns.

It isn't simple speaking of cornrowing
or thin braids, but copperbrown people
whose women still part their course half
down the middle,
whose faces have weight and
force around the eyes;
a people who still select clothing
and houses, friends and lovers
in the Indian way.

The Mirror and the Hollywood Indian

Like coups, deceptions too catch us.
Once we belonged to nations and to tribes.
The idea of being part-Indian
belonged only to those who sought no alternatives.
On the homestead or the reserve
we knew what our names meant.
Leaving Nanticoke, Cherokee village,
Brandywine, the fringes of Robeson county,
the enclaves of Lenape stretched from
Jersey to Kansas, the Piscataway—
places, land that knows who we are,
Mashpee, the Ramapoughs, Schoharie county.

Then came the movies:
Italians and wigged huns

war-whooped and died at the feet of John Wayne,
bonnets streaming, yelling heap big
bad mouths; then along comes
a blue-eyed Geronimo; then we have
a speechless X Brand leaping off
rooftops in Derringer's New Orleans.

Into our mirrors we sought
that definition our families claimed,
hidden from many of us by snub noses
and rough hair.
We sought the Hollywood Indian
and did not see him.
We refused to see the eagle in ourselves.

Council Decisions

Is leaving our homeland what is left us?
Is leaving this our ancestry,
our bones soiled dust back to the womb?
So many decide to go.
Some stay.
We face upriver from this basin,
the Chesapeake.

The Haudenosaunee* fingers beckon down
the long river that snakes through high ridges.
Tuscarora have come this way and split their party,
some heading east to a mysterious Minisink refuge.
We cross parties of our brothers
the Lenape, moving too, westward.
We, Nanticoke and Conoy, band our flight northward.
Brother nations all.
The arrows we hold make no direction.
The circle our spirit makes softens like snow.

Up this great snake river
We guide our canoes laden with memories
and sorrow,
river water spraying our bitter faces.
We leave behind our family splinters

and seek Haudenosaunee welcome
at Otsiningo, a place where rivers meet.

We don't always understand Haudenosaunee
but respect them; know them well
over the firestick people who aim
to make us slaves, who push us from
our homes the way sea winds
drive the gulls to the mountains.
We aren't strangers to the river
but alien we are to forced movement
of upheaval, advanced by our sky
filling up with odd and ominous white clouds.
With our lands pillaged
Who do we say "Hakemey" to?
Who can we greet with welcome?
Faded spirits linger along the river.
At Otsiningo our turkey and turtle clans
observe the Haudenosaunee welcome and listen
and renew the pipe of friendship.
What will appease the faded spirits
as they wander up and down the Susquehannock's river
like lost hunters drifting on the White Path?

The Spirit World touches
living delegates
to pilgrimage to Otsiningo,
place where Chenango meets the Minquas' river.
We go in advance of blackberry moon.
We find no answers of family ties
but peace and the spirit of gathering,
the smiles of friendship and
the laughter that breaks winter.
Haudenosaunee gather there and
we Conoy and Nanticoke and others all
renew the council songs.

*"Haudenosaunee" is a spelling of the traditional name of the Five Nations of the
Iroquois, which met with Conoy and Nanticoke at Otsiningo in the early 18th
century.

Grandfather's Warclub

A crude piece of polished wood,
seasoned and too short to be a cane,
lives with my mother,
having outlasted my father,
and her father its giver.
One does not hold it
by its head, a smooth knee-bone;
its handle, nearly two-feet long,
is to brandish
the curious long-headed knob
harder than a stone.
It is grandfather's warclub,
Mother's father's father
patterned upon legacy
the Mohawks learned on the Piscataway.
Its name is Conoy, and I have
never seen it in flight,
though I'm sure
grandfather remembered it,
1927 or thereabouts,
when Berwyn jailed him
to segregate its schools.

Spiderwoman Theater

Spiderwoman Theater was founded in 1975 by three sisters—Lisa Mayo, Gloria Miguel, and Muriel Miguel (Kuna-Rappahannock)—the daughters of a Rappahannock woman from Virginia and a Kuna man from the San Blas Islands of Panama. "Spiderwoman" refers to the Hopi deity who created men and women through her ingenious art of tapestry and who continues to assist humans in maintaining balance in all things. The sisters were born and raised in New York City, and their writings and dramatic productions reflect the situations of urban Indian people. Their plays, such as *Sun Moon and Feather* (featured here in the anthology) and others that have been produced through their group, mirror modern-day Indian life with rollicking humor and sharp satire, as well as genuine pathos. In their formative years each of the sisters pursued her own artistic direction. Lisa trained as a mezzo-soprano, then studied dance with Uta Hagen and musical comedy with Charles Nelson Reilly. Gloria studied drama at Oberlin College. Muriel began her career as a dancer before joining Joseph Chaiken and his avant-garde improvisational company, Open Theater. In addition to *Sun Moon and Feather,* which premiered in 1981, Spiderwoman has written, produced, and enacted *Women in Violence* (1975), *Reverb-ber-ber-rations* (1991), *Power Pipes* (1992), and *Winnetou's Snake Oil Show from Wigwam City* (1999), as well as other plays. In 1997, an honorary Doctor of Fine Arts was awarded to each of the three sisters at Miami University. During this same occasion, a commercial video of *Sun Moon and Feather* was made during a live performance of the play at the university. Muriel's daughter, Monique Mojica, also a playwright and actress, is the author of *Princess Pocahontas and the Blue Spots* and *Birdwoman and the Suffragettes: The Story of Sacajawea.*

Sun Moon and Feather

About the Play: Sun Moon and Feather *premiered at the New Foundland Theater, New York, in 1981. It was directed by Muriel Miguel. Since then, it has toured extensively, including performances at Theater for the New City, New York; New York Feminist Art Institute; Women's Theater Festival, Boston; Trent University, Ontario, Canada; Helsinki, Finland; Frankfurt, Germany; Harbor Front, Toronto, Canada; First Indigenous Women's Conference, Adelaide, Australia; Sister Fire, Washington, D.C.; Centro Cultural de la Raza, San Diego, California; the New WORLD*

Theater, Amherst, Massachusetts; The Onandaga Indian Reservation; Aspen Institute, Colorado; At the Foot of the Mountain, Minneapolis, Minnesota; the Arts Festival of Atlanta; Arizona State University; the Oneida Nation; and Miami of Ohio University, among others.

Characters

Lisa Mayo/Elizabeth
Gloria Miguel
Muriel Miguel

Setting

A large patchwork backdrop, made of cloth pieces called *molas*, and including material from our tribe. Attached to the backdrop is a white bed sheet which serves as a movie screen. The projector is placed in the audience. It is an old projector, 16mm, used for film without sound. What we hear is the sound of the projector.

The feeling is of being at home looking at home movies.

Authors' Note

The title *Sun Moon and Feather* is taken from parts of our native names. The play is performed on three levels. A taped discussion on poverty and home movies filmed by our Uncle Joseph Henry accompanies the staged performance.

I

Pink gels wash the backdrop and stage. There is a chair center stage facing stage left. Another chair stage right midstage. Next to the chair is a small basket; in it is a small mola, a Kuna rattle, a calabash, and a rag doll. Also a pair of shoes. Another chair is placed stage left downstage, facing toward mid-stage.

Audience out, stage lights dim, Poverty tape on. No one is on stage. Only the tape is heard. Five beats. Mozart's K.546 Adagio and Fugue in C minor on. (Poverty tape.)

You were only 13
He didn't believe she was 13
I said she was 17
And he said look at the moon.

And she was only 13
I was 15
And you know
I looked at the moon
We were lost in Brooklyn
Remember the guys who left us off?
Way way in another part of town
Oh God
That was really terrible
That was really treading on thin ice
We ended up in the depths of some god awful neighborhood.

Hello pretty one you have 10 cents for me?
Oh my. I have everything except for 10 cents
What do you need 10 cents for
For the machine
It's only 10 cents
No two quarters and a 10 cents I don't have 10 cents
Oh yeah
What you oughta do is take another 60 cents.
Just in case your coat doesn't yet dry
I had a lotta change but I don't have 10 cents.
They didn't give me that.
I don't have 10 cents either I only have two nickels
Oh I probably have it.
Look in that bottle
There's 10 cents on the floor in that big bottle of money
How do you know that Gloria?
She's been looking at my bottle
Can I take a dime from there
Yeah I was going to see what I have in there
Have you another two quarters

I have no more dimes
She has lots of dimes
Here these are dimes
It's the same as 10 cents
Yes *(Laughter.)*
Hurry up and wash your coat
What did you give her?

These are all hers she has lots of dimes
You have plenty of them.
I didn't know one dime was the same as 10 cents that's all *(Laughter.)*
A dime and 10 cents are the same.

(Poverty tape continues.)

LISA

So we were talking about that layer of worthlessness, selflessness, coming out of being poor, being dirty, not having enough to eat.

GLORIA.

There wasn't much hope. When you came home after school to a cold house, no food, a drunken father, a depressed mother, a neighborhood that's very hostile to you.

LISA

What is there? It's horrible. How did we make it?

GLORIA

A dirty house with bedbugs.

LISA

We used to clean the house ourselves. When we tried to clean the house they would get so upset. Mama gave up. Mama gave up a long time ago.

MURIEL.

I used to wish that we had six o'clock dinner like everybody else. At six o'clock I would be sitting around and all the kids would be gone in to eat. I would still be sitting on the stoop.

LISA

Where was our family? When did you eat?

MURIEL.

Anytime somebody made food I ate. It was strange because in a way that was good, you weren't programmed like everyone else was. That's how it is in Italy. Six o'clock dinner. You hear the sound of knives and forks, clinking of dishes. It smells so good. Didn't it smell so good? I wished I could stay and have school lunch because it was so impossible, she would give me these meals. I would have tomato soup for a month. And the reason I hate oatmeal. I had oatmeal for breakfast and oatmeal for lunch, for I don't know, for months. Whenever I see oatmeal or smell it I get so angry, I hate oatmeal.

Halfway through the tape the film comes on. The film is beautiful. It shows all of our uncles and our father. Beautiful Indian faces. Then shots of the lovely islands that they come from. The San Blas Islands, home of the Kuna nation. The juxtaposition of that sad tape and the lovely island where they come from. The worry about money in the city against a coconut culture. The wonderment: How did they get here? How did they survive?
(Poverty tape is on and film is on.)

LISA *enters wearing a light green, low-cut nightgown, hose to match, and silver high heels. She sits on center stage chair. There is a sad aura about her. She sits looking straight in front of her like she is looking out a window. Ten beats later* MURIEL *enters stage right wearing a tea-dipped rayon dress over a many-tiered petticoat that shows through an opening in front of her skirt, ruffled sparkly blue socks over light pink hose and back med-high Baby Janes. She wears a pop bead necklace and has one side of her hair caught up in a pony tail with a bow. She sits in chair stage left mostly out of the light. She is watchful.* GLORIA *enters from audience. She is wearing a tattered dark blue lace dress mended in places with red patches. Her hair is in ponytails on the sides of her head. She is barefoot and is dragging a red net.*

(Mozart tape is on, simultaneous with Poverty tape and film) GLORIA *is play-acting as if she is alone in a room. She is dragging the net with great effort as if it is a heavy burden, i.e., Jesus Christ with cross. It is a child's fantasy, and on another level a dance a la Isadora Duncan, and on another level transformation with one item. It is very, very, very dramatic.*

She climbs up on stage, drags the net stage left and upstage to center stage where she trips. The film goes off. She lowers the net, unloading a heavy burden. She puts the net over her head and it becomes a bridal veil and she walks downstage center. She becomes a Madonna, unveils one hand, and begs for pity and mercy. With both hands she claws and searches the net for an escape, then pushes the net as if under great pressure and fights until the pressure wins and bends her knees. She takes the net off. The net becomes a rope and she twists it around her body. She pulls both ends, squeezing the life out of her, then hangs herself. Next she throws it on the floor. The net becomes blood on the sand and she steps back in fear. She runs on it and pokes it with her toe. She lifts up the net with her toe. Then she carries the net in her arms like a dead child. The net becomes a majestic cape and she walks like a queen around in a circle. She walks downstage center and puts the net across her right arm and raises her arm. The net becomes a curtain to hide behind. She pulls the curtain back and peeks out fast. She peeks out again and slowly pulls the curtain back and slowly looks out and gets scared by ELIZABETH (LISA).

While GLORIA *is pushing the net* ELIZABETH *starts to move. All the next action is performed simultaneously.*

ELIZABETH *gets up and goes to stage right. She pulls in a duffel bag that contains a sleeping bag, seven stuffed dolls and animals, and a long pink cloth. She pulls with great effort like it is laden with burdens and responsibilities and places it center stage. She is very excited and busy. Then she gets a chair stage right with a basket and places it center stage. She takes her chair and places it stage left. Both chairs are now facing downstage. She gets a second duffel bag and places it next to her chair. She opens up the first duffel bag and takes out the sleeping bag and places it between the two chairs downstage. She takes out the stuffed animals and dolls and places them on the sleeping bag. She places two stocking dolls near her chair. She takes out the pink cloth very quietly and sneaks up behind* GLORIA *and scares the shit out of her.* GLORIA *screams and* ELIZABETH *laughs uproariously. Both tapes go off and lights bump up.*

GLORIA

Don't laugh! That's not funny. She always made fun of me. You're too slow, dummy. Here, let me do it. I'm much better than you are.

LISA

Dummy. Here take this. *(Hands her the pink cloth.)*

GLORIA

What's the use? Who cares. Doesn't matter anyway. *(Takes pink cloth. From this point* GLORIA *tries to do everything opposite of what* LISA *wants. She twists the cloth, punches the dolls, throws the napkins and plates.)*

LISA

(Tries to get GLORIA *to fold cloth.)* Pull it out now. Hold it still. Gloria don't twist it. Now take this end. Take it, hold it tight. Gloria do it nice. Now put all the dolls on here. Put them on nice. No don't do that I said put them on nice. *(Crying.)* You can't do that. Now everybody has to have a place. You hear me? Don't throw them like that. It's not nice. *(Goes to second duffel bag and pulls out brown paper towels.)* Gloria, do you see what we have here? *(*GLORIA, *sitting on floor near chair, has taken out her ponytails and put on her shoes; she places the mola on the floor and puts the doll in the calabash. She undresses the doll, washes the doll, and the doll pees. She spies the paper*

napkins that LISA has, takes one and wipes the doll's bottom.) Gloria, look, pure damask linen napkins. All hand rolled. Wonderful. Everybody must have one of these. Do it nice. I said nice. *(Takes out two empty plastic plates.)* Gloria, Gloria, look, do you see? This plate has cream puffs all piled high and filled with whipped cream and all covered with chocolate. And this plate has crumpets. These are crumpets. They are warm and the butter is melting. Gloria you must give everybody one. One cream puff and one crumpet. Gloria, but nice. Oh God! You're going to ruin this party for me. I said do it nice, you hear? *(Takes plastic cups from duffel bag.)* Gloria. Gloria look. Look at this—absolutely the most delicate china that was made in the world. So delicate. It's so fine you can see straight through it. And it's all hand-dipped. And we're the only family in North America with hand-dipped china. *(Gives them to GLORIA who throws cups at dolls. LISA takes out a small plastic measuring cup.)* Gloria, look, a cream pitcher and it's blue and white, it's Delft and the cream is so thick you can eat it with a spoon. Gimme your hand. *(She gives GLORIA the cup.)* Everybody must get cream. Don't ruin my party. *(Takes out plastic double-end measuring cup.)* Gloria look, do you see what we have here? Gloria this teapot comes all the way from China and it has all sorts of writing on it in gold AND it's from the Ming dynasty. Gloria, look, it's a magic teapot. This teapot is never empty because if it's empty, you just turn it over and it's full again. So wonderful! Now everybody gets tea. *(She puts tea in the cups on the floor.)* You must keep your pinky up like this and talk fancy. *(Sits down with a panda and a stocking doll, a napkin and a teacup. Gives tea to her dollies and whispers to them.)*

GLORIA

(Playing with doll.) Elizabeth, do you remember when Aunt Ida and Uncle George and Uncle Frank used to talk to you and leave me home? I used to sit at the window for hours wondering, why couldn't I go? There you were all dressed up with a big bow in your hair, going out and I had to stay home. I used to think there was something terribly wrong with me.

LISA

(Playing with her dolls.) I was sitting in the backyard with my dolls and my baby carriage and Aunt Lizzy came in to the yard carrying a bundle. She went over to the baby carriage and put the bundle in it and said, "You're not the baby anymore." I went over and I looked in and there was a baby in there and I wanted to smash it. That was the first time I ever saw my sister Gloria. *(Throws doll at GLORIA then waits five beats.)* My family lived in a big compound in Brooklyn and they never went out of the house. My grand-

father bounced me on his knee and my grandmother sang hymns and folk songs and she said I was one of them.

GLORIA

(Still playing with her doll.) Sunshine, bright sunshine. Morning glories. Beautiful red and yellow morning glories. They grew all along the backyard fence and up the side of the house. My mother and I would pick them and put them in bowls of water and decorate the house with them. I helped mama clean the house. We had fun together. *(She sings and splashes the doll in imaginary water in calabash.)* Ramona wooshie wooshie wooshie woo. On Sunday afternoon all daddy's friends and relations from San Blas would visit and I was allowed to play with them. They would talk Kuna. I didn't understand them. *Ige benuga, be a beni. E be nueti.* They called me Tuli girl. *(Sings)* Tăge. Tăge.* *(Film up: scenes of the family in the backyard waving and playing with baby MURIEL.)*

LISA

I am the granddaughter of Elizabeth Ashton Mourn, a beautiful Rappahannock Indian woman from West Moreland county, Virginia. My great-grandmother Felicia was a midwife and she taught my grandmother how to deliver babies. My grandmother delivered me and both my sisters. *(Sings to herself.)*

> Oh are-re-vy.
> My mother gave me to the witch
> Oh Why
> Oh are-re-vy
> *(Continues softly under GLORIA.)*
> The dust goes up in the sun
> The sun shines on my hands
> Oh Why

(MURIEL gets up, walks upstage, crosses stage right, and stands in front of the film. She watches.)

GLORIA

See here! That child belongs to me. She's no savage. She's a Spencer. She belongs here with me. She belongs here with me. *(She cradles doll and taps heavily on doll's chest with rattle and sings Kuna lullaby).* Lay Lay Lay Lay Lay Lay Lay. *(Sings as a young child.)* Lay Lay Lay Lay Lay Lay Lay. *(Sings as a mother.)* Lay Lay Lay Lay Lay Lay Lay. *(Sings as a grandmother.)*

*Tăge: Pronounced ta-gay.

(MURIEL walks center stage, sits on sleeping bag and pink cloth, grabs stuffed toys, and bangs them on floor, crying like a hurt child.)

MURIEL

I am the only child of my two sisters. I am covered with love and very lonely. I have two friends Paby and Kalleewiko. No one else can see them. I am the only child of my two sisters. My mother never talks to me. I live in a house with my mother and father. I'm covered with love and very lonely. I am the only child of my two sisters. *(Covers her head with cloth.)*

LISA

(Grabs MURIEL to her knee, removes cloth.) I want her to be happy. *(Takes tissue, cleans MURIEL's nose.)* I wanted her to be an Indian and carry on the tradition of the family, so I could leave.

(GLORIA gestures that she wants MURIEL. LISA throws MURIEL to GLORIA; GLORIA cleans MURIEL's face, smooths her hair.)

GLORIA

I wanted her to be happy. I wanted her to be clean. I wanted her to be educated. I wanted her to be cultured. *(She and LISA fight over MURIEL. They pull her by her arms like she is a doll.)* Let's take her for a walk. *(Pull.)*

LISA

Oh yeah? *(Pull.)*

GLORIA

I'll take her to the ballet. *(Pull.)*

LISA

I'll teach her folk dancing. *(She swings MURIEL upstage. MURIEL stays there at backdrop, back to audience. LISA is upstage left, back to audience.)*

GLORIA

(Downstage center.) The day Muriel was born, I met my father coming down the steps. He was carrying a large white basin. It contained blood. I helped my father bury the placenta under a tree in the backyard. *(She sits center stage right.)*

LISA

(Turns, walks downstage.) When I left my first husband, I went to live with my younger sister Muriel. She got me my first date. I came home all excited, "He wants to make love to me." She said, "So? Do you like him?" I said, "I'm

not sure." She said, "Well, if you like him, make love to him. If you don't, don't. Why do you have to make things so complicated?" *(To* GLORIA*)* How does it make you feel when your baby sister steals the limelight? *(Sits stage left.)*

GLORIA

I don't care. She can have the limelight. I'm really very proud of Muriel. But sometimes I feel lonely when I'm with her. I think my presence makes her face something she doesn't want to face. I fear I'm part of the burden she wants to drop. I don't know why but I'm afraid I'll lose her.

(Film off. MURIEL *does a strange little dance rubbing her legs and crouching like she is in agony.)*

MURIEL

Jerry. Jerry. The car turned over and over. I felt his body shake against me. Elizabeth, Gloria, he's dead, he's dead!!! *(Freezes.)*

GLORIA

I wrote your name on the sand. Suddenly a wave came and washed it away. Your name isn't there anymore.

Oh, why is there always such an air of sadness about me?

*(*MURIEL *relaxes and stands behind* GLORIA*'s chair.* LISA *sees how sad they are and tries to cheer them up. Again it is a transformation. Out of nowhere she starts to pluck an imaginary guitar.)*

LISA

(Sings.) Plunky Plunky Plunky Plunk

*(*GLORIA *looks at* MURIEL, *cheers up, and plays an imaginary muted trumpet.* MURIEL *reluctantly gets pulled in, plays an imaginary bass.)*

GLORIA

(Sings.) We three, were all alone

MURIEL

(Talks.) Were all alone.

GLORIA

(Sings.) Living in a memory

MURIEL

(Talks.) All memories

GLORIA

(*Sings.*) My echo, my shadow and me

MURIEL

(*Gestures.*) My echo, my shadow and me

GLORIA

(*Sings.*) We three, we're not a crowd

MURIEL

(*Talks.*) Not four, but three

GLORIA

(*Sings.*) We're not even company

MURIEL

(*Talks.*) I love you baby

GLORIA

(*Sings.*) My echo, my shadow and me

MURIEL

(*Gestures.*) My echo, my shadow and little old me

(*All three sing and dance.*)

What good is the moonlight
The silvery moonlight, that shines above

LISA

Plunky Plunky Plunk

ALL

I walk with my shadow, talk with my echo.
But where is the one that I love.

(ALL *repeat chorus singing and humming in harmony.* LISA *and* MURIEL *continue to hum while they clear the stage of cloth sleeping bag, plastic cups, etc.* GLORIA *does not participate; she just watches.* LISA *and* MURIEL *find plastic cups and toast each other. Everything is placed stage left.*)

GLORIA

I'm leaving. (*She is ignored. A little louder, still ignored.*) I'm leaving! (*Shouting, startles* MURIEL) I'm leaving!!!

MURIEL

Why don't you just go. *(To* LISA.*)* She always does that. *(*GLORIA *exits behind white sheet.)*

*(*LISA *discovers net and plays with it while she sings and hums Massenet's Élégie.* MURIEL *is still clearing the stage. She watches* LISA *and is frustrated that* LISA *is not helping.* MURIEL's *and* LISA's *lines are from Chekhov's* Three Sisters.*)*

MURIEL

I have a craving for work. Just as one has a craving for water on a hot summer day. I have a craving for work. If I don't get up early and go to work, give me up as a friend.

LISA

Father trained us to get up at seven. Now Muriel wakes at nine and lies in bed til twelve thinking and looking so serious.

*(*MURIEL *sets up three plastic bags stage left next to her chair. She pulls out old-fashioned, circa 1950, purses, gloves, hat and one brocade jacket for* LISA.*)*

MURIEL

You still think of me as a little girl. That's why it seems so strange to see me serious.

*(*LISA *does double take, realizes she hurt* MURIEL's *feelings. She tries to find a way to express her love. She sings, tweaking* MURIEL's *nose, pinching her cheeks, pokes her in the belly, and finally kisses her.)*

LISA

> For I love you truly, truly dear.
> Life with its sorrows.
> Life with its fears, fades into dawn:
> When you do appear
> For I love you truly, truly dear.

MURIEL

(Excited.) Gloria's coming! Gloria's coming! *(Film on.)* I can hardly wait to see her!

*(*GLORIA *punches sheet from behind. She makes grand entrance. She is walking down a huge staircase. She hears applause; everybody loves her. She tap dances a la Fred Astaire.* LISA *and* MURIEL *compete for her attention.)*

LISA

I saw a bird of paradise and thought of you.

MURIEL

I saw a red nose and I thought of you.

LISA

I saw Gloria coming down the stairs and I was so happy to see her.

GLORIA

(Tap dancing.) Are you happy to see me? That makes me so happy to know that you're happy to see me.

MURIEL

I made a beautiful cake just for you.

GLORIA

(Takes cake, dumps it, does a few ballroom turns.) A beautiful cake just for me?

LISA

Now that I've met you, I don't care if I die tomorrow for I will have fulfilled all my fondest hopes and desires.

GLORIA

(Stops dancing.) Say it over and over. It's like diamonds in my ears.

MURIEL

I'll fight battles for you, stop bullets for you, lie for you, steal for you, die for you, all this I will die with the greatest joy.

GLORIA

(A la Katherine Hepburn with a few tango steps.) Love me but don't die for me or I'll be bereft of feeling.

LISA

I trust you so implicitly, we don't have to be together.

GLORIA

I love you so much, I'd stay in a room forever and only go out for fresh air and water.

MURIEL

Of all my girls, I love you most, Gloria. That's my girl.

LISA

(Pokes MURIEL in the belly.) And she has a beautiful voice and don't you forget it.

(*LISA and MURIEL go upstage to backdrop, backs to audience.*)

GLORIA

I love you Mimi Mama. Never let me go. (*Moves center stage.*) He said "Goodbye, Desert Rose," and gave me a long lingering kiss. He walked down the street, out of sight and I never saw him again. I never get that kind of love anymore. Maybe I get that kind of love and don't recognize it. No! No! If I did get that kind of love I'd be happy. I wrote your name on the water and the sand washed it away. (*Crying.*) Oh! I'm all mixed up. My life is a failure. What's the use, who cares, it doesn't matter anyway.

(*LISA at first is laughing at GLORIA then becomes concerned at GLORIA's reaction. GLORIA is bawling. MURIEL thinks it is amusing, does not care, thinks GLORIA is silly.*)

LISA

There. There. Calm down. (*To MURIEL*) Get her some water, she's crying. (*Gets a chair for GLORIA, and one for herself; both sit stage right. MURIEL still laughs.*)

GLORIA

You don't know how I suffer. I suffer. I really suffer. I suffer in my bones, my bowels, my kidneys, the ends of my hair, my fingernails.

LISA

I suffer much much more than you. You don't know what suffering is. My ears suffer, my eyelashes, my belly button suffers.

(*MURIEL reluctantly brings water.*)

LISA

Here's your water.

GLORIA

(*Snarling, slaps MURIEL's hand.*) I don't want your old water.

(*MURIEL watches the two of them then walks downstage. She happily tells what she sees.*)

MURIEL

She's crying. She's suffering. Great big balls of water are dripping down her cheeks. She's suffering. (*She giggles, walks back to them, and watches. Then she realizes she has the space to herself and tells her own story. She walks stage left and mimes opening a door.*) I opened the door. Oh! Hi. Nice to meet.

(Ogles make-believe person.) Oh you're with her. I'm tired. I'm going to bed. *(Sits on the floor, looks up surprised.)* It's all right you can come in. I'm not very tired. *(Indicates stage left.)* You can sit over there. *(Follows with eyes from stage right to stage left, stares.)* She is really very beautiful. *(Seductive.)* A Leo. You know a lion. *(Growls, laughs.)* An actress. Spiderwoman Theater. It's a feminist theater group. She's really very beautiful. If I look at you, will you look at me? If I touch you, will you touch me? Does she like me? *(Follows with eyes stage left to stage right.)* Hey, where are you going. It's all right. You can stay.

LISA

When I first saw them together, I felt sick to my stomach.

GLORIA

Whatever happened to the blond fellow, the one with the long legs?

MURIEL

(Following with eyes stage right to stage left.) Are you stoned or drunk? Oh both. Yeah I'll smoke. *(Lies down on back, throws legs up and wiggles.)* I'll just lie here and we can talk. *(Sits up fast, follows with eyes stage left to stage right.)* Hey where are you going? It's all right. You can stay.

LISA

When Gloria first found out, she cried all night.

GLORIA

What happened? What went wrong? I don't want her to be that way.

LISA AND GLORIA

Gay.

MURIEL

(Looks stage left.) Look at me. Do you like me? *(Follows with eyes stage left to stage right.)* Hey where are you going? It's all right you can stay.

GLORIA

It doesn't matter. I love her anyway.

LISA

I love her.

MURIEL

(Follows with eyes stage right to center stage on knees, arms up, moving downstage.) You're leaving? *(Arms up for a hug, lips pursed for a kiss. Disappointed, drops arms and shakes hand.)* Good night.

LISA

(*To* GLORIA, *demanding*) You have to listen to me. I am sister number one. I am twenty months away from you. (*Measures with hands between her and* GLORIA.) Like this. (*To* MURIEL.) And you, you never listen to me. I am years away from you. (*Measures between her and* MURIEL.) Like this. (*Fast transformation.*) Oooo!! Let's have a tea party!

(ALL *run stage left to plastic bags,* ELIZABETH *dons jacket, hat, and gloves. She gets purse and plastic measuring cups, pours tea.* GLORIA *dons hat and string of beads. Gets purse and plastic cup.* MURIEL *dons hat and gloves, gets purse and plastic cup.*)

LISA

(*With a make-believe English accent.*) The Queen is coming to tea and we must talk very fancy. Hold your pinky up like this. We must talk on lofty subjects. I was so cunning. My Aunt Ida had a little round box and in that box she kept my brown silky ringlets all tied up with a pink ribbon.

(MURIEL *pays no attention, hums to herself, drinks tea.*)

GLORIA

Yuck.

MURIEL

There she goes again.

GLORIA

Why bring her up?

LISA

Why not? She's my friend, isn't she?

GLORIA

That's not necessarily true.

LISA

I really don't agree with you.

GLORIA

I have to think my own thoughts.

LISA

That's the way you think. I don't.

GLORIA

That's my truth.

LISA

I've got to get out of here. *(To* MURIEL, *startling her.)* You never listen to me.

GLORIA

(To MURIEL.*)* You turned your back on me.

MURIEL

(To GLORIA.*)* What were you doing behind me?

GLORIA

You walked in front of me.

MURIEL

I really hate that about you.

GLORIA

You didn't want to be with me.

MURIEL

(Jumps up, goes toward GLORIA.*)* Do you think I left you out on purpose?

GLORIA

(To LISA.*)* You didn't give me any tea.

LISA

I did too.

MURIEL

No you didn't.

GLORIA

You always leave me out.

LISA

Oh yeah?

GLORIA

Yeah.

MURIEL

Yeah.

LISA

Why are you two so mean to me?

GLORIA

Tell the truth.

LISA

If I let you, you two will put me into the ground.

GLORIA

You two don't understand me. You never understood me.

LISA

Oh yeah?

GLORIA

Yeah. (*GLORIA throws bag. Big fight. MURIEL holds LISA; GLORIA kicks and scratches LISA. MURIEL yells.*)

MURIEL

Leggo, leggo.

> (*LISA breaks away from MURIEL. Throws her upstage. Throws MURIEL's chair upstage center and throws herself on floor, yelling and crying.*)

LISA

I hate you bitches. Hope you both die!

> (*GLORIA gloats. Takes gloves off, throws them on LISA.*)

GLORIA

Elizabeth. Elizabeth. Daddy's coming.

LISA

(*Still crying.*) Don't talk to me. Get away from me.

GLORIA

(*Kicking LISA.*) Is he drunk? Elizabeth is he drunk?

LISA

He's drunk! He's drunk!

GLORIA

Tell Mama not to fight.

LISA

Don't fight Mama. Don't fight.

GLORIA

Get the baby!

LISA

Get the baby. Hide the baby.

(GLORIA gets MURIEL and places her on chair center stage. LISA and GLORIA stand in front of MURIEL to hide her.)

GLORIA

Daddy came home drunk and he started to fight with Mama.

LISA

Don't fight with Mama. *(MURIEL makes fighting sounds.)*

GLORIA

We were in the bedroom. There was a noise in the dining room. Daddy was drunk and Mama began to fight with him. Then Mama called, "Girls, girls, help me. Help me." We ran into the dining room. Daddy had one leg out the window, both legs out the window.

LISA AND GLORIA

Don't jump Daddy. Don't jump. *(MURIEL still making angry noises.)*

GLORIA

Mama jumped up and pulled the window down. Mama grabbed Daddy by the waist, we grabbed Mama, and we pulled and pulled him down to the floor.

(LISA, GLORIA, and MURIEL stay in tableau of pulling position for three beats, then MURIEL pops up.)

MURIEL

(Takes off gloves, clears space.) Okay. Line up.

(They line up, LISA stage left, GLORIA stage right; MURIEL goes into the middle.)

GLORIA

Oh no! Muriel. I belong in the middle, that's my rightful place. *(She gets between LISA and MURIEL; MURIEL goes to the other side of LISA.)* Muriel, I belong in the middle. Mama always said Gloria is second born, she belongs in the middle. *(MURIEL steps out of line, looks at situation.)*

MURIEL

Gloria, it would look better if I were in the middle.

(LISA and MURIEL line up together; they look smug. GLORIA looks enraged. GLORIA waits two beats, then lines up with MURIEL in the middle.)

MURIEL

Every summer my family went to the beach. We had a beautiful red and white bungalow on a beautiful beach by a beautiful bay.

(*GLORIA gives MURIEL an incredulous look.*)

GLORIA

Cedar Beach. A dilapidated bungalow in New Jersey on a dirty beach off a dirty polluted bay.

LISA

There was a fish house and twice a day there was a godawful odor.

MURIEL

My father bought a great big red and white boat with a great big windshield and a great big motor.

LISA

That boat was a little bigger than a rowboat and it had a motor in it that never worked.

GLORIA

And Daddy and Uncle Joe set about to make the boat seaworthy.

MURIEL

My father would stand at the helm of that boat with his brown safari hat and his wooden staff and he'd look out over the ocean. He was going to sail the seven seas.

LISA

The only trouble was 'em—

ALL

It never went into the water.

GLORIA

It just stayed in the backyard.

MURIEL

And every summer, my father would paint it, caulk it, pet it, hose it down; then all our friends and family would come. (*ALL push very hard stage left.*) And we would—

ALL

Puuush it. To the other side of the yard.

GLORIA

Then we would pose by it, on it and under it. (*ALL strike poses like being photographed by boat.*) And Daddy and Uncle Joe would stand at the helm and pretend.

LISA

And then next summer, my father would paint it, caulk it, hose it down, then all our friends and all our family would come. *(ALL push stage right.)* And we would—

ALL

Puuush it. To the other side of the yard.

GLORIA

Then we would pose by it, on it and under it *(ALL strike poses.)* And Daddy and Uncle Joe would stand at the helm and pretend. And the next summer, my father would paint it, caulk it, pet it, hose it down; then all our friends and all our family would come. *(ALL push stage center.)* And we would—

ALL

Puuush it to the other side of the yard.

MURIEL

Then one summer, it was ready to go into the water.

LISA

My mother gave a party. She made potato salad, punch, and sandwiches.

GLORIA

All our friends and family—*(ALL push downstage center.)*

ALL

Puuushed it into the water—*(ALL stare at the same spot on stage.)*

MURIEL

It started to take on water—

LISA

It was like a sieve—

MURIEL

We had to bail out the water—

GLORIA

And then it sank.

(ALL staring at the same spot.)

LISA

Then Daddy said, oh well. Next summer. *(ALL shrug.)*

(*LISA and MURIEL go upstage, clean up stage. GLORIA goes center stage. LISA and MURIEL stand very close together upstage center.*)

GLORIA

To squeeze, squeeze o, squeeze as, squeeze a, squeeze amos, squeeze ais, squeeze at.

> *GLORIA tries to squeeze in between MURIEL and LISA. She pries them apart, lets them go and they rebound off each other. She finally squeezes in. She stares eye level stage left which makes LISA and MURIEL look.*
>
> *The look: This is about a hostile environment. Having your antennae out if one sister feels threatened. They give the impression of being three cats using all their senses to smell out their enemy. Using only their eyes and a slight turning of their heads, they spot five places out in the audience, then a slow count stage right using only eyes then a quick return to center audience. They gather all their energy and walk as a unit towards the audience. They are strong but also menacing, invulnerable. The soft spot: The sisters are vulnerable, sometimes naive and innocent. The question here is, should you let your guard down? Do you take the risk? What happens when you do? This is all performed in sound, movement, and words, simultaneously. They use questions that have previously got them into trouble or hurt.*

LISA

Why did you ask that question? What's the matter? You have a funny look on your face. (*Gets punched in the stomach.*)

MURIEL

Oh! You look funny. What's wrong? (*Gets pushed in chest.*)

GLORIA

Is that true? How is that possible? My thoughts are— (*Gets hit on shoulder, hit in belly, spun around. This is repeated until GLORIA as catalyst starts next segment, picks up chair, and sits center stage.*) Bored. Bored. Bored. Bored.

> (*LISA and MURIEL place chairs on both sides of GLORIA. They crowd each other. MURIEL shakes her leg and disturbs GLORIA who tries to stop her. LISA places her hand on top of GLORIA's. GLORIA places her hand on top of LISA's. They get tangled up. They are pulling and pushing against each other.*)

GLORIA

When I grow up I'm going to marry a man from far away, from way across the sea AND he's going to take me away from all this and I'll never come back again.

LISA

I'm going to marry a rich man and he's going to give me things like a fur coat and a refrigerator full of food.

MURIEL

I'm going to get me an apartment.
I'm going to get me an apartment.

(They slowly relinquish their grip on each other and do a tap chair dance and sing.)

ALL

(Sing.)

> Give my regards to Broadway
> Remember me to Herald Square
> Tell all the gang at 42nd Street
> That I will soon be there
> Tell them of how I am yearning

(They separate. LISA takes chair downstage right, GLORIA takes chair center stage left, MURIEL faces downstage right.)

> To mingle with the old time throng
> Give my regards to Broadway
> And say that I'll be there ere long

(MURIEL is upside down in chair kicking her legs, singing, and continues to sing while LISA decides to entertain audience with GLORIA.)

MURIEL

(Sings.) Long long long long.

LISA

Hey Gloria we have a captive audience—let's you and me play "Indian Love Call."

GLORIA

Oh yeah.

LISA

Okay? I'm Jeanette MacDonald and I've got this long red hair and big green eyes.

GLORIA

Elizabeth. Elizabeth? Let me be Jeanette MacDonald.

LISA

No!

GLORIA

But you always take the biggest part.

LISA

No I don't.

GLORIA

I want to be Jeanette MacDonald.

LISA

You have some nerve. It's my game.

GLORIA

I want to be Jeanette MacDonald.

LISA

Harum Scarum Lady.

GLORIA

I have a high voice.

LISA

No!

GLORIA

(Begs.) Please.

LISA

Oh all right, but I'm Nelson Eddy.

GLORIA

I don't care who you are.

MURIEL

I'll be the horse. *(They ignore her.)*

GLORIA

(Simultaneously with LISA.) I'm Jeanette MacDonald and I have great big green eyes and long red hair that comes down to there. And I have a low-cut white dress that goes down to there and goes in like this and out like that and lace all around the bottom. And I'm standing on a mountain *(stands on a chair)* and I look down and there he is on a big white horse and I go like this.

LISA

(Simultaneously with GLORIA.) I've got a Royal Canadian Mounted Police uniform on. A big red jacket. I'm wearing black leather boots up to here. I have a big tan hat with a leather thong under my chin. I've a beautiful white horse and I'm standing at the foot of a mountain.

GLORIA

(Sings.)

Oooo Oooo Oooo

(Plays make-believe piano.)

> tootle tootle doo
> tootle tootle doo *(Twice.)*
> So echoes of sweet love notes
> gently falls
> Through the forest stillness
> are fond waiting
> Indian lovers call

LISA

(Sings.)

> When the lone lagoon
> stirs in the spring
> Welcoming home
> Some swanny white wing
> when the maiden moon
> shines in the sky
> Drawing her star-eyed
> dream child nigh

GLORIA

(Sings.)

> That is the time of the moon and the year.
> When love dreams to Indian maidens appear.
> And this is the song that they hear

LISA AND GLORIA

(Sing.)

> When I'm calling you oooo ooo
> Will you answer too oooo oooo

GLORIA
(Sings.)

> That means I offer my love to you
> To be your own

LISA
(Sings.)

> If you refuse me
> I will be blue and waiting all alone

GLORIA AND LISA
(Sing.)

> But if when you hear my love call
> ringing clear

GLORIA
(Sings.)

> And I hear you answering
> echo so clear

LISA AND GLORIA
(Sing.)

> Then I will know
> Our love will come true
> *(GLORIA gets off chair.)*
> You belong to me
> I belong to you

(They run to each other and dramatically kiss three times.)

LISA

Oh how the music is playing
so gaily, so bravely and one wants to live

GLORIA

Oh how the music is playing.
They are leaving us, one is gone entirely,
entirely forever.
We'll be left alone to begin our lives
over

(ALL *three sit in chairs,* MURIEL *upstage center,* GLORIA *center stage,* LISA *downstage right. Transformation: The inside of a limousine coming from the cemetery.*)

MURIEL

I guess there will be no more funerals for a while. I wonder who will die next.

LISA

So much heaviness. So much responsibility. Mama's dead now. There will be even more responsibility. *(Pause.)* Father died one year ago today the fifth of May.

GLORIA

Mama. Mama. I'll never hear that voice again.

LISA

It was cold then and snowing. I thought I'd never live through it. *(To* MURIEL.*)* You were lying in a dead faint.

GLORIA

(Hums song "Trees" by Joyce Kilmer.) Mama would want me to sing that song. I don't remember the words. *(Sings hesitatingly.)* I think that I shall never see, a poem as lovely as a tree. *(Hums.)*

LISA

But now a year has passed and we can speak freely. You have a light dress on. Your face is beaming. The clock was striking then too.

MURIEL

She's dead. She died a long time ago for me.

GLORIA

(Hums.) Poems are made by fools like me but only— *(Hums.)*

LISA

I remember as though it were yesterday. They carried Father along. The band was playing but there were very few people following along behind. It was raining though then. Heavy rain and snow.

MURIEL

I'm crying. I'm crying.

GLORIA

Imagine. I'm already beginning to forget her face.

MURIEL

God grant it will all work out.

GLORIA

Just as we won't remember either.

MURIEL

Weather is beautiful today.

GLORIA

They'll forget us.

MURIEL

I don't know why my heart is so light. This morning when I got up I remembered it was my birthday and I remembered when I was a little girl and Mama was still alive.

GLORIA

No. She'll go on in us, in me and my family.

MURIEL

Such wonderful thoughts thrilled me. Such thoughts.

GLORIA

I'm the only grandmother now, the only grandmother in the family.

LISA

It's warm today.

(Film on. Lights dim. They sing "We Three" in the dark until the film ends.)

Carolinas, Tennessee, and Kentucky

Early Writings, Oral Storytelling, and Contemporary Tribal Affairs

Wilson H. Welch

Wilson H. Welch (Cherokee) was born on the Cherokee Reservation in North Carolina around 1875. He graduated from Carlisle Indian Industrial School in 1898. No further information on him could be obtained.

A People Who Would Not Be Driven

You may be surprised if I tell you that there are about two thousand four hundred Cherokee Indians in North Carolina alone, and together, nearly as many more in the States of Tennessee, Georgia, South Carolina, and Florida. When they were discovered by the early settlers they were found all along the southern coast, from the Atlantic to the Pacific, but later when the settlements began, these Indians moved eastward and settled in the several States of North Carolina, Tennessee, Georgia, South Carolina, Alabama, and Mississippi, and remained there until the treaty was made in 1809 between the United States Government and the North Carolina Indians. This treaty provided that all the Indians residing in the State of North Carolina should make their homes at the head of the Arkansas River, the place to be called the Cherokee Nation.

In order to have every one of them go, it was necessary to send soldiers; but some of the people hid among the mountains, and all of the others were taken to the place now called the Indian Territory. After that the number increased by some coming from the other States until there were just as many as there were at first. Another treaty was made in 1835, providing that all the Indians should go to the Indian Territory. Again some of them went to the largest mountains and hid among the rocks until all the soldiers had gone. Then they came back to their own homes. When the danger was all over, they bought a piece of land from a certain wealthy man, and appointed him to look after them, something like a chief. He gave them more land, until they had large tracts for their own use.

"A People Who Would Not Be Driven" (1898) from *The Red Man and Helper*.

The Eastern Band of Cherokees are a self-supporting people and are not considered Reservation Indians. Most of them are citizens of the United States, and all of them dress in citizens clothes. My people are on an equal footing with the white people in everything except schools; they vote and pay taxes as any citizen to the United States does. Two years ago, a Cherokee was appointed clerk in the Legislature at Raleigh.

In 1885, a school was established under the management of the Friends from Indiana. Before this time, the children went to the public schools, and five years ago the Government took charge of this school.

Their country in the southwestern part of the State is very mountainous; the Smoky Mountains being a part of the Blue Ridge, are about ten miles from the school. The chief occupation of the people is farming, but some have blacksmith and carpenter shops, while others are school teachers. The farmers raise fruit—apples, peaches and plums, and vegetables such as cabbages, potatoes, sweet-potatoes, turnips, peas, and peanuts. All raise cattle, sheep, and horses for their own use and for market. Pottery and basket-making are some of the oldest industries.

The Cherokee is the only tribe which has its own alphabet, that consists of eighty six letters, and was invented by an Indian. These people who would not be driven from their homes have made wonderful progress within the last sixty years. The Western Band carried the alphabet with them; and today they print a paper in the Indian Territory, using the letters of this alphabet on the outside, while the inside of the paper is printed in English. It is about the same size as our school paper, "The Red Man."

When the Civil war began all the Eastern Band who were old enough went to war and fought, some on the Union and others on the Confederate side. These people knew that they could make progress without being driven to the Indian Territory; so they determined to stay where they were, surrounded by the white people and influenced by them. The Reservation Indians could do the same if they scattered among the free inhabitants of the United States. You might think that turning loose this large number of ignorant and unprepared people would threaten the peace of our communities. Until recently, not a year has passed but that we have admitted to our shores more ignorant immigrants than the whole number of Indians.

Many Indians are in the United States, but not of it. My people are here and are citizens. Why not let all the Indians immigrate to the United States?

Frell McDonald Owl

Frell McDonald Owl [Frel McDonnel Owl] (Cherokee) was born at the Cherokee Reservation in North Carolina on March 1, 1899. He attended Hampton Institute, Phillips Andover Academy in Andover, Massachusetts, and Dartmouth College, from which he received a B.S. degree. Owl devoted his professional life to Indian affairs, serving thirty-three years as a teacher, administrator, and agency superintendent. Following his retirement from government service, he returned to Cherokee and devoted his remaining years to numerous community programs. In 1969, Owl was awarded an Honorary Doctor of Humane Letters degree by Dartmouth College, thus capping a life of exemplary public service. He passed away on May 18, 1980.

The Cherokee Indians

Hampton, 1920

To some people the land of the sky in the Old North State suggests gorgeous scenery—beautiful mountains, sparkling streams, dense growths of fir, rhododendron, and laurel. To me, the Land of the Sky suggests home, a home in the land "where the weak grow strong, and the strong grow great."

For ages before the advent of the white man, this land sheltered a large tribe of Indians, who, historians tell us, were friendly and lived a life of happiness. The Cherokees, or "Hill Dwellers," undoubtedly were masters of the East, for the tribe numbered twenty thousand and controlled the present mountainous regions of North Carolina, Georgia, Alabama, and Tennessee.

Early in colonization white men made their way into the Cherokee country in search of gold, and soon we find the settler and the Indian at war. The tribe struggled desperately to hold its dearly loved land, but weakness and unjust treaties forced the Indians to abandon large areas again and again. During the peaceful period after 1800 many educated Indian leaders, such as John Ross, the Ridges, and others, came to the front. These men, with the advice of statesmen, formed the Cherokee National Government.

In 1813 the Creek tribe declared war on the United States. After several bloody battles, General Jackson, then in charge of Government troops, sent a hurried call for help to the Cherokees. The complete defeat of the enemy at Horseshoe Bend was due largely to Cherokee warriors who swam a river and attacked the Creeks in the rear while the hard-pressed General Jackson attacked the front. This was the last battle of the Cherokees in the East.

"The Cherokee Indians" (1920) from *The Southern Workman*.

The country was startled in 1821, when Sequoyah, an uneducated Indian, invented the Cherokee alphabet. For years he had pondered over the fact that white men could transmit messages on paper; and it was his belief that Indians could do likewise. His many experiments created much humorous talk, but his final success of producing an alphabet of eighty-six characters gave him much joy, for his people were enabled to read and write as he had dreamed and hoped they would. His only daughter, a well-educated girl, deserves much credit for its success because it was she who convinced many doubtful Indians that it was a useful undertaking. A printing press was set up, and in a short period the Bible, other books, and newspapers were extensively read throughout the tribe.

For a number of years following this event the Cherokees lived peaceably, but ill feeling still existed. Georgia claimed a portion of the Indian land, and when gold was discovered on it the State took steps to secure the territory. Indians were driven from their homes by maddened citizens, who demanded that they be moved west. The removal of the Creek tribe had given many people the idea that the West was the place for all Indians. The Cherokees unanimously resented this, but after many years of trouble and suffering they were forced to bow to the orders of the white man.

In 1836 the President sent a message to them saying, "After two years you are all expected to be settled in your new homes in the far West." Two years passed and the Cherokees had shown no signs of moving. Suddenly seven thousand Government troops appeared to round up and drive them over a wintry trail from their beloved homes to the wild West. Colonel Z. A. Miles of the Georgia Militia and a member of the expedition said many years later, "I fought throughout the Civil War and saw men shot to pieces and slaughtered by the thousands, but the Cherokee removal was the cruelest work I ever knew."

Many Indians were determined not to go, and for years hundreds lived in caves eating nuts, berries, and roots while soldiers scoured the land for them. Finally, in 1842, these Indians were permitted to remain in the East, on land in the western part of North Carolina. The tribe today numbers over 2000 and owns more than 6000 acres of land. The majority of the band are of pure Indian blood, and many cannot speak English.

For a dwelling the picturesque log cabin is commonly used. Of course the day of feather and blankets has passed, but in many homes food is always prepared in iron pots over a fireplace. Some delicacies, such as bean-bread, corn-bread, chestnut-bread, sweet hominy, or "cunahanna," and other Cherokee dishes, white people have never successfully made in their many attempts, not even during the days of Hoover's reign. "Cunahanna" is made of whole corn, corn meal, beans, walnuts, hickory nuts, and wild honey. This dish is very delicious, but three days are required to make it. The Cherokee women are widely known for their beautiful basket, pottery, and bead work, while a few men still possess rare ability in making wooden spoons, napkin rings, and canoes.

This mountainous country would seem useless to many as farm land. Corn and wheat are the principal products, but recently cattle raising and fruit growing have been introduced with great success. An annual Indian fair is held each fall, and last year at the County Fair the Cherokee exhibition received first prize.

Practically all Cherokee children are prepared for higher institutions at the splendid Government boarding school, located on the Ocono Lufty River in the heart of the reservation. The auditorium on the campus furnishes a place for meetings, including those held by the Indian council. The members of this council are elected every two years, and they transact all tribal business. The religious spirit of the tribe has recently been strengthened wonderfully by the appearance of the first missionary for years. Up to this time all religious work was done by native ministers.

The Cherokee have sent many of their number to Hampton, and the result is that the leading and best-educated members of the tribe are Hampton men. I unwillingly left the "Land of the Sky" to follow the trail of one sister and three brothers through Hampton. Many times I have yearned to give it all up and go back to that loved land of every Cherokee, but I could not. My life at Hampton has broadened me and prepared me for the rough and steep trail that is waiting for me just outside of Hampton's gate. I realize that the time has come in Indian history when men of character and efficiency are needed, for the Indian must bear the load of a man in the near future. Hampton and Hampton's friends must encourage Indians to seek and receive her training, for such training is essential for the future Indian as a true American citizen.

Henry M. Owl

Henry M. Owl (Cherokee), another member of the redoubtable Owl family, was born at the Cherokee Reservation in North Carolina in 1897. He graduated from Hampton Institute (one of six Owl siblings to attend the school), attended Columbia University, and then earned an M.A. degree in history from the University of North Carolina. Henry Owl was employed by the Bureau of Indian Affairs, for most of his public life, and worked in Montana, Washington, and Oklahoma. The father of Gladys Cardiff, he passed away on March 3, 1980. The address below was delivered on Commencement Day at Hampton, May 29, 1918.

The Indian in the War

In the midst of the gigantic struggle for the obliteration of autocracy and for a world-dominating democracy, the Indian can be seen, as a patriotic citizen, striving to do his part in the great cause. There can be no doubt that he is a loyal and patriotic American. He has not only proved his patriotism in this war but he has proved it in every war that our country has waged.

The red man shed his blood for American independence in the early days of Washington and Lafayette, and since the uniting of the states into an independent sovereignty, loyal Indians have volunteered and given their lives in the service of a Government which they have learned to respect and support.

Indian treaties have been broken by our Government, and some that have been kept have been detrimental to my race; but my people are longing for a brighter future and in the crisis that now dominates the world, every energy will be exerted for the perpetual prosperity of our country. The red man, cooperating with his fellow-countrymen, will fight to the bitter end for an ensured and humane peace, for we cannot enjoy such a state of existence until we successfully abolish that detestable autocratic government which is a tyrannical injustice to civilization.

Today we read accounts of how the Indian, in past history, has fought against our Government detachments for a cause he thought just, but we cannot find that he has ever allied himself with a foe in an international struggle, thus proving himself to be a traitor or a contemptible slacker. My people are fast discovering the futility of tribalism and are gradually stepping into the body politic as citizens worthy of recognition.

The Indian has always been conspicuous as a fighter because of his dexterity

"The Indian in the War" (1918) from *The Southern Workman*.

and fundamental vitality, which is an ancestral heritage. Long before our country was forced to arms, many of my race crossed the border and joined the Canadian army. Their fighting qualities were appreciated, and they formed an important factor in the expeditionary forces. In France and in Flanders they have contributed much to the glorious record of the Canadian forces. Reports have come back telling of their daring exploits in the battles of Vimy Ridge and Hill 70. Some have won military medals for gallantry on the firing line, and before this conflict is over, we shall hear of more valiant Indians.

While America was still a non-belligerent country, there happened to be traveling in Germany a number of Indians who were hooted, stoned, and beaten through the country by mobs. The Indians are not fighting Germany for that atrocity, but they are giving their utmost support to uphold that honor and humanity which the Stars and Stripes have so long sustained. We shall not hear of an Indian battalion making a spectacular attack or a wonderful raid, for the War Department has decided that there shall be no separate Indian units. But, nevertheless, the Indian is in the ranks, on the seas, and in the trenches where the peal of cannon is loudest, side by side with the white man and fighting for the same goal. When the conscription law became effective last year, only those Indians were drafted who had been declared competent as citizens, consequently much the larger portion of those now in the service are volunteers.

In western North Carolina, where my home and reservation are, we have over 130 in the service and only about one-third of that number were drafted. The Cherokees are stationed at Camp Jackson where the "Spirit of '76" exists among the soldiers. Some complexities arose when the Cherokees went to the board for their examinations and at first it would not permit them to go, as they were not considered citizens. After a more thorough investigation, however, and consultation with the War Department, their status was decided. Several cannot speak English. They would not apply for exemption, and my brother, who was also drafted, frequently acts as their interpreter. Consider the disadvantages that would naturally confront them in precarious circumstances among strange people; but, regardless of their difficult situation, they are conforming to the principles of military life and are making excellent soldiers. Conditions at Camp Jackson are not exceptional, as there are cantonments all over the land where Indians are striving to learn the essential rudiments of the different military activities, in order to become efficient soldiers in modern warfare.

Boys who enter the army from schools such as Hampton, Carlisle, and Haskell, where military training constitutes part of the school curriculum, make good records which are an honor to our race and to the schools. We are proud of our Hampton representatives in the service, some of whom are actually on the firing line taking chances with the Hun.

The Indians are not only fighting with the rifle but are also manifesting their patriotism at home. In the Red Cross work, Indian women, young and old, have joined the society and, with needles as weapons, are constantly knitting for the soldiers. Many Indians have given freely to the various war funds, over $9,000,000 worth of bonds of the first and second loans being purchased by Indians. Can you conceive of an Indian living alone in a log cabin who is possessor of $800,000 worth of bonds? Other large purchases have been made by full-blood Indians throughout the country. In the Y.M.C.A. work the Indian is also a participator. On many reservations patriotic meetings have been held where large amounts were donated for the Y.M.C.A. fund.

As farmers the Indians have resolved to increase their production of food stuffs. The last official report on production showed a marked increase, and this year their determination is to excel all previous reports. In a message to the Great White Father in Washington, Medicine Owl, chief of the Blackfeet tribe in Montana, expressed the sentiment of the Indians when he said: "We will plant more corn to feed your soldiers and we will raise more goats and sheep that your soldiers may be clothed; and if you call us to arms, we will go to the front and fight for you!" This illustrates the spirit of the Indians today in the disastrous era throughout the world.

We must all pledge allegiance and rally to the flag and, if need be, make the supreme sacrifice in its cause, in order that we may do our part in helping democracy to illuminate and rule the world.

Lula Owl Gloyne

Lula Owl Gloyne (Cherokee) was born on the Cherokee Reservation in North Carolina in 1889. After completing her primary education at the Cherokee Boarding School and her secondary schooling at Hampton Institute in 1914, she went on to become an obstetrical nurse, later graduating from the nurses training program at Chestnut Hill Hospital in Philadelphia. During World War I, she served as a nurse, first in the American Red Cross, and then with Army Medical Corps with the rank of second lieutenant. After the war, she returned to the reservation and devoted her life in service to her fellow Cherokees. In 1985, Gloyne was nominated for the Distinguished Women of North Carolina Award and was named a "Beloved Woman" by the Cherokee Tribe, one of only three women in recorded history ever given this distinction. She died on April 17, 1985. Her daughter, Mollie Blankenship, was the first woman elected to the Cherokee tribal council, and another daughter, Mary Gloyne Byler, is a well-known writer, bibliographer, and educator. The selection below was written and published under the name Lula Owl.

Life Among the Catawba Indians of South Carolina

Long ago when Indians roamed over the South, as well as over the North and the West, the Cherokee and the Catawba were the two largest tribes of the Carolinas, the Cherokee being the larger and more powerful of the two.

My father was a Cherokee and my mother is a Catawba, so, you see, I have a right to be equally proud of both tribes, although I do rank as a Cherokee and not as a Catawba. The fact that I am called a Cherokee, instead of a Catawba, will perhaps seem strange to those who know anything at all about Indians and their customs, because it is customary for Indian children to go by their mother's tribe or nationality rather than by their father's. However, this custom is not always kept among the Cherokees; for if a Cherokee man married an Indian woman of another tribe and continued to live on the Cherokee reservation, their children would be enrolled as Cherokees and would be entitled to all Cherokee rights. The children of an Indian mother and a white father are also Cherokees, but the children of white mothers and Indian fathers are not enrolled as Cherokees, and they are not entitled to Cherokee Indian rights—such as Indian money, land, and the privilege of attending Indian schools that are supported by the Government.

"Life Among the Catawba Indians of South Carolina" (1914) from *The Southern Workman*.

It is about my mother's tribe, the Catawbas, I am going to speak. Indian history tells us that during the year of 1760 the Catawbas were continually having petty warfare among themselves, as well as with the Iroquois and other Northern tribes. The colonial government tried to persuade them to stop killing each other and go to killing the French. The Indians were always friendly with the English, and during the Revolutionary War a number of them became valuable scouts for the English army.

During all these wars the tribe kept getting smaller and less powerful. At two different times smallpox broke out among them and more than one-half of the whole tribe died of it.

In 1763 the Catawbas were confined on a reservation fifteen miles square in the northwestern part of South Carolina. The Indian soon rented their land to the whites for a few thousand dollars, and later sold all of it, except a single square mile on which they now reside. This small reservation is situated about eighty miles north of Columbia. The nearest large town is Rock Hill.

The tribe has grown so small that its number now averages about ninety-nine. A few Indians enlisted as soldiers in the Confederate Army and fought until the close of the Civil War. Since then the state government has had them in charge. Each year the legislature of South Carolina provides a sum of money that is equally divided and paid to every Catawba Indian residing in that state. The money is paid out to the Indians by a capable agent who is appointed by the legislature to act as a wise white father to the Indians.

Sylvester Long

Sylvester Long (Lumbee) was born in Winston, North Carolina, on December 1, 1890, of triracial parentage. He attended Carlisle Indian Industrial School from 1909 until his graduation in 1912. While attending St. John's Military School at Manlius, New York, he assumed the name Long Lance. He graduated from St. John's in 1915. During World War I, Long served in the Canadian Army. Following the war, he became a newspaper reporter and, soon after, he further modified his name to Chief Buffalo Child Long Lance and claimed to have been born and raised as a traditional member of the Blood band of the Blackfoot Nation in Alberta. In 1928, Long published a fictionalized autobiography, *Long Lance*, at the same time he was involved in U.S. and Canadian Indian affairs. He appeared, under the name Long Lance, in several motion pictures, most notably *The Silent Enemy* (1930). He died by his own hand in Los Angeles on March 20, 1932. In 1933, *Redman Echoes*, a collection of some of Long Lance's and his friends' writings, was published in a very limited edition. Donald B. Smith's *Long Lance: The True Story of an Impostor*, a sympathetic, but thorough, biography of Long, was published in 1983 and later revised and expanded as *Long Lance: The Glorious Impostor* (1999). Long's writings appearing in this anthology were written and published when he was a "Cherokee" at Carlisle.

Origin of Names Among the Cherokee

Nov. 11, 1910

Sylvester Long, Cherokee

Among the interesting legends of the Cherokee is the one concerning the naming of children after animals and birds. Long ago, when all Indians belonged to one great family, the children were not named until they were old enough to kill a certain number of the animals after which they wished to be named. The larger and fiercer the animal or bird, the more sought was its name. Thus the bear, wolf, eagle, and hawk were considered very good names, and those possessing these names were supposed to be endowed with great skill and prowess as hunters and warriors.

During this period there lived a young chief, Eg-wah Wi-yuh, whose greatest ambition was to be the father of a brave son—brave enough to earn the name of some fierce animal. At the birth of his first child he was greatly disappointed to find that he was born blind. So grieved was he over his afflicted son that for

"Origin of Names Among the Cherokee" (1910) and "Virginia Dare or the White Fawn" (1912) from *The Carlisle Arrow*.

five days he neither ate nor drank anything; neither did he allow anyone to enter his tepee. On the fifth night he fell into unconsciousness, and while in this condition a large bird entered his tepee and carried him away. He awoke to find himself sailing through the air on the back of a large bird. He had not been awake long before he discovered that they were traveling toward the moon, which already appeared many times larger than he had before seen it.

On reaching the moon he was surprised to discover that instead of being the planet which he thought it to be, it was in reality a large opening in a thick black crust. After passing through the moon he saw, on the other side, men walking around with large holes in their heads instead of eyes. On regaining his faculties he asked the bird what all of this meant and where he was being carried? He was told that he had died and his spirit was being carried to Guh-luh-lau-eeh—Happy Hunting Grounds—to be judged and sent back to the place they had just passed. The bird, on being further questioned, explained that this place was built by the Great Spirit and intended for the spirits of animals and birds, but owing to the cruel custom of killing animals for their names, the Great Spirit has sent a curse upon the Indians. He had given the animals the real Happy Hunting Grounds and had driven the spirits of the Indians to the place which they had just passed, to have their eyes eaten out by the birds, and tormented by the animals they had wantonly killed on earth for the sake of assuming their titles. He was further informed that they were on the way to Guh-luh-lau-eeh, the real Happy Hunting Grounds, where the great chief of the animals and birds dwelt, which was reached by passing through the sun. The moon, he said, was for the wicked spirits of the Indians to pass through during the night, and the sun for the spirits of the animals to pass through during the day. The Great Spirit covered the earth with the black sheet long enough for the evil spirits to pass into their torment, and the white one long enough for the spirits of the animals and birds to pass into Guh-luh-lau-eeh, thereby producing day and night. On passing through the sun he was amazed at the beauty of the place. He was carried to the large wigwam of the Great Chief of animal and bird kingdom. On discovering that his subject was not dead, but had merely fallen into a stupor, from which he had already recovered, he was greatly annoyed and ordered the bird to carry Eg wah Wi-yuh to the fiercest animals of the kingdom to be devoured and his spirit sent to the land of evil spirits to be tormented by the animals and birds. Wi-yuh asked if there was anything he could do to save himself. The Great Spirit told him yes, there was one thing he could do to save himself, and that was to go back to the earth and abolish the custom of slaying innocent animals and birds for their names. He told Wi-yuh that if he accomplished this one task he would make him the ruler of the animal and bird kingdom, and would give back to the spirits of the Indians, Guh-luh-lau-eeh, and allow them to "hunt as much as they wanted" among all the animals and birds in that kingdom. He promised that if the young chief would name his blind child after the first animal or bird he would see on looking from his tepee the next morning after returning to his home, instead of adhering to the old custom, and thereby set an example for the other Indians to follow, he would cause the child to gain its eyesight.

On returning to the earth, Wi-yuh told his people all that had happened and they did not believe him, but the next morning when he named his child for the first animal he saw when he looked from his tepee, his son instantly gained his eyesight. Every one now believed him, and from that day to within recent years, the Indians have named their children after the first object they saw on looking from their tepees when a child was born.

The following day Wi-yuh disappeared to Guh-luh-lau-eeh.

Virginia Dare or the White Fawn
Sylvester Long, Cherokee

White Fawn is the name given by the Indians of North Carolina to the first white child born in America.

It seems that sometime during the fifteenth century when the white people were settling along the shores of Roanoke Island, the Croatoan Indians who inhabited that locality were very friendly towards the white settlers. Some of the Indians even threw aside their paganism and received Christian baptism. They were a great help to the early immigrants, in that they would often protect them from the attacks of the hostile mainland Indians who knew little of the white man and desired to know less.

Therefore, it was with great reluctance that Governor John White bade his faithful little colony farewell and sailed away for the motherland to secure supplies and bring over other immigrants to join the colony. It happened that soon after the settling of Roanoke Island, a girl baby was born to Governor White's daughter, who had married one Ananias Dare. So fair was the little one that the Indians called her the White Fawn and her mother the White Doe. White Fawn was the recipient of many beautiful presents from the natives and, no doubt, helped to strengthen the bond of friendship between the two races.

Three years had passed since Governor White took leave of his fair little grand-daughter, and now as he was returning, it was with a keen eye that he scanned the shores of Roanoke Island as his small fleet drew near, for some sign of a prattling little girl who, perchance, might be building mud-houses or watching the approach of the strange-looking sea wagons, the like of which she had never before seen. In vain did he scan the Island for even some sign of civilization, but his gaze was met only by the bleak, sandy shores and the tall pines in the background, which seemed to have a message which they were eager to impart to him as they stood drooping amidst the wild silence of the unconquered forest.

After landing, the Governor and his party went directly to the little village of Raleigh, where he had left the busy planters three years before, but to his disappointment he found the cabins empty and weeds growing within. On a nearby tree they found carved the letters C R O A T O A N, this being the last sign of the lost colonists ever seen by a white man. It is thought, however, that they joined the Indians of the mainland and that the present tribe of Croatoan Indians of eastern North Carolina are their descendants, owing to their having features similar to those of the white race and on account of their extremely religious nature.

A popular legend among these Indians is that White Fawn died while in infancy, and that her spirit entered a beautiful fawn which could be seen on moonlight nights standing on the shore of the Island looking far out over the ocean, as if longing to return to the land from which her ancestors had emigrated.

Nan E. Saunooke

Nan E. Saunooke (Cherokee), from the Cherokee Reservation in North Carolina, was born around 1889. She attended Carlisle Indian Industrial School, and it was while she was a student there that she wrote and published her work in the school magazine, *The Red Man,* in 1910 and 1911. No further biographical information could be obtained.

How Medicine Originated Among the Cherokees

There are many customs and traditions among the Indians of our land. The customs and traditions differ among the various tribes. Once, in ages gone by, the Cherokees knew nothing of medicine nor the herbs used as such. They remained ignorant of the medicinal quality of plants until a great Indian brave came and lived among them. He was unlike them in habits and dress. He wore a dress of stone which no arrow could pierce. He had a finger that was shaped like a needle, and with this he killed little children.

After years of havoc among these people they decided to kill him. His wife, after hearing of their plans, told them that those who wished to learn about medicine should be at the place where her husband was to be burned. This knowledge made them still more anxious to capture and kill him. He was caught, after a long and weary pursuit. The whole tribe assembled to see him burned, but only the elders of the tribe were privileged to learn the art of healing.

While he was in agony he chanted the words that have since been used in healing any disease among the Cherokees. At the same time he told what herbs should be used.

Thus the Cherokee medicine man received his knowledge to heal. The medicine men of my tribe are very quiet around the sick. They do not dance or sing, as other medicine men do.

When healing a person, it is customary for them to rub their hands together and talk among themselves; and with all respect to the one who bequeathed this knowledge, medicine men never fail to warm their hands over live coals before using them.

This art of healing is handed down from father to son.

Many of you in the winter evenings have heard the sizzing sound of damp

"How Medicine Originated Among the Cherokees" (1911), "Why the Turkey Is Bald" (1911), and "The Story of the Corn" (1910) from *The Red Man.*

wood in the fire. The Indians of my tribe tell their children that the sound is the dying sigh of the originator of the Cherokee medicine man.

Why the Turkey Is Bald

The Indians of our country have many legends connected with certain peculiar habits or customs prevalent among them. If one should chance to visit the home of an old Indian he would perhaps notice a turkey wing hanging near the fire. This the Indian uses to fan his fire into a flame and make it burn brightly, or perhaps in the sultry days of summer, to fan himself. If asked why he uses the turkey wing instead of the wing of any other bird, he would no doubt relate the following story:

Many years ago the fire of the world was nearly extinguished; this happened just at the beginning of the winter season. The birds of the air were filled with anxiety, for their intuition told them they would need heat to keep them warm through the winter.

A bird council was held and it was decided that birds which could fly the highest should soar into the air and see it they could find a spark of fire anywhere. The efforts of the eagle, lark and raven were in vain. The honor was left to the little brown sparrow, who spied a spark of fire in the hollow of an old stump, in the heart of a deep forest.

The birds flocked around the stump and tried to decide who should pick the spark out. But all their efforts were in vain; to their dismay they saw the spark growing smaller and fainter. The turkey then volunteered to try and keep the tiny coal alive by fanning it with his wings. Day after day the turkey kept fanning; the heat became greater each day, until the feathers were singed off the turkey's head. If one notices carefully he will see lumps on the head of a turkey that appear as blisters. It is believed that the turkey was so badly burned that all turkeys since have had bald heads and wear the blisters as a memento of the bravery of the turkey. The faithful turkey lost his beautiful feathers but he gave back fire to the world; so in his honor and as a memorial of his faithfulness, the Indian uses the turkey wing to make his fire burn.

The Story of the Corn

The Indians of my tribe relate this legend to their children from generation to generation:

Many years ago there lived an old woman with two sons. Every day she would disappear for a certain length of time; when she returned she would bring with her corn, beans, and pumpkins.

As her sons grew older, they wondered where she got these things. They planned to force her to give them the secret, or kill her if she refused. Discerning the little boys' intention, she called them to her and gave each a little earthen jug and also a bow and arrow. She then instructed the boys as to what they should do after taking her life: She told them to drag her body over the fields and bury it there; then they were to take the bows and arrows and earthen jug and shoot insects all night. They were told if they went to sleep during the night the corn would not come up until one week after planting.

The boys shot the insects and watched the corn grow to maturity. They remembered the corn was tasseling, when the younger boy said he was sleepy and believed he would lie down awhile; but alas, the little lad fell asleep and his brother did likewise. When they awoke they could see no corn. The corn did not again appear until seven days. Then little green shoots came up. The boys had to keep the fields free of weeds as a punishment for falling asleep at their posts of duty. The Indians believe that no effort would have been needed on their part to get this grain had the boys fulfilled their duty and not slept.

David A. Harris

David A. Harris (Catawba) was a chief of the Catawba Tribe of South Carolina when he wrote the letter entitled "History of the Catawbas." At the time (1905), he was living in Rodney, South Carolina. No further biographical information could be obtained.

History of the Catawbas

Chief David Harris, of the Catawba Indian tribe, writes to "The State" of Columbia, South Carolina, to tell of the troubles of his people. His letter, which is reproduced just as it was written, will be found of much interest:*

Will you allow me a space in your paper In gard to my tribe which is known as Catawba tribe. this Space is to those who is true and kind feeling to the Red men in the State of South Carolina who did everything they could do for the white people to be friends and stand right to the fellow men, they have share homes to the white people, and shads Blood in wars not only one wars but many wars. our mens leaves homes wife and little children to go in to the war for the white race, and those mens who went to the war. They had not anything for his wife or children live up on, you all may unstand that they had a great feelings to his white Brethern.

Once our tribe was Noble tribe, the Catawbas are now reduced from habits of Indolence and Inebriation to very few, our number does not exceed 130 of every age in the nation and out of the nation in 1905. Some years after the first settlement of Carolina our tribe could once mustered 1,500 fighting men. This would give the population of the nation at that time between 8,000 and 10,000 souls. About the year 1743 the Catawbas could only bring 400 warriors in to the field. Composed Partly of refugees from various smaller tribes who about this time were obliged by the State of affairs to associate with tham on account of their Reduced numbers. Among these were the Watteree Chowan, Congaree, Nachee Yamassee and Coosah Indians. At present not 50 men can be number in the list of their warriors.

The remains of this nation now occupy a territory 15 miles square laid out on both sides of Catawba river and including part of york and lancaster

---

"History of the Catawbas" (1905) from *The Indian School Journal.*
*Editor's note, appearing as given here, prefacing Chief Harris's article.

districts. This tract imbraces a body of fine lands timbered with oak etc. these lands almost all leased out to white settlers for ninety nine years, renewable at the rate of from $15 to $20.00 Per annum for Each plantation of about 300 acres. The annual, income from these lands is estimated to amount to about $50, the Catawbas have two villages one on each side of the river. The largest is newtown situated immediately on the river bank to the other, which is upon oposite side thay given no name, but it is generally called turkeyhead.

Our tribe never did lease Kings bottoms. This bottom was reserve for their children, but our tribe did not keep record of this bottom so the white Peaple got this bottom in their Posession.

In year 1780 our tribe occupy an extent of contry on both sides of the river equal to 180 square miles or 115,200 acres, the Catawbas were a Canadian tribe, the Connewayos were their hereditary enemies and with the aid of the french were likely at last to overwhelm them, the Catawbas judging correctly of their perilous condition determined on english settlements they set out from their ancient homes.

About the year 1650, crossed the st lawrence, probably near detroit, and bore for the head waters of Kentuck river. The Connewayos all time kept in full pursuit, the fugitives embarassed with their women and children, saw that their enemies would overtake tham, chose a position near the source of the kentuck and there awaited the onset of their more powerful adversaries. Turning therefore, upon their pursuers with the energy desperation sometimes inspires, thay gave tham a terrible overthrow. This little nation, after this great victory without Proper regard to policy, Divided into two bands. The one remained on the Kentuck which was called by the hunters the Catawba and were in time absorbed into great families of the Chickasaw and Choctaws. The other band settled in botetourt county, Va., upon a stream afterward called catawba creek. They remained there but few years, their hunters Pressing onto the south Discovered the catawba River in South Carolina.

In year 1735 the nation had in reservation only 30 acres of their large and fertile territory not a foot of which was in cultivation. In history of South Carolina ramsey Solemnly invokes the People of South Carolina to cherish this small Remnannt of a Noble Race, always the friends of the carolinians, and ready to peril all for their safety. Our tribe never have shed a Drop of american Blood nor stolen Property to the value of a cents. Thay have lost everything but their honesty.

Our tribe never has known to one of the members ever been to the penitentiary or never done Enough to be pounishment by the law of the land, those who want to no more about our tribe can write me. Answer all letters and hoping those men of the legislature will consider of our conditun. I will represent my tribe by visit ever town and city in the State of South Carolina befor Legislture meet in year 1906. All those who are friends to the Catawbas would be glad to hear from tham.

DAVID A. HARRIS,
Rodney, S.C., Catawba Indians.

Freeman Owle

Freeman Owle (Cherokee) is widely known for his oral stories from Cherokee culture and history. He is a highly dedicated missioner with the Global Ministries of the United Methodist Church. Owle was born on the Cherokee Reservation in North Carolina in 1946. He received his bachelor's degree in social work from Western Carolina University and a master's degree in 1978 from the same institution. He taught for fourteen years in the Cherokee school system on the reservation before turning to the church. Some of his stories, recorded during oral presentations, appear in the anthology *Living Stories of the Cherokee*.

Introduction to the Nantahala Hiking Club Gathering

Thank you very much for inviting me here tonight.

Can everyone hear fine?

My name is Freeman Owle,

I'm from Cherokee, North Carolina,

    born and reared on the Cherokee Indian Reservation.

In 1946,

    many of you may remember,

    and maybe not,

    the A-models coming over the Smokies,

    people going up into the bear jams

    and the old cars overheating.

People backing up for miles,

    and Roosevelt on top of the mountain

    when they dedicated the Blue Ridge Parkway.

They said something to the effect that:

    "Look what we made out of this land, that for so long belonged

    to the savages."

    and I think they still have it inscribed into the rocks

    up on top of Clingman's Dome.

I'm not quite so sure that those people were the savages

    that Roosevelt may have thought that they were.

Coming down from the hills
 and fighting with their Iroquois brother over some argument,
 point of view or something,
 they moved southward.
They moved into the Cumberland Mountains.
 But the Iroquois brother still said,
 "That's not far enough,"
 and the Tsa-la-gi,
 they called themselves Tsa-la-gi,
 moved a little bit farther into Kentucky and Tennessee,
 and eventually the Iroquois brother thought they'd moved far
  enough away.
I can imagine many times
 the land and the landscape that they came upon,
 a land of virgin timber,
 a land with a stream so crystal-clear
 you could count every pebble in the bottom of the stream.
A land where the wild turkey walked leisurely,
 and a land where deer were jumping from behind almost every
  bush.
Coming down
 into the hills and the valleys of the Oconaluftee,
 the Tuckaseegee,
 and the Tennessee,
 they began to look for a place to live.
Hearing drumbeats somewhere in the distance,
 they realized that they were not the only people here.
They began to come out and to part the leaves
 and look out into the valleys of Nikwasi.
Seeing people walking in this flat field down here below,
 seeing a large mound of dirt with buildings on top of it,
 they realized they were not the first people to arrive in this area.
They came to this place called Nikwasi.
 and they met the people who lived here,
 who were blond-headed and blue-eyed.
Thousands and thousands of years before Leif Erickson and the
  Vikings,
 thousands of years before the settlers came,
 there were peoples with blond hair and blue eyes already here.

James Mooney may tell you,
    in his writings of Cherokee myths and legends and sacred
        formulas,
    that the Cherokees annihilated these people
    and they were no more.
I truly believe
    that the Cherokees intermarried with these people,
    and they are still here.
You go to Cherokee, North Carolina, today,
    and you see those folks with Eskimo-type facial features,
    and you'll also see those with the South American-type features.
And in Robbinsville, North Carolina, in a little place called
        Snowbird,
    you can still see those real dark-skinned Cherokees,
    and every now and then
    you'll see one with a reddish tint in their hair and blue eyes.
The people got along well together because they loved the earth.
And you people who hike—
    at least you have got to the point in your lives
    when you can go out into the forest,
    and you don't have to run through the forest
    to get from one end to the other.
You may have had to do that for a lifetime.
But it's now a time to slow down
    and listen to the stream as it gurgles by,
    it's time to slow down
    and listen to the call of the birds and see if you can identify it,
    it's time to sometimes take your shoes off,
    and, like a little child,
    to go and splash in the waters of the Tennessee or the Nantahala.
Once you lose that childlikeness,
    then you've lost life.
The Cherokee people believe that everything is connected,
    everything that is living is a part of the great cycle,
    and we as people, human beings, are part of that great cycle also.
Society may take you by the throat and strangle you
    to the point that you feel like you must gain success.
I grew up on the Cherokee reservation
    in the time of 1946,

when the tourists began to come,
and the Cherokees' culture began to die and began to be
    removed,
and people were asked and forced out upon the streets
because it was role-expectation theory
that you go out and you put on the Sioux headdress,
and you stand in front of a Sioux tipi,
and those peoples coming along
would stand there and have their pictures taken with you—
that's what they expected us to be.
The Cherokee people were woodland farmers,
    and they farmed for a living for twenty or thirty thousand years.
They had no need to take down their house
    and follow the buffalo herd
    because the buffalo that were here were woodland buffalo
    that stood very, very tall, usually traveled in pairs of twos.
The Cherokees have made up many, many stories
    as they've lived in these valleys.
And I'm respectful of Franklin, North Carolina.
I know that sometimes you're under a lot of controversy and
        discussion.
You are one of the very few areas that has protected your mound,
    that is located within your village.
I as an individual, and as a member of the Eastern Band of the
        Cherokees,
    commend you for this.
It's a beautiful mound.
And one of the very few, that I know of, that's still intact.
There are stories behind this,
    because when the Cherokees farmed,
    they had enough food that they were able to store their food for
        the winter,
    and then when the cold winters came
    they were able to sit down in front of the fires built in those old
        cabins
    and to tell stories.
One of the ones they tell is about Nikwasi.

The Nikwasi Mound

Nikwasi was down on the valley of the Tennessee,
  and all of a sudden the Creeks began to come up and attack
  and threaten to destroy the village of Nikwasi.
The Cherokee people rallied,
  they came to protect the village,
  but over and over again the Creeks came in greater numbers,
  and eventually the Cherokees were losing, very badly.
And they'd almost given up,
  when all of a sudden the mound of Nikwasi opened up,
  and little soldiers began to march out of this mound by the
    thousands.
And so they go out and they defeat the Creeks,
  and like in biblical times
  they kill all of the Creeks except for one.
And he goes back and tells the other Creek brothers and sisters,
  "Never ever mess with the village of Nikwasi,
  because they have spirit people who protect it."
And never again
  was this village attacked by the Creeks.
It was during the Civil War time
  that the Yankee soldiers came down from the north,
  and they were camped out
  and ready to come down and to burn
  the little town of Franklin, North Carolina.
They sent scouts down to Franklin, North Carolina,
  and the scouts went back telling their commanding officer,
  "You can't attack Franklin, North Carolina.
  It is heavily guarded, there's soldiers on every corner."
And the soldiers went around,
  toward Atlanta, Georgia, and burned everything in the path.
But Franklin, North Carolina, was not touched.
And then the history and the reality was
  that every able fighting person left Franklin
  to fight in the Civil War.
There were no men here.
The old Cherokees say it was the Nunnehi, the Little People,
  that again protected
  Franklin, North Carolina.

Kathi Smith Littlejohn

Kathi Smith Littlejohn (Cherokee) is an educator and storyteller living in Cherokee, North Carolina. She holds a bachelor's degree in education from Western Carolina University. Her stories have appeared in *Living Stories of the Cherokee* and in several newspapers and journals. Littlejohn is currently the director of the Health and Human Services Department for the Eastern Band of Cherokee Indians. Since the mid-1990s, she has been in the vanguard of a growing number of Cherokee storytellers, including Robert Bushyhead, Lynn King Lossiah, Dewey Arch, Lloyd Arneach, Freeman Owle, Edna Chekelelee, Marie Junaluska, Fred Bradley, and Carl Lloyd Owle, who are revitalizing the art in the public forum through their performances and recordings.

The Origin of Legends

Today, I'm going to tell you some Cherokee legends.
We were just talking a little bit about what people did a long time
    ago.
They didn't have books did they?
They didn't go to school,
    so they needed legends to teach people
    about different animals
    with stories
    and how things came to be
    and about the rules that everybody was supposed to go by
    so they would treat each other with a lot of respect
    and take care of one another.
That's why we have legends.

Why do you think I'm here today?
To tell us legends.
What are legends?
Very good, a tale that was long ago that was true.
But does anybody know how the legends came to be?
How did we get legends?

From your grandfather, very good.
And I'm gonna tell you the first legend
   about how we got legends,
   because at one time there were no grandfathers.
In fact, it was such a long time ago.
   they were young themselves.
A long long long time ago,
   there was a group of people
   that lived by themselves in the world
   with all of the animals.
And they could all talk to one another,
   they could talk to the animals,
   and they had the same language,
   and everybody got along.
And then one day,
   as people will do,
   they started to fight.
One thing led to another.
   and this person wasn't talking to this person.
Another thing happened,
   and this person pushed this person.
Somebody wasn't very nice to somebody,
   and somebody stole something from somebody,
   and they were really really angry at one another.
So angry that they hit each other,
   and they were going to kill one other.
The Creator didn't like this at all.
And so
   he sent them
   —divided them up into groups of four—
   and sent
     one group to the north,
     one to the south,
     one to the east
     and one to the west.
All around to the corners of the world.
And once they got there,
     they were very confused,
     because they didn't know how to live

in this part of the world.
They weren't familiar with these things.
They didn't know where the water was.
They didn't know what kind of plants these were.
They didn't know how to get ready for the winter
        because they didn't know what the winter was gonna be like.
So the Creator left very sorry for them,
        and he wanted to help them,
        but he wanted them to learn their lesson.
So he sent them a gift.
He sent them dreams
        that told them about each of the animals,
        what to eat,
        what to do,
        what kind of plants they could use for medicine,
        and what kind of plants, if they ate them, would make them sick,
        how to catch that kind of fish,
    how to look at these different kind of animals and use them.
So they began to learn,
    and they began to grow,
    and they began to live in their new home,
    and they got along with each other this time.
Then he sent them another gift
    so they would never forget these things.
He sent them legends,
    about all of these animals
    and all of these plants.
So that each time they told the legend,
    they would remember these animals
    and take better care of them
    and take better care of each other.
And that's how the legends came in the world.
Okay? Now you know? Okay, let's tell another legend.

Why the Turtle's Shell Is Cracked

Now, how many of you know what a turtle looks like?
Are you scared of turtles?
No.
Why?

They're not scary, they don't bark, they don't run fast, do they?
Did you know,
> that a long time ago.
> that the turtle was the most ferocious warrior on the face of the
> earth?
He was twenty feet tall.
He was so big and strong,
> and he was mean,
> and none of the other animals liked him.
They were all afraid of him, even the wolves.
One day
> a wolf met the turtle out in the woods,
> and he thought,
> "Here comes that mean old turtle.
> I'm not even gonna get out of the way.
> I'm sick and tired of him ordering me around.
But sure enough,
> the turtle said,
> "Get out of my way."
The wolf said,
> "No, no, I was here first."
And the turtle killed him,
> cut off his ears,
> stuck 'em under his belt,
> stepped over the dead body,
> and walked on.
It didn't matter to him.
And he walked all day.
And he was real hungry,
> and he thought,
> "The next time that I come to a village,
> I'm gonna tell them that they have to fix my supper."
And he walked down into the village,
> and it was a wolf village,
> and he said,
> "Hey you, you. You come here and fix me something to eat now."

Well, they were all so scared of him,
> they ran and made him a big bowl of soup,
> and they gave it to him,

and he pulled out those wolf ears
    and used them as spoons,
    and he ate every bit of that soup,
    he didn't even care that they were wolf ears.
And the other wolves got so upset and mad,
    they said,
    "Look at him.
    He's using the ears of our brother to eat with.
    What is he doing?
    No, not me, I'm scared."
They didn't know what to do.
So they decided that they would hide in the night,
    and the next morning
    all of them would jump on him,
    not just one or two.
So they went out, and they hid,
    and the next morning when he woke up,
    he thought it was awful funny that nobody was there,
    so he began to hurry,
    he thought they were gonna trick him.
And he went all the way down to the edge of the river,
    and he turned around and here they came:
    two hundred snapping snarling wolves,
    and they were gonna jump on him.
So he jumped out,
    so he could jump into the river and swim away,
    but he missed the water,
    and he crashed onto the rocks,
    and he broke into a hundred pieces.
But, being the mighty warrior that he was,
    he sang a magic song,
    and the all pieces came together,
    and he swam away.
But ever since then
    the turtle is very small,
    and if you look at his back what do you find?
Cracks.
And that's where
    those pieces came together that day.
And that's how come the turtle's shell is cracked.

Gregg Howard

Gregg Howard (Cherokee-Powhatan) became, in a very short period of time, one of the most widely respected performers of Cherokee oral stories in the United States. His work is featured on several audiocassettes, most notably *Tales of Wonder* (1998), *Tales of Wonder II* (1999), *Grandfather's Stories* (2001), and *Cherokee Scary Stories* (2004), and his work is beginning to appear in written form in anthologies and journals. Howard was born May 25, 1936, in Central City, Kentucky, and for many years he lived in Dallas, Texas. He was the founder and director of Various Indian Peoples Publishing Company, which specializes in the production of Native American language tapes and videos. In 1997, Howard was named Storyteller of the Year by Wordcraft Circle of Native Writers and Storytellers. He made numerous storytelling visits to elementary and high schools in Texas, Oklahoma, and Tennessee. Howard passed away on April 23, 2009.

The Underground Panthers

Etiyu (a long time ago) Ganohalidohi (a hunter) was in the woods one day in late winter when suddenly he saw Tlvdatsi (a panther) coming toward him. Ganohalidohi at once prepared to defend himself. Tlvdatsi continued to approach and Ganohalidohi was just about to shoot when the animal spoke. Then it seemed to the man as if there was no difference between them, and they were both of the same nature. Tlvdatsi asked the hunter where he was going and Ganohalidohi said he was looking for a deer to feed his family.

"Well," said Tlvdatsi, "we are getting ready for Itsei Selu Alsgisdi (Green Corn Dance) and there are several of us out after a buck, so we might as well hunt together."

Ganohalidohi agreed and they went on together. They saw a deer and then another, but Tlvdatsi made no sign and said only, "Those are too small. We want something better."

So Ganohalidohi did not shoot, and they went on. They saw another deer, a larger one. Tlvdatsi sprang upon it. He tore at its throat and finally killed it after a hard struggle. Ganohalidohi got out his knife to skin the deer, but Tlvdatsi said the skin was too torn to be used, and they must try again. They saw another large deer and this one Tlvdatsi killed without trouble. The panther wrapped his tail around the deer and threw it across his back.

"Now," he said to Ganohalidohi, "you come to our townhouse."

Tlvdatsi led the way carrying the captured deer upon his back. He led the hunter up a little stream branch until they came to the head spring when it seemed as if a door opened in the side of the hill to reveal the finest *detsanunli* (dancing ground) the hunter had ever seen. There were green trees all around and the air was warm as in summer.

There was a great company of panthers there getting ready for the dance, but somehow it all seemed natural to the hunter. Ganohalidohi danced several rounds and then said it was growing late and he must be getting home. So the panthers opened the door and he went out. At once he found himself alone in the woods again, and it was *gola* (winter) again. Ganohalidohi was cold and there was snow on the ground and on the trees.

When he reached the settlement he found a party just starting out to search for him. They asked him where he had been so long and he told them the story. It was then he found out he had been in the panther townhouse several days instead of only a short time, as he had thought.

He died within seven days after his return because he had already begun to take on panther nature and so could not live again with men. If he had stayed with the panthers he would have lived.

Nigaha (That is all)

Davie's Tale

A tale discovered in an old Welsh journal by a friend of mine who was studying the Welsh language in Wales. The journal was about Evans B. Jones, who traveled with the Cherokee in the early 1800s. The tale, which appears to be an excerpt from a longer story, was translated from the Welsh language into English and is now once again being told.

Etiyu (a long time ago) a village was having a dance. Awina (a young man) fell in love with Ata (a young woman) not of his clan who was a stranger there. When she left, he followed her. They went far up the mountain to her house and the young man was welcomed.

The following day it was revealed to Awina that they were expecting the girl's two brothers. After awhile he heard a deafening sound, then a roar, and riding up on the backs of giant rattlesnakes were her two brothers, the Thunderers. They looked happy to have another man in the family and said he could help with the work. But they were rather restless and complained of a strange smell in the house. Humans did not exist among them so they were ignorant of the smell of man. Despite that, Awina succeeded in losing his smell very quickly, and so he was invited to play a ball game with them. To measure his manhood in the meantime, he was asked to put the "horses" in the stable. So great was his fear of failing to prove his manhood, he led the snakes away without any sign of fear whatsoever.

In the morning Awina was invited to mount the back of a third snake and follow the two brothers as they rode away. He climbed up on the snake in fear and he rode with them until they came to a playing field. As soon as they arrived, they took their sticks and began to play stick-ball. This was the third test because they played with a human skull. Awina took fright at seeing it fly at him with its mouth open, but thinking about his wife, he swallowed his fear and played well. Therefore, he proved his worthiness to become the third Thunderer. Every now and then you can hear him with the brothers as they travel through the air and make their sounds above.

Nigaha (That is all)

Lynn King Lossiah

Lynn King Lossiah (Cherokee) is a widely known storyteller and artist living in the Piney Grove area of the Cherokee Reservation near Cherokee, North Carolina. The author of *The Secrets and Mysteries of the Cherokee Little People*, she and her husband, Ernie Lossiah, the book's illustrator, are the proprietors of Lossiah Arts, located on the reservation.

They Want You to Believe in Them

If you do things deliberately to prove you do not believe in them, like disturb where they might live, or mock their singing and drumming, or even dispute someone who does believe in them, the Little People will help you to believe.

On a clear moon-lit night two young men were walking down a dirt road. A hard day of work had tired them and they did not relish the long walk home. As they were passing a cornfield, one said, "You know, if we cut through the field, we'll get home a lot quicker.

"Well what are we waiting for?" his friend replied, and they both turned into the field, each following a row of corn with a few rows between them. The road disappeared behind tall stalks of corn as sharp green leaves sliced at their faces and rubbed at their shirt sleeves.

The young men had not walked long before they heard the rustle of corn stalks ahead. They heard the sound of scuffling and quiet laughter, growing louder as it drew closer. Suddenly, out of the darkness between the rows of corn a party of Little People tromped right through the midst of the two young men, leaving them speechless. Thirteen in all, they marched noisily along, one or two poking their heads through the stalks to glance curiously at the young men, but otherwise paying them little attention.

The two men knew it was a band of the Little People that they saw. Many wondered about this since it is believed that the Little People show themselves only to the Cherokee, and one of the young men was white. Whatever the case, the men watched as the little group left the cornfield, crossed the dirt road and vanished into the darkness near a mountainside.

*   *   *

A stranger once came to Cherokee during the hunting season. He wore a red bandanna under his beat-up old hat and had a scruffy black beard that was always itching him. He fancied himself an adventurer and loved to brag about his latest kill, bouncing to emphasize the dangerous points.

Most people listened with a raised eyebrow as he'd work himself up to a crescendo and then jump in his pickup and drive off in search of game again.

One day, his search led him far into the hills where paved highways ended and dusty mountain roads snaked their way into the mountain coves. He drove until dusk and set up camp near the foot of a tall cliff that glowed white from the evening sun.

After a meager meal of cold beans and bread he grew restless. He wanted to hunt, but it was getting too dark. To satisfy himself, he loaded his rifle and started shooting randomly into the forest, aiming at the limbs and leaves and anything else that presented itself. He became especially attracted to shooting into the white cliff side.

"What are you doing?" asked an old Cherokee man who appeared without warning. "Practicing," replied the hunter, taking a bead on a particularly round stone in the cliff.

"Do you not care that people live nearby and might be sleeping?"

"No people around here as I can see. Where did you come from anyway?" asked the hunter with a grin.

The old man nodded toward a nearly concealed log cabin. A dim light in the window was the only noticeable evidence that a cabin was there.

The hunter glanced unconcerned in that direction then took a few more shots as the old man stood silently watching. The hunter had almost forgotten that he was there when the old man spoke again. "You're disturbing the Little People."

The hunter looked at the old man and frowned. "The little what?"

"The Little People," the old man repeated and pointed upward to the cliff. They live around the cliff where you are shooting. It won't be good for you if you anger them."

It took a moment for the hunter to comprehend. Then he laughed out loud and said, "I don't believe in such tales, old man." He continued to shoot and nothing the old man could say would persuade him to stop.

The hunter turned in defiance toward the old man, but he wasn't there. The hunter wondered how it could be that the old man could appear and disappear so silently and without his notice. He prided himself on being a more alert and aware hunter.

Soon the hunter grew drowsy and settled down in the back of his truck for the night, but before he could drift off to sleep, he was fully awakened by a bright glow. He thought that the old man had returned and was shining a lantern in his face. He sat up and opened his eyes.

The glow was coming from the edge of the road. He struggled from his tattered blankets and out of the back of his truck. He hesitated, trying to believe his eyes. His curiosity led him toward the light. A welcoming path that he had not noticed before lay before him, vanishing into the deep woods toward the cliff. The path glowed as if illumined by a full moon, but he was aware that it was a moonless night.

"What is this?" he questioned to himself, unable to resist stepping into the strange scene before him.

The path twisted and turned, and it did not take the hunter long to realize that he was lost. Strains of beautiful music, mixed with laughter, drifted in and out, first sounding closer then further away as if carried on the breeze. The sounds, always moving, frightened the hunter. Panicking, he wanted to run back down the path, but it seemed as if the path had changed. It wove itself differently through the trees. Terrified, the hunter scrambled as fast as he could, tripping over tree roots and stones, scuffing hands and knees, picking himself up and stumbling on until he burst once more into the road and fell toward his truck to secure himself.

He looked toward the old man's cabin. Led by the small light in the window he ran onto the porch and pounded on the door. The old man responded as if he had been expecting him. After sharing coffee that he had already prepared and listening to the hunter's story, the old man showed him a fully prepared bed where he was to sleep for the night. The hunter accepted everything graciously.

The next morning they walked to the campsite. Everything was as he had left it. Then they walked a short distance until the hunter was sure of the location of the path's entrance. What they saw was an impassable wall of undergrowth.

"I believe you," said the old man grinning. He turned away from the hunter and headed for his cabin.

The hunter watched the old man walk away. He looked back at the interweaving of briars and bushes, then looked defeatedly toward the old man. He quickly packed his things and left and was never seen in the Cherokee mountains again.

Teresa Morris

Teresa Morris (Tuscarora) is a teacher and historian living in Emerald Isle, North Carolina. Her book, *The People of the Neuse*, a history of remnant Tuscarora people of North Carolina, was published in 1997. She maintains several web pages—teresamorris.com, peopleoftheneuse.com, and tuscaroranc .com—for the dispensation of information about North Carolina Tuscarora history and current events.

When the Roll Is Called Up Yonder . . . Will You Be There?

This is a message posted at the Tuscaroras.com discussion forum on September 27, 1998.

Remember this: Not all of the Ska-roh-reh Roots are to be called out on the Roll Up Yonder. Why?

Not all of the Ska-roh-reh moved away after the Tuscarora War to upstate. Why? For starters all kinds of reasons . . . some due to age, others not having enough money to pay for access to traveling between what is now known as states, poor health, age, just to name a few.

Remember this: Here in North Carolina, we do have our own stories to share, songs to sing that proudly honor our native roots right where we are. This is good, and shows we are alive and well. It also shows we are MOVING FORWARD.

For those of you wanting to connect with that part of your Tuscarora past and future but have difficulty in doing so remember this: I, for one, consider the native paths and roots of my ancestors. Where in fact did they call home?

A. You do not have to have your name on any roll to be Tuscarora.
B. You do not have to have your name signed off by any individual to celebrate your Tuscarora Roots and Shoots.
C. Here in North Carolina there are those of us who are in fact DAILY building that educational and spiritual bridge from here to there and beyond eternity for those individuals and or families that have been "hungry" to know more about their ancestors walking the walk and talking the talk BUT Have not had a vehicle let alone access to honor that part of their purpose in their lifelong journey.

If you go to the Carlisle Rolls or any other Rolls and discover none of your "familiar" surnames or names are listed when the roll is called up yonder does not mean you are not Tuscarora. What it does mean is that for a variety of manmade reasons that go along with the manmade paper trails certain names made it to the paper trail while others refused to have their names associated with cliques.

Tuscarora Migration 90 Years 1713–1803

This is a message posted at the Tuscaroras.com discussion forum on February 26, 1998.

May 1713, with all h— breaking out at Ft. Neoheroka, a lot of bloodshed was spilled on NC Soil. King Tom Blunt's followers became manipulated by the whites and the hostiles were homeless . . . wandering about. Initially, the hostiles formed small bands and scattered into the woodlands/pocosins/swamplands where mosquitoes were so big you could saddle them just to survive. They lived off of whatever the Creator placed in their tracks. Many became so weak other hostile Indians moved in. But the strength of these people was carrying ancestral fires never to be extinguished . . . forever they will burn and serve as reminders. Opportunity presented itself and those rose up and came together in tribal strength. Some "talked" into believing they should leave NC, fled to the Virginia frontier. Some proceeded on to join their Iroquoian relations. Bottom line . . . NOT ALL MOVED from NC. And just because others migrated to Virginia and Pennsylvania did not cause them to become extinct.

Some Tuscarora lived in the Valley of Virginia. A village was located on the Tuscarora Creek, also known as present-day Berkeley County, West Virginia, near Martinsburg. Other Tuscarora settled in central Pennsylvania. There were paths known to be traditional paths for the Tuscarora to travel back and forth from the North to the South. Some built their lodges/cabins along a river called the Juniata River around 1762. Others lived in Schuylkill County near Tamaqua and others in Wyoming County. This is known as Wilkes-Barre. Others lived among the Mohawks and the Shawnees at Oquaga, Windsor, Broome County, NY. Others lived near Oneida Lake, 1736. Some migrated westward into the Genesee Valley and the Niagara countryside.

Many of the Tuscaroras were said to have lost their "national identity" during this moving about. Fact is: They remained TUSCARORA.

Redbird James

Redbird James [Bonnie James, Red Bird Feather James] (Cherokee) lives in Millington, Tennessee, where she is active in several Indian organizations, most notably the Tennessee Indian Cultural Society. James was born in Fort Worth, Texas, of parents who were Tennesseans. Her husband, David [Hawk] James is a Wyandot writer, and both are active members of Wordcraft Circle of Native Writers and Storytellers. She is currently at work on a novel.

Something Old Is New Again

As far back as any oral history of our people goes, there have always been special gatherings of the people, each according to their own traditions. For many of the Southeastern people, these were done at special times of the year—for new crops, for gathering the crops, etc. At these times a celebratory dance was given called the Stomp (which is a subject all to itself). As the times have changed and people were intermixed tribally and racially, fewer sacred grounds for these dances are left, but the feeling of wanting to gather together with other Native people to pray and sing and dance is still there. One solution to this has spread to the East from the Plain—we call it the powwow.

Now there are many wonderful writings out there on the origin and ways of the powwow, but for simplicity let's say it is a gathering of the people where a circle is formed (all things we believe are based on the circle) and people of all Nations are welcome to come and dance. Most wear the remarkable regalia of their individual Nations, as varied as are the Nations themselves. These events last from two to seven days and are a coming home place for many suburban Indians. A time of getting to know new friends and reestablishing bonds with old ones: a family reunion, if you will, of First Nations people.

One of the many things necessary to have a powwow is a drum. Without the drum, there can be no dancing, and for us dancing means both celebration and prayer. In the old days of the Eastern tribal people, when the Stomps were held, only one man carried a small drum as everybody danced. With the adoption of the powwow, the large powwow style drum was also adopted. A drum measuring 24" to 36" in diameter sits on a crossed wood stand and around it sit four to fifteen men, all beating out the song simultaneously and singing. In some cases, the wives, daughters, and sisters sit or stand behind the men singing with them.

This powwow way has taken a huge place in the world of many of the Southeastern tribes. Roughly 300 powwows a year are held in Oklahoma, Arkansas, Alabama, Louisiana, Tennessee, Florida, Georgia, Kentucky, and the Carolinas. This, of course, means that many of the people accustomed to a different style of music have had a choice. To have a powwow drum in the past meant you learned and sang one of two ways—Northern (based on the songs of the Lakotas, Dakotas, Omahas, Blackfeet, and other Northern tribes) or Southern (which were the songs of the Poncas and Cheyennes and other Southern tribes). The Omaha people were actually the originators of the powwow.

The problem was they were ALL plains songs. While we truly appreciate and honor the Plains people and their ways, and the struggles they endured, these ways were not the ways and struggles of our people of the East and do not tell our story

From this desire to do things in an intertribal powwow way AND to tell our stories in OUR languages comes the style known today as Eastern Woodlands. Many of the old stomp songs have been gently reworked to become powerful powwow songs and now many of the Cherokee, Choctaw, and Seminole people are singing new songs as well in the languages we know and understand. From the stirring songs that honor the flags representing our Nations to the songs honoring the Trail Where They Cried, we are now able to bring together our Brothers and Sisters from all Nations to sing and celebrate, to laugh and pray in a way that all understand.

I am proud to say of the handful of Eastern Woodlands drums (which means all people East of the Mississippi) that have been brought into existence in the past twenty years, my family (which includes Cherokee, Choctaw, Creek, and one Wyandot) is proud to be the keepers of one such drum. Everywhere we go, from Kentucky to Florida, Oklahoma to North Carolina, we hear over and over that to hear these songs and to be able to dance to them in the sunlight is a blessing and that the feeling is one of finally being home. Sometimes old ways can be gently shaped into something new. The importance is in retaining the honor.

Alliance for Native American Indian Rights

One of the hardest working groups of Native People in the State of Tennessee in these times is the Alliance for Native American Indian Rights. Until I joined the organization myself and started really talking to the members, I had no idea of the huge part this organization plays in both the past and the future of the indigenous people of this area.

A Nashville-based nonprofit organization, it was originally incorporated in

1989. At that time, ten Native people from the West Tennessee area wanted to specifically address the alarming growth of grave desecration and looting acts in this part of the state, as well as the huge artifact trade going on here.

Though it is an intertribal organization made up of members from all over the country, most of the active participants are people who live in West Tennessee and whose ancestors lived in this area.

While it also promotes Native American history and culture through gatherings and a yearly powwow, its main goal is protecting from desecration the sacred grave sites, to provide for reinterment when necessary, and to work toward strengthening local and state legislation to include much stronger penalties for the digging and selling of artifacts. One of our goals is to see the state abolish the "termination of cemeteries" statute. One of our slogans is: Graves don't have an expiration date.

In 1999, the Alliance became involved in a series of lawsuits against the Tennessee Department of Transportation, known to us as the Kelly Town Site court battle. The state was trying to destroy at least six burials, during a road-widening project in Middle Tennessee. We are charging that the state is discriminating against Native people in Tennessee by disrespecting our culture and going against the equal protection clause of the constitution.

After being granted a temporary restraining order in August 1999 (something that had never before been accomplished here), some members of the Alliance were given "interested party" status in the multiple suits pending. This status had never been given in Tennessee to a minority group undertaking such an effort.

At this time there are at least five sites being closely monitored by the Alliance and at least three individual court cases pending concerning the sites themselves and the repatriation and reburials that must follow. The Kelly Town Site case is now in appellate court. Meanwhile, we pray, sing, watch, and wait.

Tennessee Commission on Indian Affairs

In the Fall of 2001, I was privileged to be part of a history-making event in Tennessee. For the first time, the native people of this state came together to hold a democratic election of the persons to serve on the proposed Commission of Indian Affairs. In previous years, there had always been one person chosen to be the commissioner over all the people and the organizations of the state. Believing this to be too much for one person to handle, it was decided that a Board of Commissioners would better suit the needs of the people. People of Native heritage from all across Tennessee began planning the whys and wherefores of such an undertaking. It was decided that the state would be divided into seven districts—four would be metro-based in the large cities of

Memphis, Chattanooga, Nashville, and Knoxville, and the other three would be grand divisions covering East, West, and Middle Tennessee.

It was decided that on Saturday, August 25th, 2001, each of these divisions would hold separate caucuses and nominate four regional representatives and elect ten to fifteen delegates to the Tennessee Native American Convention This first convention would be held in September. As I live in West Tennessee, I was one of the four nominated for this district. Many of my family members were elected as representatives to the convention.

The convention itself was held on September 22, 2001, a beautiful fall Saturday. The chosen location was Old Stone Fort State Park, near Manchester, a somewhat central location and a sacred site of the early Indians of the area. With opening prayers by an elder and gathering songs by The Medicine River Singers Drum, the open air convention was off to a history-making start. After socializing and registration, each candidate was given time to declare to the gathering what he or she would be able to offer the people if elected. It ran the gamut from meek and quite, hard work to AIM-style kick-ass rhetoric. When all had their time to share these thoughts, we got down to the business of voting. Ballots were passed to the 200 assembled as they sat in a circle around a central fire. People were given the opportunity to offer tobacco to the fire as they prayed for wise decisions, as well as to give thanks for the gathering itself.

As the day wore on and each division announced their candidates, and as each candidate spoke, small rumblings were sometimes heard about this one being a wannabe or that one not being sober. However, all in all, it was an event filled with hope and promise. By evening the ballots had been tallied and the new board of commissioners-elect were announced. It was a group of fine Indian men and women ready to work for their people in this state.

Three delegates from each division were then named advisory council to this board. I was given one of those seats.

As those present gathered around the drum, songs of victory were sung, and the rest of the evening was spent around separate campfires with discussion and more songs.

As a commission board member, one of the first major things on the agenda was to declare a "New Broader Commission," a five-year, ten committee plan designed to give Native people more say in such areas as correct education, historical markings at sacred places, grave site protection, and better available health care for the impoverished.

Throughout the state, individual committees were meeting, decisions being made, plans being set out. We were well on our way to doing the things for the Indians of Tennessee that some had only dreamed about. Then the governor stepped in.

In 1999, Governor Don Sundquist and some of his staff decided that there were not enough Native American descendents in the state to warrant having an office of the Commission of Indian Affairs. We had been led to believe that if we did provide a commission made up of native people, he would then appoint a person to also be on this commission and it would be reinstated. We went ahead with the meetings and elections and had already started appointing committees. We were careful to keep his office updated. We were becoming, to say the least, cautiously optimistic. When the bill to reinstate the commission came before the state House and Senate, it passed to a majority vote. We almost started to relax. Yet, when it went to the governor's office, the complaints started: He thought there weren't enough Indians (voters) to warrant the office, despite the fact that on the 2000 Tennessee census over 15,000 people marked their forms as either Native American or mixed Native American and other races.

The governor said that there was no blood quantum proven on the newly elected commission seats, even though all of the persons elected either held tribal recognition cards or were personally recognized by their individual communities as being Indian. We and he had also been informed by the state's attorney general that demanding such would be against our constitution.

Another complaint was that there were no appointees on the commission from his office, which could only have been solved if he had appointed someone. It was something we agreed to, but which he never followed through with.

Lastly, he said that he thought that the commission should be placed under the Department of Health (not Environment and Conservation where it had been) because to the eyes of the people in his office we were mostly after social services anyway, instead of being a force for positive action in the state.

On the last day at the last hour, then the governor vetoed the bill that would reinstate the Indian commission. Not only this, but his timing was perfect because he did so as the state congress was recessing for an extended period of time, thus making it impossible to be appealed. His words on the matter were that if the Indians in this state needed representation, he would appoint people to do so. He would take one person from the Cherokees in North Carolina and one from the Chickasaws of Oklahoma—meaning that we would not be allowed to have any say directly about what relates to the Indians of Tennessee.

Despite this, the commission has moved forward, still meeting and planning. Although we have been told that by law we must use the words "PROPOSED commission," we are working together to improve our place and to restore our heritage to this state. Maybe next year they will see us.

Contemporary Writers

Gladys Cardiff

Gladys Cardiff (Cherokee) is the author of *To Frighten a Storm* (1976), which won the Washington State Governor's Writers Award for a first book of poetry. Cardiff was born November 23, 1942, in Browning, Montana. Her parents, from the Cherokee Reservation in North Carolina, were career employees with the Bureau of Indian Affairs, serving on the Blackfeet Reservation at the time. She holds a Ph.D. from Western Michigan University. A second book of poems, *A Bare Unpainted Table*, appeared in 1999. She has been published in most of the principal anthologies in contemporary Native American literature: *Carriers of the Dream Wheel*, *Songs from This Earth on Turtle's Back*, *Wounds Beneath the Flesh*, *That's What She Said*, and *The Remembered Earth*. Cardiff is currently a professor in the English department at Oakland University in Rochester, Michigan, and is completing a new poetry manuscript, "They Hide Now in Deep Pools." Her appearance in the present anthology unites her as a fellow writer with her father, Henry M. Owl; her aunt, Lula Owl Gloyne; her uncle, Frell McDonald Owl; and her cousin, Freeman Owle.

Beautiful Zombies

Kanane'ski Amayehi, Fishing Spider, speaks:

There are things more terrible than death.
To see the turtle tribe swim by,
huge eyes half-dead yet brimmed with tears,
following, always following
some hazy possibility

is to see the manner of my own
predation magnified. Dim-buzz
punching fang and venom volt,

and all the senses washed away. But theirs
is a communal self-inflicted bite.

As they were once, they were the watery
world's artisans. They studied
the designs of water, the surface tension
of still pools, wind-dapple and deep
whorl of moon-called water.

And as they learned, the patterns grew
upon their bodies so that they and water
seemed one. Their numbers increased, their forays
lengthened. If one was hurt, it thought
into itself the intricacies

of water, and sewed itself back up.
Everyone knows only a turtle
can loose a turtle's bite. They thought:
"We are living calendars. Time
and we are one. Time heals our wounds."

They no longer studied water. Their bodies
thickened, became deeply
engraved. They slowed down, forgot the trick
of mending themselves. They live a half-
life of perpetual noon. They cast no shadow.

Prelude to Love

Given another unknown face: first, hair;
                    then what the eyes are doing; then
monkey-wise, the covert volley, eyes to mouth, mouth to eyes,
                        do they match?
Let's say yes. The hoped-for, pleasurable, reassuring mouth.

But this is a photo, a portrait. Long hair, black eyes—
my gaze skips the rest.
                    Whose wouldn't? Except for a necklace, no,
not a necklace, except for her earrings, she's naked.

Bare breasts, sepia pale, pushing out from the portrait fully,
contoured against her, plum shadows curving under. How they fall
a summer's day of leisurely scoops and burdens from shoulders
        to ribs,

plum space where her arm curves in, a last light sash of sepia
        ribcage

                                        cropped.
Whose genuis is she? How is she beautiful, erotic,
and yet so like a bare, unpainted table?
Her hair is straight and long, and parted in the middle.
Her face is broad. Her gaze, flat. Her mouth, unsmiling.

But how extravagant her earrings are. Finger-weaving.
Looped through large hoops at her ears,
long lattice-work strands drape like braids over her breasts,
the two ribbons held in a V by a third,
hooked, one ear to the other,
which hangs like a loose chin strap, or martingale.
The whole of it makes a breastplate.

She's posed as if she's in a mission,
standing under the arch of a mission window, looking out.
Almost courtly, the arousals, almost Spenserian, to be so
        framed,
                                her neather parts
concealed *in secret shadow farre from all men's sight,*
space pulled up like a high-waisted Empire gown. A Victorian
        postcard,
not the racy, *raw mementos*, the private snaps that came
in the 1890s with the new handhelds, with the "Facile"
        and Kodak Falcon.
The sill is a blank place to nail a plaque with a legend:
                        Dangers of the Indian Country,
part of a series. Frontier Exposures. File it backward in time,
archival, colonial nude. Or as, perhaps, a prelude to love.

Going Home to Cherokee

for Donald

It's Don's turn at the wheel. Denise is by his side.
We've been driving all day, bumper to bumper,
through Dollyland, Pigeon Fork, the Gainesville bottleneck.
It's been alien, mile after mile of false fronts,
bungee jumps, gun and car museums, theme parks

and eateries, souvenir shops. G. Love is singing, wry
and gravelly, "My baby ain't sweet like yours."
The road becomes loopier. We climb up and wind down.
Even the Smokies are a slog. Except for Clingman's Dome,
we neglect the overlooks. We settle for glimpses; distant,
blue wooden slopes, brown screes, black cataracts, yellow balds,
the white peaks standing like mystics who will remain
long after the travelers have departed.
From now on, we'll be on Indian land.
I've been frank about how the gauntlet doesn't end,
goes right into town, becomes Cherokee skyrides,
motels, billboard appeals. The water slide is neon blue
and flaunts a single engine prop plane crunched at the top
in a simulated wreck, one wing flailing against green trees,
blue sky. What was tacky and bizarre before
has a new edge now. We drive past Saunooke Village,
the Teepee, the Indian Princess. Chief Big Eagle waves.
He's Cherokee, but his garb is Plains-style; the red tunic,
black bicycle shorts, the blue feathers, garish.
"Faux-Sioux," I quip. Like this stretch into town,
he is what he is but not what he seems.
"I can't go there," Don says. It's the Bear Park.
Live Bears! Feed the Bears! My son is shaking his head.
Denise rests her hand on his thigh. She glances back at me.
I think how he must love the way her short hair
curls around her ear. *Bittersweet*, I think, reminded again
about the part of motherhood that is reeling,
reeling out, letting go. We pass Best Western and the Bingo Hall.
We cross to the other side of the Oconoluftee
and turn down the drive that flanks Mollie's plot
of sweet corn. Taller than a man, in rows, the prop
roots mounded, sword-shaped leaves. Green
feather capes, headdresses, gold topknots.
We're on Mollie's allotment, Parcel #12, Upper Cherokee,
Qualla Boundary, Swain County, Cherokee, North Carolina.
Our side of Rattlesnake is in shadow. Late afternoon.
Up, up, up, deep trees. From this side of the river
all the way up its slope is Owl family land.
Tomorrow, I think, we'll stand on the porch

and I'll point up, about there, where a few slants
of sun will be angling across the posts
of the wood crib, crossed in an **X**, all
that's left of his grandfather's childhood home.

A surprise going in, like a boat. The trailer
roomier than it appears from outside.
Nook kitchenette. Neat living room, shag,
dark narrow hall. Denise slips her hand,
small and pale, into his. I remember Mollie's voice crackling
through the phone last week. Just calling to chat.

I hope the trailer will be okay. I've sent a map.
Be careful! The tourists drive so fast.
Slow down when you see my corn, the turn's right after.
How we talk is what I love. Nuance.
A kind of propriety. Ear-work. *I was cleaning.*
I used to work real hard at cleaning house.
You know how people used
to think in the old days. Thooose Injuns.
"Shiftless," I say. And then we laughed.
Lace curtains lift. Cool breeze. The master bedroom
is sunny. For you, Don; for you, Denise.

We hear the crunch of tires. Mollie's here.
How can I say what it is like to see her face?
This face is one I sink into, whether it's
a stranger's in the post office or a history
professor at Kalamazoo. It's my father's face,
and my brother's. My sister's broad forehead.
Deep mouth lines, slightly hooded eyes, and, yes,
chiseled lips. A face inclined to quiet.
Things pass swiftly across it. Faces capable
of keeping what's thought to the barest nudge.
And now, my cheek against the warm flat
of hers, I think maybe we look a little silly,
a woman in her eighties, one in her fifties,
leaning, propped against each other, grinning
like crazy. But we don't care. And that's my son
walking, to see him one might say, walking
easily, toward us, his hand outstretched.

Khv:na

Rustling through the leaves below my window
while I am rising from doughy sleep,
your pip, pip, falling from the eaves,
because it is early light, and nothing much is about
to disturb you—for this little time,
I like you.

I know how you are.
You carry yourself like an only book.

Even the grouse, who had a good voice once,
and who wears forever some of your feathers,
could not teach you how to enter a field
with a beautiful victory cry.
Any noise for you is his drumming.
A door slams, or dog bark, or lawn mower sets you off.
You of the gutturals, the bray,
the nerve-rending screech, go lurching,
silly as a blown cabbage on stake legs
the color of burned bone, driving through the underbrush,
the scalplocks fastened around your neck, bouncing,
bobbling your red wattles,
the jut of your powerful neck, your naked
immune-to-death blue cobbled head,
your talons ripping wet clods and tossing them out behind you.

Gobbler in every sense, a "lord ful fat"
Chaucer would say, "that stemmed as a furnais of lead."

I've seen you snitch the cat's discards,
wagging the small purple lump of bird or mole
crazily through blackberry trailers and foxglove stalks.

A ruckus of gabbling. You swayed over a hen,
the hen going quiet, her neck seized in your beak.
Your bronze feathers cracked and cracked.
Hers glistened and cracked; some fell out
as she sank under the freight of you.
Fan-tail, redness, commotion, quiet.

Khv:na. I am learning to say it.
Khv:na khane:ke. Turkey, he is speaking.
It is too beautiful for you.

Two Plots: Qualla Boundary, Cherokee

Steep, narrow, as any rural mountain road is,
this one winds up Rattlesnake,
past cousin Dan's cantilevered house.

On the side of this mountain, the space allotted is carved and fitted,
like the yellow stones of Yellowhill Baptist, Grandmother Nettie's
small country church. Only the bell-steeple is made of white wood.

Some things won't fit in a photograph, though the sense of things
    suspended
would be true. After the car doors and gravel, we were hushed
    in the grass.
If there were birds, I didn't hear them. A faint breeze blew
    across my ears, felt, but not heard.

But, here, under the cross, it is the sun that is most fitting,
laying our portion across our shoulders as we look off into space.
Here, two little cemeteries are fitted on either side of the road.

On this side, one stands, shelved on a small green apron
downside of the church. It hardly has room for itself.
Small, white, regimental wood crosses are packed in rows
to the verge and open sky.

Across the way, a little bigger, starting right on the shoulder
of the road, the other cemetery dissembles, yellow and overgrown.
In the shadows, crosses and headstones, dull bronze plaques,

and inconspicuous flowers strewn like afterthoughts. Members
of my family are buried here. Their graves are well-marked.
The nestling hackberry and huckleberry respect the preference
of others, here, not to be noticed, except by a few, and pokeberry,

too tangles, pushing up against the side of Rattlesnake.
Steep, blue, sheer, thick with trees, stolid, you think, solemn,
until, leaning back, one notices the tops barely swaying. White pine,

pitch pine, sweetgum, like coming home after a boat trip,
grabbing the sides of the shower stall so you won't fall down,
blackgum, cucumbertree, silverbell, and hemlock,
    and shining sumac.

Pamela Masotti

Pamela Masotti (Cherokee) is a poet living in Texas. She served as an editor of *Coastlines Literary Magazine* while attending Florida Atlantic University.

Jukebox

The family took the names from the white man. They were forced to take these names: Ray, Frannie, Jane-Leigh, and Ray, Jr. They had their original names, still, but never called each other by them. It was forbidden in this house. Ray wanted to have his family fit in and not make any noise to attract themselves any unwanted attention. Even though Ray was trying to get his family to fit into the new world of the whites, he still wanted to hold on to whatever he felt suited him best. He still wanted to be able to denounce bad health diagnoses from doctors. He still wanted to drink his drink whenever he wanted and to curse the "stupid white man."

They lived in an old, rickety wooden-frame house. They had to go around to the back of the house to relieve themselves. This didn't bother them, though. They never knew any different. They just walked out to the outhouse and squatted over the bucket. Then, they would take the waste and bury it. It was routine; just like taking baths. They heated the bathwater over the fire in the winters and they went down to Flat Rock Creek during the summers. But these were not problems because they never knew any better.

They did have problems, though. Just like the next family, this family had its share of problems. Ray had complete control over his family and everything they did. The wife and kids didn't much mind this, though. Every father had control over the family around this time—particularly around these parts. Country people and natives that overtime became country people, too, followed the same patterns. The father ran the house, while the mother cleaned and cooked and gardened. The kids—well, these kids were some of the first to go to school. The white man's school. These kids were known as "first generation educated Injuns."

Frannie would cook and clean and garden. Ray would farm and sell and drink. Farm and sell and drink some more. He only came home to eat and sleep and beat the shit out of his son and his wife. Usually this happened after he drank some more.

Whap! Whap!

"Aaaaaaah!" Ray, Jr., wails out as his father whips his eighteen-year-old ass. Ray, Jr., is always getting a beating from his father and the water hose. Well, sometimes it is the belt—the end with the hook—but usually it was the dust-covered old water hose. That water hose had no other purpose to it. The family had no running water, so what was a hose doing around their house, anyways? Originally, it was traded at the market for some watermelons and squash. Ray seemed to think that the hose could be used as strong rope—or maybe even someday could actually have real, wet water running through it.

"How can you beat me? All I want to do is go to a real job over in Raleigh."

Ray, Jr., never questioned his father's beatings before. At least he never questioned his father about them before. But Frannie, she was different. She and Ray, Jr., would sit on the stone front step, wondering if the beatings would ever end.

"Sugar, I'm not sure if that day will ever come. Your daddy just gets too drunk and comes home to take it out on the two of us."

"How come he never lays a finger on Jane-Leigh?"

"I don't know. Maybe because she's a girl?"

"But you're a girl, too, Mama."

"Yeah, but he is stuck with me. He probably doesn't even think of me as a girl anymore. Used to, though. He used to think I was beautiful. Now, he just doesn't think of me—at least I don't think so."

"But what do you mean by saying that he is stuck with you? Isn't Jane-Leigh, also?"

"Well, if I know your father's scheming, drunk mind, I believe he will soon be trying to trade his only daughter. She's so pretty that I'm sure the thought's crossed his mind. Maybe that's why he never beats her."

"So, Daddy, can I use the truck to run in to Raleigh for the job interview up at the plant?"

"I guess so, boy. First, you must drop me off down at the Jukebox. Then you can go to your stupid, white man interview. Why do you want to work for him? Can't handle a real day's work in the fields anymore?"

"I thought you wanted us to be more like them, Daddy?"

"I never said that!"

"Well, maybe you didn't say those exact words, but you do always talk about how some of their ways are better than ours."

"Don't question me, boy. Just get your ass up there in the truck and let's go."

The Jukebox is a rundown shack the local red men call their home away from home.

They go there to hide out from the family, work, and facing the reality of their simple worlds. They go there to get wasted on the pure grain alcohol they make. Just about a mile and a half down the path past Flat Rock Creek, the Jukebox can be found. Ray, Jr., although old enough to follow his father in the door and get a drink of his own, decided a long time ago to never step foot in the place.

"Okay, Daddy. I'll drop you off down at the Juke. But remember what the doctor told you?"

"You think I really give a rat's ass what the white man says about my health? They know nothing about medicine. My drink is my medicine. I work too hard to stop my only pleasure in life."

"As much as I understand what you are saying about their knowledge of medicine, I still think you should listen to the doctor's advice. Think about it, you are the first from our family to go and see a real doctor. That should say something."

"Boy, you are in rare form today. What did someone put a quarter in you? Don't you ever shut up? Do you want another beating?"

Ray, Jr., doesn't know how to respond to this. Instead, he flinches away from his dad and stares straight ahead at the road.

Just a month or two before, Ray went to the doctor. He was having trouble seeing and thought that he may need glasses. The doctor ran some tests and told him that he had blood on his retinas. This could be caused by only two things: One, damage to his eye from time out in the fields. Or, two, liver trouble.

Just before dusk, Ray, Jr., pulls up in the rusted out Chevy. As he walks towards the house, he smells his dinner cooking. He walks in and sees Jane-Leigh and Frannie boiling corn and stirring another pot over the fire. Ray, Jr., walks over to hug his mother's neck.

"Whatcha making? I'm so hungry, I could eat a horse."

"Be patient, Ray, we have to wait for Daddy."

"He's not home yet?"

"No. And I will tell you what, if he does not get in here soon, we'll eat without him. I can't keep this food hot all night over a dying fire. And I am sick of making all this food and then we end up eating after we waited for two hours for him to come home."

The three sit down at the table together and start their suppers. There is a certain lightness to the conversation—something different from times in the past. Each of the three feel a bit more liberated today than days in past. Ray, Jr., had stood up to his father for the first time ever. Frannie had decided to start supper right after she finished the cooking. Even Jane-Leigh is not as shy and quiet as she normally is during supper. They are actually cajoling one another.

"You shoulda seen that guy who interviewed me. He was strange. He took his hair and had it greased down, covering a balding spot. Anyways, I hope I got the job."

"I'm sure you got that job, sugah. You are a fine boy—well, a man now, I guess. Besides, you're my son." She looks at Ray, Jr., with a bright smile across her leathered face.

Two days pass and there is still no sign of Ray. Ray, Jr., goes around looking for him in the fields and over by the Jukebox, but he is nowhere to be found and no one has seen him lately.

"The last place I saw your daddy was at the Juke."

Ray, Jr., questions some of his father's friends, but they can't help either. When he arrives at the Jukebox, he sees the usual trucks and bicycles parked around the shack. He doesn't want to go inside, but no one is outside for him to ask about his father's whereabouts.

Ray, Jr., steps on a dusty wooden floor. Everyone quiets down and looks towards the door. They all wave at Ray, Jr., or tip their hats a bit. Ray, Jr., looks around, deciding who he should approach. He walks over to the guy leaning against the wall in the left-hand corner of the room. Johnny Red is a distant cousin of Ray, Jr.'s. The same age as Ray, Jr., this guy followed his father from the fields right on into the Juke. He doesn't have the aspirations that Ray, Jr., has. He is already a drunk.

"Hey, Johnny Red, have you seen my daddy around?"

"Huh? No. I haven't seen him in a while. Did you try some of the fields?"

"Yeah, but they told me that this was the last place they saw him so that's why I came here."

"Did you look around outside of here? Sometimes men have been known to wander off when having one of those nights of drinking."

Ray, Jr., thinks to himself. He decides that he will take a quick walk around the vicinity surrounding the shack. If he doesn't locate his father, he will head on home. Maybe his dad skipped town on him and his mama and sister.

He says his good-byes to his cousin, then walks out the door. He circles the building, hoping to find his father passed out somewhere with his back against the wall of the shack. No luck. He moves out a little further into the woods and comes across a little makeshift covering under some pine trees. He lifts the flap of the cover and walks in. When his eyes adjust to the dark, he sees a body hunched over, leaning against the tree. The weird thing is that the body has a jacket or some sort of coat flung over it. Ray, Jr., reaches slowly to remove the jacket from the head of the body. It hangs there like a coat on a hook on the back of a door. When he finally gets a good grasp of the collar, he pulls down the coat quickly, revealing a man slumped over. He shakes him vigorously and calls out his father's name. Then he yells, "Daddy, Daddy." No answer.

He puts his hand right in front of his father's mouth and feels for his breathe. His daddy is not breathing. He throws down the coat and runs back to the truck. He hops in and speeds down the clay path, blowing up red dirt that clouds the path trailing behind the truck.

Ray, Jr., tells his mother what he found.

"Yeah. I was waiting for this day to come. I knew that liquor would kill him sooner or later."

"So, what do we do now, Mama?"

"Don't worry. I'll figure something out."

Two more days pass. One night, there is a knock at the door. It is the police. Jane-Leigh gets nervous and starts pacing and ringing her hands.

"Girl, what's wrong with you? Answer the door!"

"But it's the po-lice. Should I open the door?"

"Of course, girl. Why wouldn't you?"

The policeman barges his way past Jane-Leigh and into the center of the kitchen. He tells Frannie of the news of her late husband's body being discovered. She sits down and starts to cry.

"When was the last time you saw your husband?"

"Four days ago."

"Why haven't you been looking for him?"

"Well, my son did. I figured that he was just out again wasting money on his drink."

"Are you aware of where we located your husband's body?"

"Probably down at that shack in the woods."

"Yes. How did you guess?"

"Well, that's where he spends most of his time and he was dying of cirrhosis of the liver, according to his doctor. So, I figured that he probably passed out and died in his sleep somewhere."

"He did not die of natural causes. He was shot in the stomach and bled to death."

"What? You are lying. The only enemy he had in this town was himself. I probably qualify as the next in line as one of his enemies before someone else in town would."

"So are you suggesting that you could have been involved in your husband's death?"

"I am a woman, for god sakes. I wouldn't know the first thing about killing someone and we don't own no gun. Plus, like I told you, he was gonna die soon anyways. I was just waiting around for that to happen."

"Well, alright. We'll be in touch."

Ray, Jr., can't believe how quickly they accept the answer from his mother.

She is practically telling them that she is the one and only suspect. He knows his mama doesn't have it in her, though.

Jane-Leigh gets out of the chair and walks over to her mother and wraps her arms around her neck. She plants her face in her mother's bosom. Frannie just gazes out past Jane-Leigh, past the wall—almost to an unidentifiable space. Somewhere unattainable.

Later that evening, Ray, Jr., sits on the front stone step with his mother, listening to the crickets and watching the sky. The clouds move quickly like a storm is approaching.

Frannie closes her eyes and lifts her head towards the sky above. She takes a long breath in. She smells rain again.

"Mama, what should we do about Daddy?"

"What do you mean, sugah?"

"Should we go get his body and provide him with a burial ceremony?"

"Your daddy has been dead for a long time, Ray. Don't you worry about that body, you hear?"

"Yeah, but what about tradition?"

"Your daddy never allowed us to practice our traditions, so we are not gonna start again—especially by giving him a proper burial."

"I don't understand. He was our family. He was my daddy—your husband."

"Don't you worry anymore, you hear? We don't need to do a thing with him. It's all over now."

She pulls her son close, placing his head in her lap as she rubs his back. Even though Ray, Jr., is curled up in his mama's lap, he knows that he must now become the man of the house. For the first time in her adult life, Frannie takes a big breath in and exhales out loud. Ray, Jr., feels the movement of her heaving chest and breathes the same way. He knows that it is all over now. He realizes that his mama has always been the head of the house. She makes things safe for him. She takes care of the evil. She is his protector.

Allison Adelle Hedge Coke

Allison Adelle Hedge Coke (Cherokee-Huron) was born in Amarillo, Texas, on August 4th, 1958. Her father's family lives in North Carolina, where she spent part of her girlhood, but she has also lived throughout the Great Plains and in California. Hedge Coke holds an A.F.A. from the Institute of American Indian Arts and a master's degree from Vermont College, as well a professional performing arts certificate from Estelle Harmon's. She has published poetry in numerous anthologies, such as *Reinventing the Enemy's Language*, *Gatherings*, *Dissolving Boundaries*, *Sister Nations*, and *Visit Teepee Town*, and has co-edited *Voices of Thunder*, *It's Not Quiet Anymore*, *Working Clans*, and *Radio Wave Mama*. Her poetry collection, *Dog Road Woman*, was published in 1998 and was an American Book Award winner the following year. Her autobiographical memoir, *Rock, Ghost, Willow, Deer*, came out in 2004. Two more books of poetry, *Off-Season City Pipe* and *Blood Run*, were published in 2005 and 2007, respectively. She currently holds the Paul W. and Clarice Kingston Reynolds Chair of Poetry at the University of Nebraska at Kearney.

Off-Season

Early, on grayest morning, when we
nettled deep in between rows,
tobacco and sweet potato,
both two seasons away from planting,
you reasoned I belonged there,
flowing like creek water
below our bright leaf fields,
then showing only golden stubble and root.
You said I'd never make it
swinging hammers and teething
saws for Inland Construction.
I raised my back wings, those muscles
wrought from priming rows, muscles
which cradled my ribs and sides. I
chucked tools in the flat bed, headed
north, to the city sprawled out like

scattered masonry and split rails, Raleigh,
smoked factory winds and speak easy halls.

A white chicken fell off a Tyson rig,
just a bit ahead of me on Saunders Street.
I called her "Hooker"
from walking down the red light street.
The Inland guy hiring was big and red,
sat behind a door laid flat for a desk on cinder block.
He chuckled much like you
at the sight of me, but the fields and breaking horses,
justified my ninety pounds of lean.
Next day he had me start out on a crew full of men.
Men who'd never seen a woman work
that way in town, first
time I had a chance to operate a back hoe,
first time I got to frame, and when I swung the hammer
full leverage, three pounds drove in sixteenpennys straight.
In six weeks, I made foreman.
Just before I drove back to you.
"Hooker" almost got pecked to death
by our bantams—citified as she was.

I laid out so much money, I beat
what you pulled in for fall. We settled in
for the long freeze. You ate ridicule and haste.
We never were the same,
until spring when the fields reclaimed
us as their own and we returned
to what we both knew and belonged to.
The off-season only an off-shoot
in what we were meant to be.
You never did know this part
of what I am. Fieldworker, or framer,
I only showed you what you said I couldn't be.

The Change

(For the sharecropper I left behind in '79)

Thirteen years ago,   before bulk barns and
fifth-gear diesel tractors,   we rode royal blue tractors with

toolboxes big enough   to hold a six-pack on ice.
In the one-hundred-fifteen-degree   summer
Heat   with air   so thick with moisture
you drink as you breathe.
Before the year the dusters sprayed
malathion over the clustered bodies,   perspiring
while we primed bottom lugs,
those ground-level leaves of tobacco,
and it clung to us with black tar so sticky we rolled
eight-inch balls off our arms at night   and
cloroxed our clothes for hours and hours.
Before we were poisoned   and
the hospital thought we had been burned in fires,
at least to the third degree,
when the raw, oozing hives that
covered ninety-eight percent of our bodies
from the sprays ordered by the FDA
and spread by   landowners,
before anyone had seen
automated machines that top and prime.
While we topped the lavender
blooms of many tiny flowers
gathered into one,   gorgeous.
By grasping hold below the petals
with our bare, calloused hands
and twisting downward, quick, hard,
only one time,   snapped them off.
Before edgers and herbicides took
what *they*   called weeds,
when we walked for days
through thirty acres   and
chopped them out with hoes.
Hoes,   made long before   from wood and steel
and sometimes (even longer ago)
from wood and deer scapula.
Before the bulk primers came
and we primed all the leaves by hand,
stooped over at the waist for the
lower ones   and   through the season
gradually   rising higher   until   we stood

and worked simultaneously,
as married to the fields as we were to each other,
carrying up to fifty pounds of fresh
leaves under each arm   and   sewing them onto
sticks four feet long on a looper
under the shade of a tin-roofed barn,   made of shingle,
and poking it up through the rafters inside
to be caught by a hanger   who
poked it up higher in the rafters   to another
who held a higher position
and   so   they filled the barn.
And the leaves hung down
like butterfly wings,   though
sometimes the color of
luna moths,   or Carolina parakeets,   when just
an hour ago   they had been
laid upon   the old wooden
cart trailers pulled behind
the orange Allis-Chalmers tractor
with huge round fenders and only
a screwdriver and salt in the toolbox.
Picked by primers   so hot
we would race through the rows
to reach the twenty-five gallon
jugs of water placed throughout
the fields to encourage   and   in attempt to
satisfy our insatiable thirsts
from drinking air   which poured
through our pores without breaking
through to our need   for more
water   in the Sun.
Sun we imagined to disappear
yet respected   for growing all things on earth
when quenched with rains called forth
by our song   and drumming.
Leaves, which weeks later,   would be
taken down and the strings pulled
like strings on top of a large dog food bag
and sheeted up into burlap sheets

that bundled over a hundred pounds
when we smashed down with our feet,
but gently smashing,
then thrown up high   to
a catcher   on a big clapboard trailer
pulled behind two-ton trucks and
taken to market in Fuquay-Varina
and sold to Philip Morris   and
Winston-Salem   for around   a buck a pound.
Leaves cured to a bright leaf,
a golden yellow with the strongest
aroma of tobacco barn-curing
and hand-grown quality
before the encroachment of
big business in the Reagan era
and the slow murder of method
from a hundred years before.
When the loons cried out in
laughter by the springs and
the bass popped the surface on
the pond, early on, next to
the fields, before that time
when it was unfashionable to
transplant each individual baby plant,
the infant tobacco we nurtured, to
transplant those seedlings to each hill
in the field, the space for that particular plant
and we watched   as   they would grow.
Before all of this new age, new way,
I was a sharecropper in Willow Springs, North Carolina
as were you   and we were proud to be Tsa la gi
wishing for winter   so we could make camp
at Qualla Boundary   and the Oconaluftee River
would be free of tourists and filled with snow
and those of us who held out forever
and had no CIBs would be home again
with our people, while the BIA forgot to watch.
When we still remembered before even the Europeans,
working now shoulder to shoulder with descendants

of their slaves they brought from Africa
when they sold our ancestors as slaves to the Middle East,
that then the tobacco was sacred to all of us and we
prayed whenever we smoked and
did not smoke for pleasure   and
I   was content and free.
Then they came and changed things
and you left me for a fancy white girl
and I waited on the land
until you brought her back
in that brand-new white Trans Am,
purchased from our crop,   you gave her
and left her waiting in a motel,
the nearest one was forty miles away,
but   near enough   for you
and   for her   and I knew   though
I never spoke a word to you
about it,   I knew   and I kept it to
myself   to this day   and time and
I never let on
until I left   on our anniversary.
I drove the pickup
down the dirt path   by the empty fields
and rented a shack for eighty dollars,
the one with cardboard windows
and a Gillespie house floor design,
with torn and faded floral paper on walls
and linoleum so thin over rotted board
that the floor gave if you weighed over
a hundred pounds,   I did not.
And with no running water of any kind,   or bathroom.
The one at hilltop,   where I could
see out across all the fields
and hunt for meat when I wanted
and find peace.
I heard you remarried
and went into automated farming
and kept up with America.
I watched all of you   from the hill

and I waited for the lavender blooms
to return   and when it was spring
even the blooms   had turned white.
I rolled up my bedroll,   remembering before,
when the fields were like waves on a green ocean,
and turned away,   away from the change
and corruption   of big business on small farms
of traditional agricultural people,   and sharecroppers.
Away,   so that I could always   hold this concise image
of before   that   time and it
floods   my memory.

Sequinned

for S.J. in the city & Marsha Stands

Don't tell me you couldn't reach down pick up
the whole gleaming garment and wear it
to fancy shawl dance back home. Dancing proud
in a twenty-four-dollar trinket city

all laid out
shimmering and shining on jet black world
traffic lights, street lamps, hot neons, cool fluorescents.

Headlights
      swim freeways electric

      minnows, glittering eyelets on bridges
bridges lacing up New York and Newark, separate
sides of a sequinned vest.   Borough lights trace out
webbed wing

butterfly designs, no wasps—mosquitoes even.
Something ready to fly off the whole metro stretch.
Some cousin calling:
Girl, leave your French brains tight   'cause
      Cut Nose is goin' ta have it out with you
over snagging her sometimes half-side last night.
She wants to take your prize and crown
      from Red Nations Pow Wow—
Her eyes painted sharp red at the corners,

red as the landing light
    on this plane's wing tip.
Her plume high and straight, the Empire State,
while yours falls
    gently over your part. But that vest—
red, green, gold, silver sparkles,
no one SPACE got more brilliance.
More elegant than bugle beads and embroidery
more stunning than satin and silk.

Girl, don't you let that city get away.
Lift it up, raise it, slip your arms through
and take it back to dance.

Ralph Salisbury

Ralph Salisbury (Cherokee) is professor emeritus from the University of
Oregon, where he taught for most of his academic career, from 1951 until his
retirement in 1994. His mixed-blood Cherokee ancestors immigrated north-
westerly from Tennessee and Kentucky in the 19th century to Iowa, where he
was born in Arlington on January 24, 1926. He served in the U.S. Army Air
Force, 1944–1946, and afterwards attended the University of Iowa, where he
received an M.F.A. in 1951. His published books of poetry include *Ghost Grape-
fruit and Other Poems* (1972), *Pointing at the Rainbow* (1980), *Spirit Beast
Chant* (1982), *Going to the Water* (1982), *A White Rainbow* (1985), and *Rainbows of Stone* (2000), as well as an edited anthology, *A Nation Within* (1983).
He is also the author of such works of prose as *One Indian and Two Chiefs*
(1993) and *The Last Rattlesnake Throw and Other Stories* (1998), both works
of collected short fiction. *Rainbows of Stone* was a finalist for the 2002
Oregon Book Award. Salisbury has received a Rockefeller Bellagio Award, a
Chapelbrook Award, and others in his long writing career. He has also been an
Amparts lecturer in India and has twice been a Fulbright professor in Europe.

The Only Medicine Sure

*(for Chicabob, my father's mother's mother, and for John and Mary Ax, who
ministered to our people)*

My dad, did he say anything, did he say,
a prayer so old the words
were ones he
had not ever heard,
his mother's mother's breath
blown from his tongue,
with smoke from tobacco,
the Medicine Hummingbird had suffered—throat
to glow like a lighted pipeful, forever—to win
for us, from selfish or testing Gods—and did I—
my ear-drum almost burst,

from centuries of pain
aeons of evil spirits inflicted on
untold numbers of listeners in human genes—did I hear
Grandmother's parents' parents' prayers,
to be shaped, warmed and sung in my own generation?

the only medicine sure
whatever we give when we try
to give more
than the Gods alone
seem able to give.

Cherokee Ghost Story: My Father's

Their whisky, women, dancing and clouds
    of their greetings fading in cold wind,
the stranger, pale astride—
    a mount as white
    as reflected moon
    they'd turned thirsty horses toward—rode
full gallop through flesh, pierced
by arrows of enemies decades dead,
    answering gunshots echoing in
    a meteor-crater the young
    men ride,
decades of words,
    from the tongue
    of the son of one of them.

Without Thunder

Twelve, I was shocked out of dreams by what
whatever makes thunder had done to the barn
my mother's father, whom I'd only known
as chiseled stone, had built from trees—
last leaves become food
for grass—cows' grazing becoming bones
and teeth, as I drank, every day, without thought.

Fifteen, my father and brothers heard,
thunderbolt's Voice Beyond Words,
and my singed ears tuned-in

silence, more clear than radios' military oratory,
my body the barn, risen from ashes of hay
and animals, to teeter on finger, as in
fevered delirium, at three.

Eighteen and feeling the roller-coaster lift,
a bomber lightened of load, I saw, and I see
what brothers and father saw touch me, and, friends
turned into smoke, I heard,
and I hear, only my own sounds,
failing at becoming understanding.

Of Pheasant and Blue-Winged Teal

Mother's people, pictured in their stiff black best,
were filed in drawers, but Dad's killed,
buffalo, deer and bear, respectfully, and,
in an oral history
not on school shelves,
defended sacred land
against the White kids' dead,
family hunters and warriors closer to me
than any teacher across a desk,
bone fingers guiding gun dropping rainbow glory of pheasant and blue-winged teal
and Nazism's Christian-crossed planes
from sky—ghost tongues lightning from
my own dark tomb.

Ginny Carney

Ginny Carney (Cherokee) currently serves as the dean of academic affairs, along with her full-time duties as a professor, at Leech Lake (Anishinabe) Tribal College in Minnesota. A poet and fiction writer, as well as an administrator, Carney was born in Maryville, Tennessee, in 1941. A registered nurse, she obtained her bachelor's degree from Tennessee Temple University, a master's degree from the University of Alaska-Anchorage, and a Ph.D. from the University of Kentucky. Her book, *Eastern Band Cherokee Women: Cultural Persistence in Their Letters and Speeches,* was published in 2005. "A Time to Heal" is from a novel-in-progress.

A Time to Heal

Caty's dark eyes misted unexpectedly as she studied the lifeless husk of a long-gone cicada, clinging tenaciously to the bark of a gnarled, old pear tree. "Thirty years. Thirty years of married life, five young'uns to finish raisin', and I'm still a-workin' like a mule," mused the solitary woman. "Empty as that ol' locust shell, though, I reckon."

The day was muggy, typical for August. Caty wiped her clammy forehead with the back of her dress sleeve as she strained to adjust a hairpin in the bun of black hair unraveling on top of her head. Suffocating in the afternoon haze, the five-foot, full-figured woman unbuttoned the cuffs of her long-sleeved muslin dress, glanced cautiously toward the front porch and unbuttoned the high-necked collar as well. "This is a heap of foolishness," she mumbled, her black eyes snapping. "Whoever come up with the idea that womenfolk must keep their limbs covered—even in this heat—oughta be shot!" Staring absently at the empty locust shell, she contemplated, as she had so frequently these past few months, how different life might have been, living among her own people.

John was a good man, she reckoned, but he had let her know right from the start that he had no use for her "Indian ways," and as the babies had come— twelve of them in all—Caty found herself too tired to argue with the strong-willed Scot she had married, too mentally exhausted to sort through all the happenings of her life.

Something, however—she couldn't say exactly what—had stirred up her memory today, and, in spite of the stifling heat, Caty McLeod found herself leaving the orchard and her house and children behind, pulled along by some invisible force to the pine thicket on the south end of their hillside farm.

Back in the mountains of North Carolina, she reflected, a person could find relief from the heat, could find peace in the woodlands. One of the delights of Caty's listening to Wind, was crafting stories with the flair of an artist, evoking at first only a self-conscious tittering in the tops of the centuries-old trees, then sending waves of laughter through the entire forest, leaving the saplings swaying in silent mirth long after the aged ones were still.

Moving to North Georgia had been John's idea—not hers—and the red clay hills and lonesome pine trees seemed to intensify the sense of foreboding which hovered about Caty lately. She had tried once telling her husband about this fear—a kind of "warning" feeling like the one she had just before her family got spit up back in the 1830s, and like she felt when word came in the '60s of the War Between the States. John had looked at her sternly and bellowed, "Woman, where's yore faith? All this superstition is going to make heathens out of the children, and folks is a-going to think I married me a lunatic."

Since John's outburst, Caty had tucked her thoughts quietly away, willing them to remain in seclusion until nighttime, forcing them to wait for the discordant snoring of her household before permitting them to tumble forth and haunt her.

The solitude she enjoyed today, however, gave rise to a multitude of memories, and with the carefree abandonment of a young child, she entered the thicket—soothed by the sighing of Georgia pines, content in the humid stillness surrounding her.

Springing youthfully atop a large rock beneath a scaling sycamore tree, Caty surveyed the creek area for cottonmouths before sitting down and removing her heavy brogans. Water spiders skittered across the surface, and crawdads backed swiftly underneath creekbed rocks, as the laughing woman lowered her sweaty feet, caked with red dust, into the clear, cool waters of Sylco Creek.

"Today I am Wa-le-la," she whispered.

Born prematurely, she had been a miraculously spunky baby, whose lively flailing of miniature arms and urgent rooting for breast milk had brought murmurs of happiness to her anxious parents. "So tiny, so active! Our daughter will be called Wa-le-la—Hummingbird," her elated mother had declared.

The story of her birth had been told and retold so often that she knew her parents' dialogue by heart. "It was *Duna Na-Dee*, Harvest Month," Kitteuah would begin. "I remember it well. I had sat most all day slicing apples for drying, and I found myself eating more than I was putting out to dry! That night when the pains started, I thought it was 'green-apple cramps.' I never paid it much mind. It was two months till time for our little one."

"Well, you sure sent me for Ma in a hurry when the cramps got worse," Big George chuckled. "When she got here," the jovial man continued, "she commenced boiling water—there in the fireplace—so calm that I thought she was making tea. Then she squatted down beside your pallet and started singing. The words were in the old language . . . asked the Creator to give our little one a safe journey."

"And the little one did have a safe journey," Kitteuah smiled triumphantly at her broad-shouldered husband.

"Yes," Big George replied, with a twinkle in his black eyes, "but that baby was such a little mite that I didn't know whether to hold her, or stick her in my pocket!"

"As I recall, you had no trouble holding our daughter—you were so proud of her that Ma had to take her from you and remind you of your ceremonial duties."

"And in my excitement, I almost broke the clay bowl," Big George laughed. Becoming suddenly serious, the tall man reminisced quietly: "It was 1826. I remember well what it was like outside that night. Sounded like the screech owls over by the cornfield was sayin', 'She—ee is here, She—ee is here!'; it was a mite chilly, but a few crickets still twittered in the broom sedge, and a body could smell autumn in the ground fog. I looked off toward Rattlesnake Mountain . . . Moon was full and bright, and . . ." Words seemed to fail him at this point, or perhaps they became unnecessary. Any man, woman, or child in the Cherokee Nation could describe such a night. "I still recollect the drumbeat of Mother Earth's heart as I returned the afterbirth to her bosom—seemed like the whole universe was celebrating our daughter's birth."

"And I called her Wa-le-la," Kitteuah added softly.

The rumble of thunder in the west brought Caty back to the present with a start. Pulling her feet from the frolicking waters, she scrambled up the rock, almost tumbling into the creek in her haste to get her shoes on.

"Lord a-mercy me!" she muttered. "No tellin' how long I've been settin' here studyin' on the past. John's a-goin' to be madder than an old wet settin' hen, and looks like I've got me a thunderstorm to outrun, too!"

Caty huffed onto the front porch just as the first raindrops spattered the grassless yard, and ran headlong into the brawny forearm of her husband— extended like an iron bar across the open doorway.

"Woman, where you been?" John demanded, his blue eyes crackling with anger. "I don't see no sign of supper in here, and me and the younguns cain't hardly hear the thunder over the growlin' of our bellies. Out a-gallivantin' around, doing no tellin' what. The Good Book says . . ."

A deafening clap of thunder drowned out the fuming man's words, mercifully sparing his wife a sermon she already knew by heart. Brushing past John and their wide-eyed brood of children, she made her way to the fireplace, and humming mournfully in the half-light, Caty kindled a roaring fire.

Snuggling deeper into the soft furrows of her featherbed, the eleven-year-old Indian girl listened contentedly to the ebb and flow of her parents' voices as they stretched their tired bodies before the fading embers of the family fireplace. The handwoven coverlet she shared with Lottie rose in rhythmical waves beside her, draping the somnolent body of Hummingbird's nine-year-old sister, and in the far corner of the cabin floor lay a tangled disarray of small brown bodies who, when awake, were three of the most energetic little brothers Hummingbird could imagine: Jackson, Lloyd, and Samuel.

Drifting drowsily, Hummingbird's mind registered the muted sounds of a hoot-owl—probably on the lookout for a careless field mouse—and she was vaguely aware of the blue tick's restlessness outside the cabin door.

Suddenly, the hound cut loose with the deep-throated excited baying he reserved for strangers, and Hummingbird looked to her father for some clue to this disruption of her sleep. What she saw sent little shivers of alarm through her body. Instead of stepping outside to call off the dog, Big George was bolting the door with the heavy iron bar which, for as long as the little girl could remember, had never been used, except as a doorstop. Kitteuah hurried to snuff out the candle, and Hummingbird lay stiffly in the darkness, trying to make sense of her parents' unusual behavior.

Hummingbird longed to run to the strong arms of her father, to cuddle up in the warm embrace of her mother, but her instincts told her to stay put. Finally, the baying of the hound ceased, and the muffled words of her frightened parents were the all that the wide-awake child could hear.

"They're saying we all have to move out West," Big George was whispering, "and anybody who fights it . . . the soldiers . . ." Hummingbird strained to hear the rest, but her mother's quiet sobbing blotted out the terse words of Big George.

"What if they separate our family?" Kitteuah's anguished voice broke through the darkness.

"It will be over my dead body!" Hummingbird heard her father declare.

The days following that nightmare experience were fearful ones for Hummingbird, and life as she had known it seemed permanently suspended. Corn crops were overtaken by weeds, her father's blacksmith shop stood idle, young men no longer played stickball or went hunting, and women of the settlement watched over their little ones with an anxiety Hummingbird had never witnessed before. Day after day, Big George rode horseback to gather the latest news from neighboring settlements, and occasionally Hummingbird overheard details of council meetings her father attended.

More and more frequently, Grandpa Youngbird, a devout Methodist, came by to pray with his family, and Hummingbird's intuitive spirit whispered, "It won't be long now . . ."

Though Big George and Kitteuah were protective of their children, they always shared with them anything which might affect the family, so Hummingbird and her younger brothers and sisters were aware of the white man's plan to remove them from their beloved hills to a faraway place called "the West." Still, the young Cherokee girl had no way of preparing for the horrors that were to confront her when that dreaded day finally arrived for her family.

Years later, Hummingbird would repeat the story over and over to her own children and grandchildren.

"It was early morning, and the lonesome call of Rain Crow sounded closer than usual. The ground fog was heavy. I remember feeling chilled to the bone as we set out for Mayford Postelle's grist mill. We was carrying sacks of grain fer him to grind into corn meal. The Postelles was white folks . . . friends of my father for years . . . still, Mama insisted that Jackson and Lloyd walked with me that day.

"The boys and me didn't talk much, a-walkin' down the mountainside. As we hurried along the trail, we noticed the squirrels and bluejays a-makin' such a racket up ahead that we jumped down into a gully. Hid behind a big ol' log. Just in time, too, for no sooner had we hid than two soldiers—both of 'em carrying long rifles—come ambling around the curve, headed up the path towards our house. We was scared half to death, but we figured it was safer to go on to the Postelle place right then than it was to turn around and run for home. I've regretted that decision ever since . . ."

At this point in her story, Caty McLeod would always pause to dab her eyes with her apron tail, heave a heavy sigh, then continue the story in staccato tones that sent chills down the spines of her listeners:

"The boys and me never said nothing to the Postelle about them soldiers. We just waited for Mr. Postelle to grind the corn, and started back up the mountain with our meal. All the time, we was watching out for them strangers, but we never saw nothing of 'em but their tracks. When we got to our clearing, we broke into a run to see who could be first to tell Papa about the soldiers. About that time Jackson give out a scream as he tripped over our blue tick—all bloody and shot up—and I froze in my tracks as I realized that them burning embers up ahead was all that was left of our cabin.

"I dropped the sack of cornmeal, grabbed my brothers' hands and set in a-running towards what used to be home. We must have looked like three chickens with their heads cut off—running round and round, crying and hollering for Mama and Papa and Lottie and Samuel. Then I grabbed up a long stick and started digging in them hot ashes, just knowing for certain I'd find my family's corpses, but about all I found was the iron bar Papa had used to bolt the door with—red hot, but still in one piece."

Once again, the trembling woman would pause to wipe her eyes, then with bowed head and lowered voice, continue on.

"I never see'd my mama or papa after that. I heard that Papa made it to Indian Territory, but if he was alive, he woulda come back to North Carolina fer us. Some Cherokees did move back to the mountains. Told the Postelles Lottie and Samuel took sick with whooping cough and died on the Trail. Said Mama grieved herself to death, but they didn't know what had become of Papa.

"Another white family, the Wootens, took me and Jackson and Lloyd in. Finished raising us. They couldn't speak Cherokee, though, so we soon forgot most of it. Changed our names, too. That's why I'm called Catharine now instead of Hummingbird, and Jackson is David, and Lloyd is Isaac. Eh, law . . . can't go getting upset again. That was a long, long time ago, and I got me another family to fret over now . . ."

Dawn Karima Pettigrew

Dawn Karima Pettigrew (Creek-Cherokee-Choctaw-Chickasaw) wrote a novel, *The Way We Make Sense* (2002), which was a finalist for the First Book Award in Prose competition sponsored by the Native Writers' Circle of the Americas. Her second novel, *The Marriage of Saints* (2006), was a finalist for the New Mexico Book Award for best novel, adventure, or drama. She holds a bachelor's degree in social studies from Harvard University and a master's of fine arts in creative writing from Ohio State University. A former Ms. Native American Worldwide Achievement, she is a member of Wordcraft Circle of Native Writers and Storytellers and the Native American Journalists' Association. Widely published as a poet and fiction writer, her work has appeared in *Through the Eye of the Deer*, *Twenty-Five and Under Fiction*, *Higher Education*, *Gatherings VII* and *IX*, *The Mythical Midwest*, *The Urban Midwest*, *American Indian Culture and Research Journal*, *Red Ink*, *Raven Chronicles*, and *The Moccasin Telegraph*. As a journalist, her articles and interviews have appeared in such newspapers as *News from Indian Country* and *Whispering Wind*. Pettigrew is currently a writer-in-residence at Western Carolina University, and lives in Cherokee, North Carolina.

school supplies

school supplies
what cherokee children really learn at st. jude's indian boarding school

pencil
weapon of choice
arrow of the new world

eraser
bless me teacher, for I have sinned.
i have begun a continent with a preposition

english
tongue of lost pirates
in the mouths of those who know better

lunch
corn chowder is the last supper.
frybread makes a suitable host.

kleenex
God counts the tears of preschoolers
and of their mothers.
He calls them holy water.

purgatory
algebra taught by a murder
of crows

judges
they cut our hair because they fear
one of us might be Samson
blinding has gone out of style

dress code
conquistadors' women ate arsenic
to make their skin
half as pale
as the teachers wish ours to be.

locker
the helmet of salvation fits just fine
even over braids

epistles
new smoke signals
the scalping of trees

glossolalia
open mouths
swallow God's tongue
never tell the nuns what they are missing

Psalm

Aniyunwiya* singing

Help us, Creator.
The prodigal was lost,
but you have killed fatted calves
and given him all
the cattle on a thousand hills.

---

*Aniyunwiya—"Real Human Beings"; Eastern Cherokee name for themselves.

You let him take our Smokies;
he still refuses to pray,
We bow low, Creator,
we wash your feet with our trail of tears.

We come bearing salt and lard,
flour, corn, and peanut butter.
We will build your ark from our mountains.
We regret that we have no gold.
The conquistadors took it and left us smallpox.
The silver we offer is truly tin,
papered with labels, flashing heartache.
Our frankincense is the smell of cedar,
the odor of dogwood wet after rain,
and we have no myrrh.
Andrew Jackson took it.
We bow low, Creator.
Our souls are on their knees.

Help us, Creator.
Redeem this long-suffering firstborn.
Is there no feast for us?

Medicinal Purposes

Manna Redpaint and her great-grandaddy, Grady Stands
Straight, do their best to figure out the way they make
sense in Cherokee, North Carolina.

Who is this Bob Barker?
How does he have so much to give away?

I smile
squint through the famine of light in his HUD house.
I give my voice a lilt,
the sound of the sun trying to explain itself to the moon.

I think he has help, Grandfather.
His giveaway is courtesy of Proctor and Gamble.
Think of new cars as commodities.

Grandfather nods his head,
spreading the scent of sage and cedar
between me and his beloved color TV.

We are concerned,
Grandfather breathes through old ivory.
There are many men who would share their blankets with you
but you do not seem to have eyes for them.

This is bad.

You are such a pretty girl,
not pale,
not watered down like so many other half-breeds.
Your skin still shows who you are.

You are such a fine girl,
not lazy,
not complaining like so many modern girls.
Your cornbread, your moccasins tell how you are.

You are such a good girl,
not fast,
not kissing or flirting like yunega women.
Your blood on your husband's sheets will whisper what you
are.

Every day you wait
is a sad day for us Aniyunwiya.

Every day you wait
is one less warrior
one less hunter,
one less Human Being in the world.

The game show bells count coup in the background.

Grandfather's words ride bareback on the smoke in the air.
I cannot tell him.

The warriors now battle hand-to-hand
with buckets of Montana gin,
water wed to Lysol or hairspray
and charge away in Chevrolet ponies
to meet a warrior's end.

The hunters today stalk prey in K-Mart,
capture commodities from the BIA.
The trophies they gather are often illegal.
Fishing without asking is a federal offense.

I cannot tell him
there are no fathers.
So
I whisper.

Fewer people died of smallpox than of a profound,
terrible,
lack of love.

This is a lie
that is also true.

Norman H. Russell

Norman H. Russell (Cherokee) was one of the first poets of Native American heritage to become well-known at the beginning of the much-vaunted Native American literary renaissance that began in the early 1970s. He was a professor of botany during his academic career and was the vice president of academic affairs at the University of Central Oklahoma when he retired in 1988. Russell is proud of his "thirteen books of poetry," which, he says, complement his "thirteen published texts in botany." Some of his poetry titles include *Night Dog & Other Poems* (1971), *indian thoughts: the ways of the world* (1974), *Russell! The Man, the Teacher, the Indian* (1974), *indian thoughts: the children of god* (1975), and *The Longest March* (1980). *From Star to Leaf* (1995) is a volume containing selections of his poems from all his previous collections. Russell was born November 28, 1921, in Big Stone Gap, Virginia. He lives in Edmond, Oklahoma. Nicolaus P. Kogon writes of Russell's poetry as "the voice of a pantheist . . . marked by a quiet ecstasy: a still, small voice celebrating the unity of all things . . . (yet of a sensibility that) does not, however, ignore the problem of evil."

Mights and Gots Is Two Different Things

theys things i might do
and theys things i got to do
mights and gots is two different things
knowing the difference is what counts

i might buy a new tractor
i got to milk the cow
i might go to town this Saturday
i got to help the church

i might go hunting
i got to cut wood
i might let the boy have a car
i got to teach him right from wrong

knowing a might from a got takes awhile
children don't learn it right off
mights and gots is two different things
when theyve learned the difference theyve growed up.

Gods Drugstore

my grandmother comed to see me last sunday
walked with her in the field out to the pond
she likes to fish catches a few there
maybe mostly she likes to sit in the sun
asleep when there aint nobody looking

we was walking she was talking she was telling me
says ever plant we seed was good for something
little yellow flowers good for brooms
boil them up in mulleinberry tea stops you coughing
says i ought to try them sometime to save me money

well i guess thinking back they wasnt no drugstore
run to the corner or drive your car back then
when she and granddad lived here on this farm
couldnt get the doctor to come ever time you coughed
got to go to the field got to make your own medicine

well i always wondered what good
these little bitty weeds was for
grandma says theys gods drugstore
got a kind for everthing what ails you
and everone of them is free.

A Silver Pocket Watch

my grandaddy was a mean man he swore
sometimes and he wasnt always good
to my mother and when he died he said
he was going to a baptist heaven which
was even hard for a baptist to get into

my grandaddy was a railroad man he had
a gold watch i admired which he left
to my brother who has still got it
i reckon its a pocket watch with
a pretty lid that clicks when it shuts

my grandaddy didnt leave me no watch he
didnt leave nothing but the hell that scared
him so he hollered like the devil
caught his foot and pulled him off the bed
goodbye grandaddy I'll remember you i said

been saving my money went down to the store
yesterday bought me a silver pocket watch
put it in my pocket take it out all day
today watching how the hands they go around
feeling it how good and cold it feels.

Anybody Who Has Growed Up Barefoot

anybody who has growed up barefoot
has learnt to step real careful
feel the ground he walks on
anybody who has growed up barefoot
he dont fall down very much

anybody who has growed up barefoot
has learnt not to run in thorns
picks his way real slow
anybody who has growed up barefoot
he dont get hurt much

anybody who has growed up barefoot
has learnt theys places not to go
stay where he can see his way
anybody who has growed up barefoot
he dont never git lost.

Even the Stone Moves neither Swift nor Slow

it is a gray day a whispering day and it is not broken
like a trellis which steps the sky and cannot climb
at all only the smooth snaking vine which seeks not
the sky as it mounts its own body and it reaches
for itself and it seeks also itself which it continually
finds even as you and i if we open our hands from
the fingered fists which contain nothing for we much neither
hold behind or run ahead or turn our heads and then
we may hear the songs
we sing ourselves.

Cottonwood

leaf by leaf peeling and smaller
and smaller to the probing needle
careful not to kill and the looking
under the lens so great the smaller leaves
and every thing green then a moment
the last covering leaf and the small white
glistening somehow pulsing alive
tip of the stem from its hiding
exposed to the dryness of the air

with the sharp razor cutting across
so thinly the steady hands hold
and sharply the thin slice comes
into the water and under the lens
so great the gaping cells all emptied
of life and their yawning walls

dissecting the cottonwood twig
needles and razor bleeding with sap
the raw bark slipping in my fingers.

Patricia Riley

Patricia Riley (Cherokee) lives in Coos Bay, Oregon. She taught for several years at the University of Idaho and is now teaching in Oregon. She earned bachelor's and master's degrees from the University of California–Santa Cruz and a Ph.D. from the University of California-Berkeley. She is best known as the editor of *Growing Up Native American* (1993), one of the major anthologies of contemporary Native American literature. Her poems, short stories, and essays have been published in such journals as *Studies in American Indian Literatures*, *Callaloo*, *Northeast Indian Quarterly*, *TWANAS,* and *Fiction International*, as well as in the anthologies *Maroons and Redlegs*, *Understanding Others*, *On Our Own Terms*, and *Storytelling: Contemporary Short Stories by Native American Women*.

voices

it is these voices i hear
coming up from the watery ground
rising like sap through the roots of trees
whispering between the branches and the moss
voices as restless and beautiful as snakes
it is these voices i hear
it is these voices i listen to
they tell me to speak the truth
i promise   i will not lie

poem for skeletons that dance in my closet like cats on a hot tin roof

sister woman
brother man
our grandmother turned her back on her very own people
and buried alive the Cherokees who shaped her flesh and bone
because someone someplace up the line had married white
because she was just barely light enough to pull it off
because she let the white man make her feel ashamed
she lied

and she passed
black Irish   she told the white man
not Cherokee   black Irish
until the white man left her alone

and sister woman   you know as well as i
there came a point in my life
when i did about the same as she
when i came up against all those urban indians
telling wannabe jokes about whitefolks
and their always Cherokee grandmothers
i lied
and i passed
because my skin was light enough to question
because their laughter burned in my ears
because i let other indians make me feel shamed
Mohawk   i told them when they asked
not Cherokee   Mohawk
until they left me alone
and brother man   you know as well as i
mendacity has trailed us
like a hound all of our lives
for we were born into a house of carefully kept concealments
heirs to an uneasy legacy of generations
who lied about their true and genuine selves
we slept and ate in rooms where windows were kept closed
where curtains were forever drawn against the light
rooms that reeked of things swept deftly under carpets
rooms with odorous closets   their doors deliberately locked
and there we learned denial and the delicate art of subterfuge
but no more   for me   no more
for the voices came and told me
speak the truth
and i have promised them
i will not lie.

reflections on mixed blood 1

this pool of unstill waters
coughed us up

gave us a history
of muddied messages
so now we have to write our own
just so you know
we are not someone's rootless lilies
not stained   not damaged
not anyone's defective merchandise
like dandelions we resist your toxic notions
we refuse to go away
throw us in the trash
and we'll crop up again
right in your backyard
you see we are indigenous to this place
the earth demands our presence
and we insist upon it
look around   you'll see us
we blow upon the wind
we know which way it blows.

reflections on mixed blood 2

we come and we go
sometimes singing broken songs
sometimes knowing all the words
sometimes breaking our hearts in the singing
sometimes mending them
we come and we go and we're here
you say   water cannot cleanse us   wash us white enough
or stain us red enough to still your voices
you say   we are seeds planted carelessly
yet the earth remembers us
the drum beats loud in our blood
you say   it is not enough
these days you need a paper
to prove you are an indian
you say   there is no room for what we are
you say   they make no honor songs for us
you say   there will be no weeping when we go
you say   you say   you say
we say   something else

we turn our backs on what   you say
we walk away in another direction
we walk away from the things   you say

reflections on mixed blood 3

we are pools of darkness
deep with desire and dreams
we are your worst fears realized
your shadowed secrets given flesh
begotten   not made
true woman and true man
we refuse to be crucified by you
to suffer under you
to be buried by you
we rise up

look into our mirrored eyes
see what brought us to this place
see sails and strange seas
stone cities occupied
swords broken against native bone
women weeping
look into our mirrored eyes
see whose side we're on
see fields on fire   broken pottery
the arrowmaker's tools dropped in haste
the blood of innocence staining earth
we watch the night with our many-colored eyes
we look at you   we say no more   it is enough

Elizabeth Hosler

Elizabeth Hosler (Saponi-Abenaki-Chickasaw) Elizabeth Underwood Hosler was born in Barberton, Ohio, the daughter of an Abenaki-Saponi-European mother and a Chickasaw-European father. She has a B.S. from the University of Rio Grande and an M.B.A. from the University of Dayton. Her poetry has appeared in such journals as *The Moccasin Telegraph* and *Snaketalk,* and her poetry collection, *Songs From the Wolf Woman's Daughter*, was published in 2003. For two years in a row, 1996–1997, she was the winner of the *Columbus Alive* poetry contest. She is a member of Wordcraft Circle of Native Writers and Storytellers and lives in Columbus, Ohio, with her husband and daughters.

Affirmative Action

these things are divided,
segregated,
neatly boxed.

except for me.

me, with my
irish freckles over
indian cheekbones.
me with my straight hair
and light skin.

the government
man says
check one box but
i am not one way
i did not have one parent
or one grandparent

my people did not come
from one tribe
or even country
and it feels like a lie
that dishonors their memories
to check one box
and pretend that they did.

Assimilation

As a child I always thought
that my Grandfather had
grown up in a teepee,
lived among wild horses,
and hunted buffalo with
a great, long spear.

I used to dream
of him this way
instead of as an
old man sitting
in a chair and
watching TV but
he never did those
things at all.

He grew up in a frame
house on a regular
street in Greenup, Illinois
and he had a
Grandmother who was
a brown-skinned white woman
who wore a starched,
white apron and
went to church on
Sundays and,
if she ever drummed
or danced,
it was in her dreams.

Jean Starr

Jean Starr (Cherokee) was the author of two books of poetry—*Songs of Power* (1987) and *Tales from the Cherokee Hills* (1988)—and she enjoyed a long career as an educator in the California public schools. She was active in many educational organizations, including the National Education Association, the American Indian Education Program of the Sacramento (Calif.) school district, and the National Indian Education Association. Starr was born in Alexandria, Virginia, on July 6, 1935, and her childhood was spent in Florida, Kentucky, and Indiana. She earned a bachelor's degree from Franklin College and later studied creative writing at the University of Nevada. Starr died on January 18, 1994, in Sacramento, California. Along with her husband, the Oklahoma Cherokee writer Winn Starr, she devoted a great deal of her time and attention in the last years of her life to mentoring beginning Native writers through Wordcraft Circle of Native Writers and Storytellers.

Selu and Kanati

Up on Pilot Knob they lived, all alone,
Selu and Kanati with their son,
The two of them never feeling their loneliness.
All the long years together, she was all he wanted,
And she, too, needed only Kanati her husband
To be neighbor, friend, family, and lover.
In her house, so carefully tended,
She fixed good food to feed them,
And he, whose name meant Lucky Hunter,
Always brought back game.
But though the house was warm with love,
The child felt lonely.
Was it, perhaps,
That the parents were so happy in their love,
They failed to know this?
He played by the river every day,
Not far away—they thought it was safe enough.
And, from the bushes by the water's edge,

They could hear laughter.
Funny, it sounded like two children,
Laughing there.
"Oh well," they thought, "he's having fun. Why not?"
"I had fun with my friend today,"
The little boy said.
"He's coming again tomorrow."
"Well, that'll be good," said his father.
"Where's he come from?"
"Out of the water," said the boy.
"Well, who is he?" said the mother, teasing.
"Who's his family?"
"He's my older brother, he says.
And he got thrown away in the water."
Could this be? It was a strange time,
The world not so old as it is now,
And besides, Kanati and Selu
Knew of stranger things themselves.
"When he comes tomorrow, call me
And hold him tight," Kanati said.
When his playmate came,
He was challenged to a wrestling match,
And as soon as Kanati's son held the boy fast,
He called for help.
"No," cried the Wild Boy. "No,
You threw me away, you threw me away,"
For he was formed from the blood
Selu washed from the game she cleaned.
They carried Wild Boy to the house.
A child needs a family, after all,
And their son needed his friend.
But when they thought they were taming him,
Holding him there
And feeding him good food, kind words,
And the touch of soft hands,
They had only made him sly,
Obedient when in sight.
What were they to him? Something that stood
Between him and freedom.
Creatures who could force him into a box

(And that was all he saw in their neat house),
Givers of tidbits he could cajole from them.
And the child, Younger Brother?
Was he running partner, pet,
Toy for a morning's amusement?
Selu, a loving mother,
Saw a child who needed love,
Her son, knowing only kindness,
Saw no evil in Wild Boy,
And, calling him Elder Brother,
Followed where he led.
Only the father, Kanati the hunter,
Man of the forests,
Sometimes looked into those wild eyes
And wondered
Who or what he had let into his house.

Bear

That boy loved the woods.
When Yona was so little
His legs were too short to keep up,
The big boys learned to take him anyway.
He always knew
Where the fattest, ripest berries were,
Where the trout were hiding in the pools,
Where the nuts were thickest.
He began to go out all alone, whenever he could,
Finally, getting up before his parents
So they wouldn't tell him not to go,
Staying longer and longer.
His parents worried,
Especially when he missed dinner
And hadn't had breakfast. Why, that wasn't right!
But still, he was always bringing his mother
Combs of wild honey, baskets of nuts,
Fresh mushrooms, greens, berries—
Why, they could have lived
Off the trout he caught alone!
Finally they spoke to him.
"Yona, we never see you at home all day.

That shouldn't be; what's going on?"
His answer amazed them.
He simply held out his arms for them to see:
They were covered with long, brown fur.
"I can't stand sleeping
Under a roof anymore," he said.
"Eat at home?
I can eat better in the woods, and soon
I'll live there all the time."
His parents begged him to stay at home;
Clearly, something strange
Was happening to him in the woods.
"Oh, it's a better place, better than here,
And I'm changing, I'm changing.
I can stay, no matter what you say or do.
Come with me, Mother, Father,
Come with me there—
There's plenty of food in the forest.
You know that; I've brought you some.
You'll never have to work again,
Never sweat in the sun hoeing corn,
Never haul water from the spring,
Never sleep behind hot and stuffy walls,
But sleep on soft moss, live with walls of trees
And a roof of stars."
Oh, to live free, to run in the wind,
To be strong, to have plenty!
So they told the people of the village,
And they all, every one, fasted and prayed for seven days,
And at dawn they left their houses,
Left them forever.
Messengers from other towns
Found them as they walked.
But they were changing, they were changing;
They could not stay.
"Come into the woods when you are hungry.
Find us. We shall come to give you our flesh."
They sang,
And they taught the messengers their song,
And then went back on their way.

Looking back, the messengers saw only bears
Going up the mountain into the forest,
The words of the song drifting back on the wind:
"Surely we shall see each other,
Surely we shall see each other."

Strawberries

Oh, I think I married her too young, this girl.
Not yet ready to be serious and sober,
Head of the family,
Mother.
I come home, to find dinner not cooked,
Corn and squash not even picked to make dinner,
When everyone knows the best time is early,
Before the dew dries.
Here it is sunset, and where is she?
Out picking flowers.
I was angry,
But I was sad, too.
I had seen her beauty, and I married her too young.
In my guilt, I spoke impatiently.
It was not well done.

Oh, he doesn't understand.
He thinks I feel nothing for him,
Because I neglected dinner
And picked flowers instead.
I thought of him
When I followed the flowers into the forest,
Thinking of the day I saw his eyes gleam
When he looked at me,
And I knew that day he was thinking of me in his house
Cooking his meal.
Now he shows me he is sorry he thought of me.
Oh, he must show me that he loves me.
I will make him show me.

Next morning I awakened
And she was gone.
Outside I saw her footprints in the dew.
I followed, running.

Finally I saw her, too far ahead to catch,
And I longed for her to stop
So that I could speak to her tenderly,
And as I stood there, regretting it was too late,
Magic happened.
Wild strawberries grew at her feet.
She slowed, she stopped to pick them.
When I came to her
Her mouth was sweet with them.

At first, I was not leaving him, not really.
I was teasing, playing.
I wanted to see him follow, show his love.
But when he ran behind, fear came over me
Without a reason, and I ran hard.
I could not stop.
Pride would not let me stop tamely for him.
When I saw the berries, it was magic.
I stopped, and when he came,
I told him the spirits had done this,
And I told him I was glad.

Rabbit and Possum

Poor old Possum.
He never did have a lick of sense,
Even as a child, always running behind the others,
Never chosen first, too weak, too little,
Standing on the sidelines, grinning nervously,
Blinking his little eyes. No wonder
He thought it was so fine
To have Jack Rabbit for a friend.
Friend?
Fellows like Jack don't have friends, just dupes.
But nobody could tell Possum that:
He wouldn't listen.
Rabbit was full of schemes,
Mostly to prove how smart he was,
How dumb everybody else. Take the time
Jack noticed that half these village chiefs
Never went to Council, including his.
Too busy. Planting time, roof needing fixing,

Crops getting ripe, something.
So Jack went around telling everybody
He'd just come from Council
And the chiefs decided
Everybody had to make love,
Right now. Jack would be glad to help out.
(Well, *some* people fell for it.)
Of course, Possum grabbed for a girl
Just as everybody's grandmother
Arrived to break up the party
And break up
Whoever started such disreputable goings-on.
Jack Rabbit jumped out the window,
And ran away laughing.
Limping and bruised, Possum followed,
Getting to the next town
In time to hear Jack declare
The chiefs wanted everyone to fight.
He got knocked out, of course.
And after they brought him to,
Possum dragged himself on, to find
Jack had told the next town
Everybody had to get married,
But all the girls were taken,
So, again, Possum didn't get one.
Well, just then,
All those angry folks from the first town
Showed up. Jack Rabbit? Nowhere to be found.
But there stood Possum, asking plaintively
If there weren't some girls left over.
As they all pounced, Possum at last
Did something on his own: he fainted.
As he lay there with his eyes rolled up in his head,
The angry fathers, brothers, lovers, and husbands
Threw up their hands in disgust
And on second thought let him go.
No use talking to Possum.
Next time Rabbit's up to his old tricks,
There'll be Possum, trotting along behind him.
The only thing he learned from his close call was
When in trouble, pass out.

MariJo Moore

MariJo Moore (Cherokee) lives in Candler, North Carolina. She is the owner and publisher of rENEGADE pLANETS pUBLISHING, which she began in order to publish her own books, but which now accepts the works of other authors. The author of several books of mixed poetry and short fictional sketches—*Returning to the Homeland* (1994), *Stars Are Birds and Other Writings* (1996), *Crow Quotes* (1996), *Spirit Voices of Bones* (1997)—and a series of children's books—*First Fire* (2000), *The Ice Man* (2000), and *The Cherokee Little People* (2000), Moore has also recently published a collection of short stories, *Red Woman with Backward Eyes and Other Stories* (2001) and a novel, *The Diamond Doorknob* (2003). She is the editor of the following anthologies: *Feeding the Ancient Fires: A Collection of Writings by North Carolina American Indians* (1999), *Genocide of the Mind: New Native American Writing* (2003), *Eating Fire, Tasting Blood* (2006), and *Birthed From Scorched Hearts: Women Respond to War* (2008). Her articles and news stories have appeared in numerous journals and newspapers, such as *National Geographic*, *Indian Artist*, *Native Artists*, *The New York Times Syndicated Press*, *Asheville Citizen Times*, *Charlotte Observer*, *Studies in American Indian Literatures*, and *Through the Eye of the Deer*. In 1998, Moore was honored with the Distinguished Woman of the Year in the Arts for the State of North Carolina Award.

At Kituwah

This story is for Betty Maney of the Big Cove Community in Cherokee, North Carolina

Her dark head is bent low as she and the necklace she is creating are becoming one. So involved with her work, she is almost oblivious to the goings on around her. People have begun to file into the Asheville Civic Center now, wanting to get a view of American Indians. Not the "Hollywood" type they see on the movie screens and not the "Wannabes" that assemble every full moon for a sweat. These dancers, artists, and crafts people are real Indians. The kind they want their children to see—the kind to write back home about.

The belly of the civic center, swollen with colorful American Indian artwork, blankets, beads and crafts, looks as though it will burst into one brilliant stream of colored lights at any moment. The center's auditorium heart beats in slow, methodical, hypnotic thumps as dancers of many nations parade around in their brilliantly colored traditional regalia—the feathers in their black hair bouncing in unison with each meaningful step as they dance their cultures alive. The unique clicking sound of rolled-up snuff can lids tied to several of the women's dresses announces a modern day homage to their grandmothers' use of shell rattles filled with tiny pebbles.

The magical swirling colors and the high-pitched voices of the accompanying drum groups slowly rise to a crescendo bringing tears to the eyes of the most sensitive. Later, after these exhibitions of Traditional, Fancy, Grass, Jingle, and Shawl dances, Elders will share some of the wisdom they have been chosen to preserve with those who care to listen.

Soon people begin stopping in front of her table, admiring her work, asking prices, inquiring about specific pieces. Her Cherokee jewelry, along with tiny handwoven baskets, is laid out for display. A small sign over one delicate creation reads:

CORN BEAD BRACELET

"What is this corn bread bracelet?" asks a woman draped in turquoise jewelry.

A wide smile, making an already beautiful face even more so, flashes before the answer. "No, it is not corn bread, it is corn bead." Leaning over the bracelet she continues her explanation. "These are perfect for making jewelry. I just push the pin through the centers and they string naturally."

"Well!" says the turquoise woman, suddenly turning to walk away.

Looking at the bracelet for a long moment, she wonders aloud to herself if maybe she should change the sign. There may be others who will also misread it. But the sign is correct: it reads true. How could she change the truth?

After selling a few pieces of her craft, she settles back down to continue working on the necklace, humming a little tune to herself.

Rumors

It was rumored that Addy May Birdsong would sneak into your house, touch your forehead with her fingers while you were sleeping, and change the course of your dreams. I had heard this rumor for the first time when I was about thirteen. Lydia Rattler, who sat next to me in Home Room, told me this because she had heard that Addy May was related to me.

"So what?" I had said back to her. "Everybody's related to everybody on this reservation." I had never liked Lydia much because she had ugly teeth that stuck way out and because she wanted to gossip all the time like an old woman. But she sat next to me that whole school year and I learned to endure her gossip, if not her buck teeth.

When I had asked my mama about the rumor, she said that lots of things were said about Addy May because she was different than most.

"What do you mean, different?" I asked in total sincerity. It seemed to me that almost every adult I knew back then had some sort of strangeness about them—mostly caused from alcohol, or from running out of it.

"Well," my mama had said thoughtfully as she scratched her chin the way she often did when she was trying to explain something in terms that she thought I might understand, "Cousin Addy May just has a way of stirring up people. She looks all the way into their souls with these black pitted eyes of hers and it makes people wonder if she knows what they've been up to." I had to agree with the part about the black pitted eyes. They reminded me of a tunnel that a train had just gone through.

"But you don't pay any mind to what you hear about her. She's your cousin and she's had a hard life, harder than most on this reservation, and so she deserves to be a little stranger than most if she wants."

I forgot about my "stranger than most" Cousin Addy May and all the rumors about her until one night it was so hot I was having trouble sleeping and decided to crawl out the bedroom window to get some fresh air. I was careful not to wake my younger twin sisters. 'Course I loved them with all my heart, but they could be quite bothersome when I wanted some time alone.

The night air was so cool and refreshing, I pulled my braids on top of my head and let it touch the back of my neck. It made me feel so good, I decided to take a walk down the road that led up the mountain to our house. The two other families that lived on the road were at least two miles away, so I felt like I had the road all to myself. I had walked for about ten minutes, staring up at the stars and full moon, feeling proud that I was so brave to be out by myself that late at night when I saw Addy May standing there in the middle of the road with the moon shining down on her head like a flashlight. Her hair was long and loose, not braided as usual, and I remember thinking that it looked like a thick, black waterfall flowing down her skinny back. I was totally shocked to see someone standing there in the middle of the night and grateful that she hadn't heard me coming down the road.

She had her back to me, so I stepped into the darkness of the brush beside the road so I could watch her. She was wearing a long cotton skirt that was probably dark blue but looked purple in the moonlight, and a shawl of many colors was draped loosely around her thin shoulders. I watched quietly as she swayed her head. The more I watched her, the faster my heart beat. And when she started singing, I felt like it would bust right out of my chest. Her voice was beautiful, high-pitched and full of rich guttural tones. Over and over she sang her song, swaying there in the moonlight. I could hear her words distinctly:

> First I was woman
> then I was mother
> Now I am woman again.

Mesmerized by her presence and her voice, I had no idea what her song was about, but I know the words came from way down deep inside her. From the same place my moon time had begun flowing several months back when Mama had told me that I had become a woman. Addy May's words came from the connecting source to the earth that every woman has inside her and my stomach burned way down deep in that spot as I listened.

I must have stood there in the brush for at least half an hour watching her, listening to her singing, and feeling my heart trying to jump up into my throat. Then something happened that I never would have believed if someone else had told me about it. There were two female spirits come down from the sky and stood right next to Addy May's swaying body. One was real old and the other a young girl just a little older than me. With quick, jerky movements, they began to dance around Addy May, looking kind of like the white curling smoke that dances around a red hot fire, and chanting in Cherokee. I couldn't understand all of what they were saying because I don't speak my native language proper, but I heard a few words I could recognize and realized the gist of their song had to do with sorrow and grief.

As I stood there, squinting my eyes, trying to figure out what was in the bundles each spirit woman carried in her arms, and to muster up enough courage to stay and see what would happen next, Addy May turned and looked directly at me. I swear she looked directly at me and smiled right into my eyes, never missing a beat to her swaying or a word to her song. When she did that, I ran back home as fast as I could and didn't tell a soul what I had seen that night. Not even my mama. As a matter of fact, I kind of forgot about the incident for a while because my thoughts were on other things. Mostly, my new boyfriend, Roger. That is until I heard from Lydia Rattler that Addy May had been arrested for stealing a baby boy.

She had gone into John and Amanda Wolfe's house late one night and taken their baby right from his crib. The baby hadn't cried or made any noise or anything, so the parents didn't know he was missing until his mama woke up the next morning and went to check on him. He was only six months old, but he was big for his age. I had seen him in front of the Spirit on the River with his mama the week before Addy Mae stole him. Amanda had gone in there to apply for a job and asked me and my cousin Lenny, who had happened to be walking by at the time, to hold him for her while she went in the restaurant to get an application. It was really curious to me that I had actually held that same baby in my arms just a week before Addy Mae stole him.

She hadn't tried to hide him or anything, and that's why they had found out so quick that she had him. She had just taken him home with her, and when Mavis Rose had passed by Addy May's house on her way to the Tribal Offices, as she did every weekday morning, she had seen Addy May sitting there on her front porch in an old rocking chair, holding him. Mavis said later that she thought it was kind of odd, Addy May sitting there on her front porch with a baby and all, but didn't know how odd until she arrived at work and was told that the Wolfe baby was missing. Of course she told all of them at the Tribal Offices what she had seen and they called the Wolfes, who had Addy May arrested. The baby wasn't hurt or anything, so the Wolfes didn't press it. The authorities let Addy May go after a good talking to because they didn't know what else to do with her, I guess.

Mama said she probably needed some kind of professional help 'cause she had never got over the death of her two babies who had burned to death that past winter. One was a girl, about a year and a half old, and the other a boy, six months old. Her old mobile home had caught fire because of bad wiring or something and she hadn't been able to save them.

I cried after my mama told me that story. I cried like I had never cried for anybody before because I felt so close to Addy May somehow. So I went to visit her about a week after that. I just stopped by her house on my way home from school one day to tell her I was her cousin and just to see how she was doing. She didn't talk much, just nodded her head, and gave me some water from her well to drink. I can still taste that water now, all fresh and cool and sweet from that dipper gourd she used. I stayed for about an hour I guess, just sitting there on her front porch with her, not talking. And that was OK with me 'cause I felt like I just needed to be there for her. She never mentioned that night I had seen her in the road, swaying and singing, but I knew she knew. And I knew she knew that I cared about her.

I didn't get back to visit her again, but I did see her at different times, walking around, mumbling to herself. She got real crazy after the Wolfe baby incident and people just kind of left her alone and made up more rumors about her to entertain themselves. She wasn't a real threat to anybody, and the

Crowe Sisters who lived down the road from her always made sure she had something to eat.

I guess I just grew up and forgot about her for several years. There were my two kids and a husband to worry over, and I hadn't thought about her for a while until Mama told me that Addy May had died. She had got the flu or pneumonia or something, and passed away in her sleep one night.

"She's probably better off," Mama had said. I quietly agreed 'cause deep inside I knew that Addy May was with those two spirits who understood the song she was singing that night there in the middle of the road. The night she was swaying and singing in the moonlight, and I stood in the darkness of the brush, quietly watching and listening.

In These Mountains

As dreams begin to dance themselves awake
   after a day of full flushing rains
     in these mountains
   the bronze hands of women
   reach from beneath the earth
their bones glowing like neon fishes in cave waters.

Droplets pelt the underfur of delicate wild flowers
steam rises to kiss moistened lips of falling leaves
     while I wander around inside the past
       watching, waiting
     hearing the bronze women calling
       my name.

     Memories unfold from around these
       glorious ancestral mountains
     positioning themselves into low hanging fog
touching the soft breasts of those who pay attention
     as the rains fall down into running waters
stopping only when instructed so by the Thunder Being.

Sweet tobacco smells rise from the white water falling
     and I taste the aroma as it floats into my being.
This is when the memories come close enough to smell
       but not close enough to touch
         just close enough to taste
       but never close enough to touch

Marilou Awiakta

Marilou Awiakta (Cherokee) is the author of *Rising Fawn and the Fire Mystery* (1983), a children's book; *Abiding Appalachia: Where Mountain and Atom Meet* (1986), a volume of poetry; and *Selu: Seeking the Corn Mother's Wisdom* (1993), a work of nonfiction. Awiakta was born in Knoxville, Tennessee, on January 24, 1936. Her numerous poems and essays have appeared in such journals and anthologies as *A Gathering of Spirit*, *The Poetics of Appalachian Space*, *Returning the Gift: Poetry and Prose from the First North American Native Writers' Festival*, and *Aniyunwiya/Real Human Beings: An Anthology of Contemporary Cherokee Prose*. She lives in Memphis, Tennessee.

(Untitled)

The atom was poetry in my childhood—images, rhythms—a presence
    beautiful, mysterious,
dangerous . . . like the mountain. And I loved them both. Then the atom
    went awry . . . was
alien. Without knowing why I turned away. Now I know it was the way they
    spoke of it. They'd
split the nucleus in those days—neat, precise, controlled—and described it in
    heavy, concrete
prose. But the language didn't fit. Concrete won't do . . . won't do . . . won't
    do . . .

Now in my ripening years I hear, "Quark, quark . . ." a discovery in the atom's
    heart called by
the strange cry of the gull. "Quark . . ." a particle so small it can't be seen at all
    except by trace,
like the high-flying jet whose white trail against the sky is the only sign that it
    exists. And beyond
quarks may lie something so refined it has no form at all . . . except in
    mystery.

Four quarks are known so far—"Up, Down, Charmed and Strange." And if
    there're others

they may be named "Beauty" and "Truth." The language of science is coming
  round. The atom
has found its poetry again and I can feel love once more for its image and its
  sound.

Out of Ashes Peace Will Rise

Our courage
is our memory.

Out of ashes
peace will rise,
if the people
are resolute.
If we are not
resolute,
we will vanish.
And out of ashes
peace will rise.

In the Four Directions . . .
Out of ashes peace will rise.
Out of ashes peace will rise.
Out of ashes peace will rise.
Out of ashes peace will rise.

Our courage
is our memory.

Smoky Mountain-Woman

I rise in silence, steadfast in the elements
with thought a smoke-blue veil drawn round me.
Seasons clothe me in laurel and bittersweet, in ice
but my heart is constant. . . . Fires scar and torrents
erode my shape . . . but strength wells within me
to bear new life and sustain what lives already. . . .
For streams of wit relieve my heavy mind
smoothing boulders cast up raw-edged. . . . And the
raven's lonesome cry reminds me that the soul is
as it has ever been . . .
Time cannot thwart my stubborn thrust toward Heaven.

Cynthia Kasee

Cynthia Kasee (Cherokee) received her Ph.D. from Union Institute College, where she also taught for a while. Recently, Kasee was a professor at the University of South Florida, but she currently lives in Cincinnati, Ohio. Her essays have been published in *Aniyunwiya/Real Human Beings: An Anthology of Contemporary Cherokee Prose* and in *Indian Participation in the Revolutionary War* and *Indian Wars of the West*, the latter two publications being encyclopedias on American wars. Her poetry has been published in *The Eagle*.

Homecoming

There is a Choctaw woman named Terry in Dayton, Ohio, who is a close friend of mine. We have many things in common, not the least of which is that we are "urban Indians." Although she is Choctaw and I am Cherokee, we also have many traditional customs and historical events we share. Her nation too was a "civilized tribe." In those days (that is, before the 1830s), our people must have believed that being considered civilized would save us from the forced exile to Indian Territory which many Eastern nations had already suffered. Of course it didn't, and the removal of our nations provided us another commonality—our progenitors were split into separate entities . . . Mississippi Choctaws, Oklahoma Choctaws, Eastern Band Cherokees, Oklahoma Cherokees.

Add up all the roots to common vines, "remnant," "removed," "urban," and identity can be a confusing thing. Of course we must also factor in a plethora of non-Native ancestors and the relative isolation of living in Ohio, and the fragmentation seems endless.

What this whole introduction has been leading to is my first trip to Oklahoma. I looked on it with trepidation, almost talked myself out of it a dozen times, and ran up huge long distance bills commiserating with Terry. Why was I so apprehensive? To understand the "race memory" of the Indian removals, I so apprehensive? To understand the "race memory" of the Indian removals, if you're not Indian, try picturing yourself as a Jew visiting Auschwitz or a Cambodian survivor returning to Pol Pot's killing fields.

I feared how overwhelming that race memory might be when I first stood as my Ancestors had, looking into an Oklahoma night sky, remembering those who had not survived our version of the Bataan Death March.

Of course, I must also have feared how I would be received, although I didn't admit that to myself at the time. If the convolutions of Southeastern Indian history aren't confounding enough, my own background is more so. After the Removal Era was over, after the Easterners hiding in the hills had moved out to live in their mountain coves, 160 Cherokees from Indian Territory journeyed back to the Smokies at the behest of their North Carolina relatives (the U.S. government soon got wind of this, stopping the repatriation tide at 160 individuals). I am a product of that repatriation, that commingling of refugee and exile. Some people couple that fact with my unlikely hometown of Cincinnati (hey, my father had to find work during the Depression, didn't he?) and snicker loudly about "wannabees," "Five dollar Indians," and "Princess Grandmothers" (sorry, no royalty up my family tree, nor those trees of other Cherokees!).

Well, as you see, I can go off on tangents rather easily. To the point, dammit, I wondered if I'd be accepted! My run of luck that first day did not do much for my confidence. I missed my plane to Dallas, which meant I also missed my connection to Tulsa. Since I was staying at the Tsa-la-gi Lodge, or the Lodge of the Cherokees (which the tribe owns), they were sending the airport van to pick me up. What a great first impression I'm going to make, I thought. Three hours late, the poor van driver wondering where I am, and you can only get away so much with using this "Indian time" excuse. I did manage to get a message to the Lodge when I got to Dallas, so at least they didn't send that driver out on an hour's drive into Tulsa too early. Even with that call, I still feel my embarrassment welling up as my plane touched down in Eastern Oklahoma.

The first pleasant experience for me was that "van." No Chevy Econoline with "Cherokee Nation of Oklahoma" painted on the side. It seems that, since I was so late, a Lodge employee had offered to pick me up on his own time . . . in his sister's car . . . with his sister in it! It seems they were trying to coordinate a Divorce Party for her for the next night, because she had just received her Final Decree. A trip to Tulsa was in order to inform friends and pick up supplies at the warehouse supermarket, so getting me at the airport was fine with them. They were a little hungry (so was I, but I didn't want to put anybody out any further), so we all went to McDonald's. We ate Big Mac's while we discussed Johnny Bench (an Oklahoma Choctaw who played for the Reds) and where the hell was his hometown of Binger, Oklahoma, anyway?

Before we arrived in Tahlequah, the capitol of the Oklahoma Cherokee Nation, I knew all about the hated ex-husband and they knew how the Cincinnati Reds were doing on their latest road trip. Still, these were two very nice people and not necessarily an indication of how others would be. I couldn't have been more wrong. As I signed the Lodge's guest register, the clerk told me, "Miss Kasee, please call your mother back home. She is so worried about you missing the plane that she's called here twice."

This was just the beginning. Next day, I sat down to breakfast at the Lodge's restaurant, only to find myself sitting one table over from Chief Mankiller, a person whom I greatly admire. Looking up from her plate, she smiled and nodded a "Good Morning" to me. As I enjoyed my onions and eggs (we call them ramps-n-eggs back East, something I had to explain to the waitress, who laughed good-naturedly after she figured out what I wanted), I began to feel a deep sense of belonging. Here I was accepted, and here I accepted others, no longer feeling defensive.

Finishing a sumptuous meal, I went back to the desk to call for a cab to take me to the Historical Society. The clerk told me the Lodge runs a taxi for its guests and she would get it for me. As my "cab" pulled up in front (a station wagon which was obviously someone's family car, judging by the toys and Happy Meal boxes!), I recognized the driver as the maintenance worker from the previous evening. Although I'd seen him as I checked in, we hadn't yet spoken. You can imagine my surprise when he smiled and said, "Hey, you're the lady who missed that plane to Dallas, aren't you?" I couldn't help but laugh, as I wondered whether it had appeared as a feature article in the local overnight newspaper!

These were my initial experiences with Western Cherokees and the rest of the visit was just as wonderful. I excitedly called Terry the second night, telling her how it was like being the long-lost guest of honor relative at a huge family reunion. As I took a walk around the grounds that night, I looked up into that Oklahoma night sky without fear. We will never forget those who didn't survive that Trail of Tears, but we as a People survived, in North Carolina, in Oklahoma, and yes, in Cincinnati. Feeling so safe and accepted, there was no overwhelming race memory of the devastation, just a prayer for those silent graves and the knowledge that we were still there, still a proud people. I laughed to myself as I thought of how Terry had reminded me of a phrase I had taught her . . . to be a descendant of a removed tribe is to be homesick for a place you've never been.

Adolph L. Dial and David K. Eliades

Adolph L. Dial (Lumbee) and David K. Eliades were professors at Pembroke State University (now the University of North Carolina at Pembroke) when they coauthored *The Only Land I Know: A History of the Lumbee Indians* (1975). Adolph L. Dial was born December 12, 1922, near Lumberton, North Carolina. In addition to a thirty-year career as a history professor and historian, he was involved in Lumbee tribal affairs and was a successful tobacco farmer. He was also the author of *The Lumbee* (1993). Dial served a term in the North Carolina State Senate and was a strong advocate for full federal recognition for the Lumbee Tribe. He died December 24, 1995. David K. Eliades was a colleague of Dial's when they collaborated on *The Only Land I Know*. He taught in the History Department at Pembroke until his retirement in 2001. Eliades lives in Lancaster, South Carolina.

A People of Traditions

When Scottish immigrants began to settle the upper reaches of North Carolina's Cape Fear Valley in the early 1730s, they were amazed to find a group of English-speaking people already living near the Lumbee River. Far from being the "savages" no doubt expected by the Scots, these Indians lived in simple houses, farmed in the European manner, and generally practiced many of the arts of European life. The Scots had found the ancestors of the Lumbee Indians. How the Lumbees came to live in such a geographically inaccessible area, in the manner they did, has long been the subject of historical speculation.

Clinging fiercely to their Indian origins, the Lumbees nonetheless have no remnants of their Indian language, which might provide clues to their relationships with other Native Americans. Only traditions and folktales remain as evidence, tales that link this unique group with the lost survivors of the Roanoke Colony as well as with the Eastern band of the Sioux Indians, the powerful and highly assimilated Cherokee, and the Tuscarora Indians. Each tradition has its supporters; each has its detractors. But each is worth examining for the clues it offers about the origins of the remarkable Lumbee Indians.

In 1584, Sir Walter Raleigh obtained a charter from Queen Elizabeth I giving him the right to possess lands in the New World not already under Christian control. Raleigh promptly sent explorers to determine the nature of the lands within his grant and to find a site suitable for a colony. The explorers examined the coastal region of North Carolina, which they named Virginia in honor of the unmarried queen, and returned with a glowing account of Roanoke Island and the surrounding area. As a result, a colonizing effort was made on Roanoke Island in 1585–1586; this attempt was abortive. Beset by internal dissension, supply shortages, and Indian hostilities, the colonists returned to England. Ironically, within a month after their departure, three ships reached the Roanoke area with needed supplies and additional colonists. Finding all settlers gone, fifteen courageous men were now left on Roanoke Island to maintain England's claim to the region.

The Lumbee Indians and the Lost Colony

Although Raleigh was disappointed over the failure of his initial colonizing effort, he was nevertheless determined to establish a permanent English "nation" in America, and so, in 1587, he sent a second colony of 117 men, women, and children to the New World, under Governor John White. This group was instructed not to settle on Roanoke Island, largely because of those Indians in the area who were angered by earlier mistreatment and had become suspicious of the Englishmen's intentions. It should be noted, however, that most Indians in the vicinity remained well-disposed toward settlers. White was told to stop at the island and see if the fifteen men left there in 1586 were still alive. While none of the fifteen could be found, the visit proved to be of momentous importance. For unknown reasons and contrary to its instructions, the White expedition remained at Roanoke Island, thus precipitating a fascinating sequence of historic events.

The John White Colony reached the New World in midsummer, too late to plant and harvest a crop. The settlers quickly realized they had inadequate supplies to carry them through the coming winter and they urged Governor White to return to England for new supplies. Although reluctant to leave, White finally consented, and sailed for home in late August 1587. Upon reaching England, John White found the mother country to be at war with Spain. The war was essentially an outgrowth of economic and religious rivalries: King Philip II of Spain, frustrated in his many attempts to bring England under Spanish control, was now so determined to destroy his Protestant rival that he ordered the construction of the "invincible Armada," a fleet of 130 ships that imperiled the freedom and independence of England. Although the English, through a combination of fast ships, boldness, discipline, and good fortune, defeated the armada in the summer of 1588, Spain remained a formidable seapower. Thus, White could not safely embark for America until 1590, reaching Roanoke Island in August of that year. The Governor had been gone for three years. When he finally landed on the island and sought the settlers, there were none to be found. The colony had disappeared, becoming known to history as "The Lost Colony." Somewhat surprisingly, most historians share the judgment of a noted North Carolina scholar, Samuel A'Court Ashe, who wrote: "When the colonists receded from White's view, as he left the shores of Virginia, they passed from the domain of history, and all we know is that misfortune and distress overtook them; and that they miserably perished, their sad fate being one of those deplorable sacrifices that have always attended the accomplishment of great human purposes." It is incredible that historians so naively accept this assumption that the colonists died of starvation, disease, and Indian hostilities, and blithely disregard evidence to the contrary.

Governor John White, based on his written account, was not unduly concerned over his failure to find the settlers. He noted that the possibility of the colony moving inland for fifty miles had been discussed prior to his departure for England. It had been agreed that if such a move were made, the settlers would so indicate with a marking. It was also agreed that if they were in danger when they left, they would signify this with a cross. While locating no inhabitants on Roanoke Island, White did find, carved on a tree, the letters C R O and on a gatepost the word CROATOAN. Significantly, there was no cross indicating distress. Moreover, most of the goods left behind were possessions of the governor, or goods which would have been burdensome on a long journey. In addition, most articles had been buried as if the settlers hoped to return and recover them at some future date. John White wrote, concerning his discoveries: "I greatly joyed that I had safely found a certain token of their being at Croatoan, which is the place where Manteo was born, and the savages of the island our friends." Though White sought the missing settlers, bad weather and the desire of the sailing master to move on to the West Indies resulted in a perfunctory search and revealed nothing. The important point is that White was confident the settlers were alive and that they had gone to live with the Hatteras Tribe of the trustworthy Manteo, whose friendship dated back to the discovery of Roanoke Island in 1584. The fact that the colonists were not seen again does not prove they perished, or ceased to have a role in history.

The fate of the John White Colony continued to be of concern to Walter Raleigh and other Englishmen for years to come. Raleigh urged every ship sailing to the vicinity of North Carolina to seek news concerning the lost colonists, though none ever returned with useful information. Then, with the successful establishment of a colony at Jamestown in 1607, two Englishmen of that colony attempted to discover what had become of the missing settlers. Captain John Smith records in his *True Relation*, written in 1608, that information obtained from Indians in the Jamestown vicinity told about men in the Chowan–Roanoke River area of North Carolina who dressed like Englishmen. William Strachey, secretary of Virginia Colony wrote, supposedly in 1613, *A Historie of Travaile into Virginia Britannia*; he cites reports of Indians that White's colonists did indeed move inland where they constructed two-story stone houses and lived with the Indians for twenty years. This peaceful existence ended with the coming of the Jamestown settlement. The further incursion of Englishmen excited and angered the "priests" who were advisors of the great chief Powhatan and who, according to Strachey, convinced that powerful leader to order the slaughter of the survivors of the missing colony. Strachey reports that some escaped, but none ever had communication with Jamestown. There are several problems with accepting Strachey's account. To begin with, it is not at all certain, and indeed doubtful, that Powhatan controlled the area where the surviving colonists were to be found.

Moreover, it strains logic to accept that a small band of whites, intermixed with Indians, could have been the objects of such hatred as Strachey describes. Logic indicates that the Indians would have turned on the Jamestown settlers, rather than upon those far removed in North Carolina. In addition, Indian societies were extraordinarily tolerant toward people who willingly joined with them, and there's little reason to believe that this wasn't the case concerning the colonists from Roanoke Island.

English-Speaking Indians

In the mid-seventeenth century, two more adventurous individuals braved the hazards of travel into little-known regions and reported their findings. The first was the Reverend Morgan Jones, who claimed to have marched to North Carolina from Port Royal, South Carolina, in 1660 and to have been captured and then befriended by Indians who spoke English. His descriptions indicate the possibility of his having been in the area of Robeson County, the central location of the Lumbees. Though Jones makes no mention of the "Lost Colony," nor of his captors having a European culture, the fact of his having found natives who spoke English certainly indicates outside influence. Unfortunately, the reliability of Jones's letter is questionable in that it was not written until 1686 and the only extant copy is a newspaper record of the letter, published in the *Gentlemen's Gazette* in 1840.

The second adventurer who traveled through parts of North Carolina in the seventeenth century was John Lederer, a German who began his expedition in Virginia on May 20, 1670, and ended it back in that colony on July 18, 1670. If the information contained in Lederer's account is accurate, it appears that he entered the state at a north-central location (Warren County, N.C.), traveled eastward toward the Roanoke River area, proceeded southwestward through the vicinity of Robeson County, and then crossed into South Carolina. The route of his march has been ascertained both by geographical features he noted and by Indian tribes with which he came into contact. He claimed to have visited, among major tribes, the Chowanoc, Tuscarora, Cheraw, and Santee Indians; the first two were in North Carolina and the latter two in South Carolina. The great difficulty with Lederer's information is that two months for such a journey through largely wilderness conditions seems too brief a span of time. It is quite possible that some of Lederer's material is factual and other information hearsay. At any rate, the most important statement he made concerning the possible fate of the "Lost Colony" came when he was in the border area of the Carolinas. Lederer wrote of his visit: "Here I made a day's stay to inform myself further in these countries; and understood both from the Usheries (Santee) and some Sara (Cheraw) Indians that come to trade with them, that two days' journey and a half from hence to the southwest, a powerful nation of bearded men were seated, which I suppose to be the Spaniards, because the Indians never have any, it being a universal custom among them to prevent their growth by plucking the young hair out by the roots." While it is possible that the bearded men were Spaniards, or that they were Englishmen from a Barbadian colony on the lower Cape Fear River, it is also possible that they were English survivors of the "Lost Colony" intermixed with Indians and removed inland from the coast.

In 1709, John Lawson, surveyor-general of North Carolina and a long-time friend of the Indians in the colony, published his *History of Carolina*. This work recounted Lawson's journey from Charleston, South Carolina, northward to the Neuse River area of North Carolina. Lawson was an observant and perceptive traveler, and his record of what he did and saw constitutes one of the best sources modern historians have on the geography and peoples of the areas of the Carolinas as yet not settled by Europeans. Indeed, Lawson's account is so reliable that he has been labeled the "first North Carolina historian."

Lawson's journal indicates that he traveled up the Santee and Wateree Rivers, across the foothills of the Carolinas to the headwaters of the tributaries of the Neuse, and then down those rivers to the coast. He apparently passed through the country of the Catawbas, the Tuscaroras, and the Corees. Interestingly, Lawson notes that as he approached the coast of North Carolina he was given two chickens by friendly Indians—a clear indication of contact with Europeans because the eastern Indians of North America had no domestic fowl prior to the coming of the whites. During his travels, Lawson gained the services of an Indian guide named Enoe-Will, a man "always ready to serve the English, not out of gain, but real affection." Based on accounts of his youth, related by Enoe-Will, Lawson deduced that he was a Coree Indian. One night after making camp, Lawson pulled out a copy of an illustrated Bible, which the guide asked to see. Lawson granted the guide's request, and then asked Will if he did not wish to become a Christian; the Indian sharply declined. However, he stated his willingness to have Lawson take his son and educate him in the ways of the whites. Lawson's comments make it clear that Enoe-Will was familiar with the ability of the English to "talk in a book" and to "make paper speak" (read and write). It is conjectured that the Coree Indians perhaps came into contact with Englishmen, possibly survivors of the "Lost Colony," prior to or during Enoe-Will's boyhood.

Further evidence of early English influence among some of the coastal Indians of North Carolina is given by Lawson in a part of his book entitled *A Description of North-Carolina*. In this part, Lawson wrote of Raleigh's missing colony; he said:

> A farther Confirmation of this we have from the Hatteras Indians, who either lived on Roanoak-Island, or much frequented it. These tell us, that several of their Ancestors were white People, and could talk in a Book, as we do; the Truth of which is confirm'd by gray Eyes being found amongst these Indians, and no others. They value themselves extremely for their Affinity to the English, and are ready to do them all friendly Offices. It is probable, that this Settlement miscarry'd for want of timely Supplies from England; or thro' the Treachery of the Natives, for we reasonably suppose that the English were forced to cohabit with them, for Relief and Conversation; and that in process of Time, they conform'd themselves to the Manners of their Indian Relations.

The sum total of these statements is that at least some of the missing Raleigh colonists survived, and intermingled with friendly Indians. There is no other conclusion that can withstand close scrutiny. What became of the survivors cannot be ascertained from the comments of these early observers, but fortunately there is other evidence.

"Lost Colony" Survivors

In 1888, Hamilton MacMillan, one of the best white friends the Indians of Robeson County ever had, an able state legislator and local historian, published a pamphlet entitled "Sir Walter Raleigh's Lost Colony: A Historical Sketch of the Attempts of Sir Walter Raleigh to Establish a Colony in Virginia, with the Traditions of an Indian Tribe in North Carolina, Indicating the Fate of the Colony of Englishmen Left on Roanoke Island in 1587." In this work MacMillan vigorously defended the tradition that at least some of the Raleigh colonists survived and joined with Manteo's tribe migrating ultimately to Robeson County. MacMillan so strongly believed this, that, the year prior to publishing his pamphlet, he succeeded in getting the North Carolina General Assembly to designate the Indians of Robeson County as the *Croatan Indians,* erroneously believing this to be the name of the tribe with which the colonists took refuge.[1]

MacMillan's position was supported by a prominent lawyer and business-man in Robeson named Angus Wilton McLean, who became a governor of North Carolina in the 1920s. Although McLean believed strongly that there was Cherokee blood among people in the area, he definitely accepted the Lumbee tradition of "Lost Colony" descent. McLean wrote, in a letter to the Commissioner of Indian Affairs in 1914: "My opinion is, from a very exhaus-tive examination . . . that these Indians are not only descendants of Sir Walter Raleigh's lost colony . . . but that they are also mixed with the Cherokee Indians." This future governor went on to say that the Lumbees "from time immemorial" have contended that they were "of Cherokee descent and they further have a tradition among them that their ancestors, or some of them, came from 'Roanoke and Virginia.' Roanoke and Virginia, of course, orig-inally comprised all of eastern North Carolina, including Roanoke Island, the settlement of Sir Walter Raleigh's lost colony." The relationship of the Cher-okee and Lumbee people will be examined shortly, but the important point is that McLean, a learned and competent man, was convinced and had long heard that the Lumbees could trace their families back to the missing Raleigh Colony.

Stephen B. Weeks, a professional historian with a national reputation, was also a strong proponent of the "Lost Colony" thesis. In 1891, Weeks published, in the *Papers of the American Historical Association,* an article entitled "The Lost Colony of Roanoke: Its Fate and Survival." After examining the evidence, oral and written, Professor Weeks concluded: "The Croatans (Lumbees) of to-day claim descent from the lost colony. Their habits, disposition, and mental

1. As noted earlier in the text, Croatan was a place occupied by Hatteras Indians and MacMillan should have sought recognition for the people as descendants of that historic tribe.

characteristics show traces of Indian and European ancestry. Their language is the English of three hundred years ago, and their names are in many cases the same as those borne by the original colonists. No other theory of their origin has been advanced, and it is confidently believed that the one here proposed is logically and historically the best, supported as it is both by external and internal evidence. If this theory is rejected, then the critic must explain in some other way the origin of a people which, after the lapse of three hundred years, show the characteristics, speak the language, and possess the family names of the second English colony planted in the western world."

In 1914, the United States Senate adopted a resolution authorizing the Secretary of the Interior "to cause an investigation to be made of the condition and tribal rights of the Indians of Robeson and Adjoining counties of North Carolina." To carry out this investigation, Special Indian Agent O. M. McPherson was sent to Robeson County. Through numerous interviews, examination of pertinent literature, and historical research, McPherson produced an extensive and thorough report both on the history and existing condition of the Lumbees. In the course of his investigation, McPherson confronted the question of the relationship of the Lumbees to Raleigh's Lost Colony. The agent wrote: "There is a tradition among these people at the present time that their ancestors were the lost colony, amalgamated with some tribe of Indians. This tradition is supported by their looks, their complexion, color of skin, hair and eyes, by their manners, customs and habits, and by the fact that while they are, in part, of undoubted Indian origin, they have no Indian names and no Indian language." When his investigation was complete, McPherson was convinced of the validity of the Lumbee claim of descent from the "Lost Colony."

But what is the specific evidence on which these prominent men and scholars rest their case? Generally, they were all convinced that the colonists were not really lost—that they simply moved to the mainland to live with friendly Indians, thus tying their future to that of their native brothers. In other words, they accepted the testimony of John White, John Smith, William Strachey, and others. The failure of early adventurers to make direct contact with the survivors did not distress them, because they realized that Croatoan, to which the settlers indicated they removed, was not a clearly defined location; some accounts and maps indicate that it was an island to the south of Roanoke, while other sources indicate that it was a part of the mainland. In fact, no one knew exactly where the settlers went. It is quite possible that the word "Croatoan" meant more than one particular place. "Croatoan" might have been the designation for a hunting area to the Hatteras people, a designation the white settlers would not necessarily have understood. Consequently, finding Croatoan might not have been as simple as even John White had supposed.

The Records of History

All these scholars were impressed by the names found among the Lumbees, clearly similar to some of those listed on the John White log. There were one hundred and seventeen settlers still on Roanoke Island when the governor sailed back to England for additional supplies in 1587. Among those settlers there were ninety-five different surnames. As counted by Hamilton Mac-Millan, forty-one of these surnames (more than forty-three percent), including such names as Dare, Cooper, Stevens, Sampson, Harvie, Howe, Cage, Cheven, Jones, Brooks, and others, were found among the Lumbees, a people living more than two hundred miles away from Roanoke Island. Even more remarkable, as MacMillan found in the late nineteenth century and as is occasionally found among some of the older residents today, was the fact that "the traditions of every family bearing the name of one of the lost colonists point to Roanoke Island as the home of their ancestors." While some of the family names that existed earlier have disappeared, the comparison of names is still striking. Admittedly, most of these names are fairly common English names, and the similarity of names would not in itself prove a connection with the "Lost Colony." But this development, added to the fact that there is no other satisfactory explanation as to why the Indians of Robeson County have English names, must be considered as additional evidence in explaining what happened to Raleigh's colonists and identifying the origin of the Lumbees.

Moreover, the Lumbees, prior to the breakdown of their geographical isolation in the mid-twentieth century, with the advent of mass media, spoke a pure Old English. Their language differed from that of the whites and blacks among whom they lived. According to Dr. Stephen Weeks, "They have preserved many forms in good use three hundred years ago, but which are now obsolete in the written language and are found only in colloquial and dialectical English." He went on to describe how the Lumbees drawled the final syllable in every sentence and how they began all greetings with "mon-n-n," which meant *man*. Weeks, as well as other observers, also noted that they usually began their traditions with the phrase: "Mon, my fayther told me that his fayther told him," and so forth. To further illustrate the old English patterns and characteristics of their speech, Weeks wrote:

> They retain the parasitic (glide) y, which was an extremely common
> development in Anglo-Saxon, in certain words through the palatal in-

fluence of the previous consonant, pronouncing cow as cy-ow, cart as cy-art, card as cy-ard, girl as gy-irl, kind as ky-ind . . . The dialectical Jeams is found in place of James. They regularly use mon for man; mension for measurement; aks for ask; hit for it; hosen for hose; housen for houses; crone is to push down and wit means knowledge.

One is reminded that these speech characteristics were present when the first whites came into contact with the Lumbees in the early eighteenth century and that they persisted to a considerable extent until the 1950s. More important, no one has yet offered an alternative explanation as to how these people learned to speak that type of English and made it their natural language, if they were not influenced by settlers from Raleigh's missing colony.

Still, all the evidence offered to this point does not satisfy the skeptics. Samuel Ashe, a writer determined to preserve the purity and romance of the "Lost Colony," even in defiance of logic, and evidence to the contrary, wrote concerning the Lumbees: "Because names borne by some of the colonists have been found among a mixed race in Robeson County, now called Croatans (Lumbees), an inference has been drawn that there was some connection between them. It is highly improbable that English names would have been preserved among a tribe of savages beyond the second generation, there being no communication except with other savages." In other words, most scholars invariably argue that if the Raleigh colonists went to live with Manteo and his people, they would, in due course, have adopted the Indian's culture, rather than the reverse occurring. This is particularly interesting, because virtually no one seems to have considered the demography of the situation. Many Indian villages consisted of as few as ten to fifteen families, and this was quite possibly the case with Manteo's village. If so, and this is more logical than assuming that there were hundreds of Hatteras people living at Croatan, then it is indeed conceivable that the English culture predominated and the Indians were assimilated by the whites. Even the skeptics are unable to explain how the Lumbees came to have their distinctively English culture. Moreover, even Ashe, noted for his white supremacist attitudes in the late nineteenth century, admitted that "many persons believed them to be the descendants of the Lost Colony; and the Legislature has officially designated them as 'Croatans'; and has treated them 'as Indians.' "

It is also important to note that there are traditions among the Lumbees that their ancestors moved from their former coastal homes to the Black River area of North Carolina in the vicinity of present-day Sampson County. The time of their removal from the Black River region to the banks of the Lumbee

River is uncertain, but all the traditions of the people point to a time prior to the Tuscarora War, and it seems likely that they were settled in Robeson County as early as 1650. All of this, though based on oral history, again seems logical, for Indians were a mobile people and certainly the whites who had joined them would have wanted to avoid conflict with any hostile people. The fact of their difference would have made this mixed group wary of other peoples, particularly if the white culture prevailed, as seems likely. Understandably, they would have moved into a largely unsettled area and continued to seek a location that would guarantee them the most isolation. Robeson County would have been viewed as the "promised land" for a people seeking to escape contact, because this county was virtually surrounded by swamps for centuries, with only a few trails cut through it. It was one of the last areas settled by whites, and one of the least desirable locations from the standpoint of most Indians. A people who sought isolation would certainly find it in Robeson, and they did. In short, geography seems to be the real explanation as to why the Lumbees retained the English language and mode of living, their legacy from the "Lost Colony."

While proof of Lumbee descent from the Lost Colony, in the form of birth records and other documents is most unlikely to be found, the circumstantial evidence, when joined with logic, unquestionably supports the Lumbee tradition that there was a real and lasting connection with the Raleigh Settlement. The survival of colonists' names, the uniqueness of the Lumbee dialect in the past, the oral traditions, the demography of sixteenth century North Carolina, the mobility of the Indian people, human adaptability and the isolation of Robeson County, all prove the "Lost Colony" theory. When one combines these factors with the determination of men to survive regardless of the century in which they live, and the fact that no one can satisfactorily explain the English culture of the Lumbees—a culture obviously adopted over a long period of time, for all traces of Indian culture could not have been obliterated in one or even two generations—no other conclusion is reasonable.

The Lumbee Indians and the Cherokees

Because the white population of southeastern North Carolina turned the name *Croatoan* into a label of disdain and even derision, the Indian people sought a name with no derogatory connotations. Because of a tradition, dating back to the early eighteenth century, that there was considerable Cherokee blood in the Indian community, the state legislature designated the people in 1913 as the *Cherokee Indians of Robeson County*. The people carried this name until 1953.

The basis for the claim of Cherokee blood is found in the Tuscarora War of 1711–1713. In what was the bloodiest Indian war in North Carolina's history, the Tuscaroras rose up to avenge the loss of lands, cheating traders, and the practice of Indian slavery. The threat to the colony was so serious that Governor Edward Hyde promptly asked for aid from Virginia and South Carolina. While Virginia offered help under conditions that North Carolina found unacceptable, South Carolina quickly responded with a force of whites and friendly Indians under Colonel John ("Tuscarora Jack") Barnwell. Although Barnwell was unable to break the power of the Tuscaroras, he did force them to sign a truce. Unhappily for Barnwell, who had been wounded in the fighting and had incurred considerable expenses, the North Carolinians were ungrateful; they wanted the Tuscaroras destroyed as a threat to the colony. Consequently, when Barnwell appeared before the North Carolina Assembly requesting financial compensation and a reward of land for his efforts, his requests were denied. The assembly took the position that he had not ended the danger to the colony and thus was not entitled to money or land. Angrily, Barnwell left North Carolina. As he and his army departed, some Tuscaroras were seized to be sold as slaves. The departure of the South Carolinians and their seizure of the Tuscaroras led to a renewal of the conflict. The power of the Tuscaroras was not finally destroyed until 1713 when Colonel James Moore, aided by his brother Maurice, defeated the Indians at their stronghold of Fort Nohoroco.

The Barnwell expedition is particularly significant, because tradition has it that this force marched through Robeson County on its way home from the fighting. Moreover, several historians and ethnologists reported that Barnwell's army included a number of Cherokee warriors. Lumbee tradition says that some of the Cherokees with Barnwell chose to stay in Robeson County after they had participated with whites in the war against the Tuscaroras. It is further related that once they had decided to stay in Robeson, they abandoned their Indian culture and mixed with the local population. This theory was advocated by Angus Wilton McLean, who, as noted, later became governor of the state, and certainly the General Assembly of North Carolina was influenced through a belief in the probability of this tradition.

There are, however, several obstacles to accepting the Cherokee theory. Barnwell, in a report dated 1712, mentions no Cherokees in his army, though he did name a number of other tribes. It is doubtful then, that "several hundred" Cherokees fought with Barnwell, as some sources claim, or he would almost surely have mentioned them as a part of his force. More likely, there were a few individual Cherokees who took part as members of both the

Barnwell and Moore expeditions, men who were perhaps involved in trade with the backcountry, or mixed Cherokees, the offspring of white trader fathers and Cherokee mothers. In addition, it is difficult to explain how the Cherokees, mountain people and bitter enemies of the Catawbas and their kinsmen, could have allied with them against the Tuscaroras. In short, it is possible that a few Cherokees did fight in the Tuscarora War and did remain in Robeson County, but these Indians were most certainly few in number and had already been largely assimilated into the white culture when this happened. All aspects of Cherokee culture would not have disappeared by the 1730s, when the Scots began to arrive, and there is no evidence indicating that these first European settlers found anything but an English culture. Indeed, it is far more likely that some Lumbees went west with the Cherokees who passed through the area, established a lasting relationship with them, and then that some of their descendants returned to Robeson County in later years.

The oral tradition of Cherokee blood is so strong among the Lumbees, and has been supported so strongly by local historians who conducted extensive investigations, that it is impossible to dismiss the claim. Moreover, it is of considerable interest that a Cherokee chief was George Lowrie, said to be related to some of the Robeson County Lowries. A reasonable assessment of the Cherokee theory leads to the conclusion that some Cherokee blood was introduced into the Lumbee community in the early eighteenth century, but on a small scale. Then, throughout the eighteenth and early nineteenth centuries, frequent contacts between the two peoples led to sporadic intermixing, as the Lumbees sought a stronger Indian connection, while the Cherokees were striving to adapt more thoroughly to the white man's lifestyle, which they accomplished by the 1820s, though it did not save them from removal. Plainly, the Cherokee connection seems definitely to have existed, to have taken place over a considerable span of time, and to have existed between the Lumbees and the more fully assimilated individuals of the Cherokee people.

The Lumbee Indians and the Eastern Sioux

The lands now occupied by the Lumbee Indians were once controlled by Indians of the Eastern Siouan linguistic family. How the Eastern Sioux became detached from the main body of Siouan Indians is not known, but they were definitely living a settled existence in the Carolinas by the sixteenth century, because Spanish explorers make reference to them. Generally, these southern Siouan people lived on the banks of rivers and led sedentary lives, based on agriculture supplemented by hunting and fishing. The most powerful and influential of the Eastern Siouan tribes was the Catawba. Other important members of this family were the Cheraw, Winyah, Keyauwee, Santee, Pee Dee, and Waccamaw. Broadly speaking, the Eastern Sioux, and especially the Catawba, were hereditary enemies of the Cherokee and Tuscarora peoples, though the reasons for this enmity are unknown. One legend explains that the Sioux were latecomers to the South and settled on Iroquoian lands, but this has not been verified by archeological evidence.[2] Generally, the Siouan peoples were friendly to the English and usually fought with them against their European and Indian enemies.

Because of Siouan domination of the lands in southeastern North Carolina, the possibility of a connection between these people and the Lumbees has long been recognized. Special Indian Agent O. M. McPherson noted, "It is not improbable . . . that there was some degree of amalgamation between the Indians residing on the Lumbee River and the Cheraws, who were their nearest neighbors." This belief was echoed some years later by Stanley South, serving at the time as state archeologist for North Carolina and author of *Indians in North Carolina*. South wrote: "Since this group of Indians [the Lumbees] is located in the area where the Cheraw were living when last heard of, it would not be unreasonable to suggest that they are probably the descendants of this Siouan tribe." The eminent ethnologist, John R. Swanton, though unconvinced that the Lumbees were descended from the "Lost Colony," was more certain that they had a relationship with various bands of the Eastern Sioux peoples. In his book *The Indian Tribes of North Carolina*, he told of the Keyauwee tribe, which was first found in Piedmont, North Carolina, but had migrated to the Pee Dee River area by the early eighteenth century, where they joined with the Cheraw and possibly several other lesser tribes. Swanton wrote: "In the Jeffreys atlas of 1761 their town (Keyauwee) appears close to the boundary line between the two Carolinas. They do not reappear in any of the historical records but probably united ultimately in part with the Catawba, while some of their descendants are represented among the Robeson County Indians, often miscalled Croatan." In a portion of his book dealing with the Woccon Indians, Swanton records that the first mention of this tribe was made by John Lawson in 1701 and that he reported the tribe to be quite large, having about 120 warriors. Swanton then states: "Lack of any earlier mention of such a large tribe lends strength to the theory of Dr. Douglas L. Rights that they were originally Waccamaw. They took part against the Whites in the Tuscarora War and were probably extinguished as a tribe at that time, the remnant fleeing

2. Both the Cherokee and Tuscarora Indians were members of the Iroquoian linguistic family.

north with the Tuscarora, uniting with the Catawba, or combining with other Siouan remnants in the people later known as Croatan."

The "Lumbee" Name

Partly because of the geographical circumstances that located them in Eastern Sioux territory, partly because some of the people wanted a more precise identity than they then had, and partly because the federal government was sympathetic to the condition of the American Indian during Franklin Roosevelt's first administration a number of Robeson Indians, led by James Chavis and Joseph Brooks, tried in 1934 to obtain congressional legislation naming them the "Siouan Indians of the Lumber River." This legislation had the support both of the Secretary of the Interior and John R. Swanton of the Smithsonian Institution; however, Swanton preferred that the people be given a more specific name than Siouan Indians. In a memorandum to Senator Burton K. Wheeler, Chairman of the Senate Committee on Indian Affairs, Swanton wrote:

> The evidence available thus seems to indicate that the Indians of Robeson County who have been called Croatan and Cherokee are descendants of certain Siouan Tribes, of which the most prominent were the Cheraw and Keyauwee . . . It is not improbable that a few families or small groups of Algonquin connection may have cast their lot with this body of people . . . if the name of any tribe is to be used [for] this body of 6 or 8 thousand people, that of the Cheraw would be most appropriate.

Though the idea of the Lumbees being of Siouan descent intrigued many, it gained the support of only a handful of the Lumbee people, and the opposition of most, because it threatened, by offering an imprecise name, to introduce a new element of confusion into their history. Thus, the bill seeking to rename the people was ultimately abandoned and died, but not before it produced some developments that would have future ramifications.

During the same period of interest in the "Siouan" bill, Joseph Brooks wrote to the Commissioner of Indian Affairs, asking what benefits his people would be entitled to if the bill passed. Assistant Commissioner William Zimmerman responded to this inquiry on June 11, 1935, calling particular attention to Section 19 of the Indian Reorganization Act of 1934. This section states:

> The term Indian as used in this Act shall include all persons of Indian descent who are members of any recognized Indian tribe now under Federal jurisdiction, and all persons who are descendants of such mem-

bers who were, on June 1, 1934, residing within the present boundaries of any Indian reservation, and shall further include all other persons of one-half or more Indian blood.

Zimmerman went on to say in his letter to Brooks, "In order to share in the benefits of this act, your people must fall within the third class." This meant they must prove their Indianness according to an artificial standard established by the Washington bureaucracy, a task of almost insurmountable difficulty unless one's family contained individuals previously recognized as Indians by the federal government.

Because of the complexity of determining "Indianness" on the basis of blood, 209 members of the Indian community in Robeson cooperated with a physical anthropologist, Carl Selezer, who used anthropometry in an attempt to determine who was Indian, according to the criterion established by the government. Anthropometry is the science and technique of human measurements. Selezer attempted to determine Indianness on the basis of anatomical and physiological features. Selezer's findings were later revealed to Joseph Brooks in a letter from John Collier, Commissioner of Indian Affairs. Collier wrote:

This answers your inquiry as to the result of Dr. Selezer's physical examination of members of the Siouan tribe. A total of 209 individuals were examined, of this total 22 were found, on the basis of the physical test exclusively, to be apparently of one-half or more Indian blood. As you know no other evidence was attainable; no geneaological evidence; no historical documentary evidence; and no etymotological evidence. It is not in my power to say whether the findings of the physical anthropologist, Dr. Selezer, will by itself be considered by the Secretary of the Interior to supply the necessary evidence for a final decision upon the question at issue, namely as to whether the 22 number of individuals can be declared Indians under the meaning of the Indian Reorganization Act.

On December 12, 1938, another letter was sent to Brooks by Assistant Commissioner Zimmerman, in which he said:

As you may recall, we accepted a total of 209 applications in Robeson County, and of these, 22 applications were recommended for submission to the Secretary. He has ruled that, on the basis of the information presented, the 22 individuals should be considered eligible for enrollment as persons one half or more Indian, and entitled to benefits established by the Indian Reorganization Act. *Please note* that no other benefits are involved. These people did not obtain tribal status or any rights or privileges in any tribe.

Although the events of the 1930s led the national government to recognize "22" of the examined people as Indians, this was done on the absurd basis of physical appearance, of whether a given individual "looked like" an Indian. This determination was made on the assumption that Indians are uniformly alike. In fact, Indians are characterized by variety and diversity of language, customs, and mode of living, as well as by physical appearance. Can you describe a Greek, Jew, or a Russian by his appearance? Only in the most superficial way can this be done, and then the exceptions will almost always equal, if not exceed, the rule. Looking back, it seems incredible that the federal government helped perpetuate the myth and the stereotype that all Indians look alike, but that's exactly what was done. Perhaps the significance of this episode is that it indicates, at least in part, why the government has so frequently bungled Indian affairs.

While the Indians of Robeson County were never designated as the "Siouan Indians of the Lumber River," the conclusion of historical research on this point is that some of the decimated Siouan tribes, losing their health to the white man's diseases and their land to the white man's greed, took refuge in the friendly confines of Robeson's swamps and ultimately were assimilated by the Lumbees with their English culture. This is a reasonable assumption, when one considers that historically the Eastern Sioux were friendly toward all European settlers. However, Siouan influence seems to have consisted of the addition of small numbers of people after they had already abandoned their tribal relationships and begun to adopt the white man's lifestyle.

The Lumbee Indians and the Tuscarora

In recent years a small segment of the Lumbee population has begun to insist that their heritage is Tuscarora, and to demand that they be recognized by that tribal name. Although the percentage of Indian people who take this stand is small (less than five percent), they have shown themselves to be determined, and at times even violent. Their position is essentially this: That if they are recognized as Tuscarora Indians, they would be entitled to all the forms of assistance provided to "recognized" tribes by the Bureau of Indian Affairs, assistance not provided the Lumbees because of their past self-sufficiency and the fact that they were not a federally recognized tribe until 1956, when the Congress denied them privileges granted most other Indian people. On the other hand, the historic Tuscaroras, most of whose descendants now live on a reservation in upstate New York, have long been recognized by the national government and receive federal aid. The discontented Lumbee group seeks to be considered as the North Carolina branch of that tribe, and thus to become eligible for similar benefits.

Yet, it would be misleading to imply that the Tuscarora faction is interested only in federal monies, for this is not the case. There is also a desire, stated by some of their leaders at various times, to end forever the speculation concerning their Indian origins. Their claim to Tuscarora descent rests on two major grounds. First, they believe that Tuscaroras moved into the Robeson area during the period of the Tuscarora War, either to escape enslavement or to avoid further hostilities, and in the process became a factor in the existing society. Second, they rely on the fact that in the 1930s, the Department of the Interior conducted physical examinations in the area in an effort to gauge the Indianness of the people and concluded that 22 of the test group of 209 were Indian by artificial government standards. Since several of the discontented faction are descended from those individuals, they claim the Tuscarora name to substantiate their position that they are Indian. Unfortunately, they have adopted the attitude that they are the only legitimate Indians in the area and insist that any funds appropriated for the Indians of the county should be used for their benefit alone.

The position taken by the Tuscarora faction is almost impossible to reconcile with the facts. It is most unlikely that there were more than a few, if any, Tuscarora Indians in the Robeson area prior to the war of 1711–1713. The records show that the first European settlers, arriving in 1731, found a people fully assimilated to the white man's lifestyle. It is therefore difficult to see how the Robeson "Tuscaroras" can claim to be the only Indians in the area, since the group from which they claim descent must have been latecomers and few in number, making little impact on the society of which they became a part. But the biggest puzzle is how the Tuscarora faction can utilize the developments of the 1930s, which were supposed to show kinship with the Eastern Sioux, and use these developments to "prove" their own descent from the historic Tuscarora. This is particularly confusing for two reasons: First, the Eastern Sioux and the historic Tuscaroras were hereditary enemies, a fact that virtually rules out any substantial Tuscarora activity or influence in Robeson, since its location is within what were Siouan lands; second, physical examinations to prove racial characteristics are, at best, of questionable value but most certainly cannot prove tribal origin. There is some evidence, however, based on oral tradition and fragmented documents, that Tuscarora blood was marginally infused into the local Indian society in the decades following the defeat of that nation in 1713.[3] In summary, Tuscarora influence was piecemeal, minor, and contributory, rather than major and formative in the history of the Indian people of Robeson County.

3. The evidence indicates that marriage was the principal method by which the Tuscarora strain was introduced into the Lumbee community in the eighteenth century.

Conclusion

The central fact of Lumbee history is that the people are Indian in origin and social status. That the Lumbees believe in their Indianness has done a great deal to shape their history and way of viewing the world in which they live. Moreover, the Lumbees, more than most native Americans, are well aware that being Indian is not merely a physical foundation, but that it is even more importantly a state of mind, a self-concept. Consequently, the Lumbees, now more than ever, are determined to achieve political, social, and economic equality with the whites, while at the same time preserving their distinctiveness as a people.

Although it is true that the Lumbees have no visible "Indian culture," such as dances or a native language, outward manifestations are not the only way to determine ethnic identity. There are traits that are characteristic of American Indians which are still found in the Lumbee community despite the tremendous cultural impact of whites in the past. No one who really knows the Lumbee people can possibly deny their firm attachment to the land, nor fail to note their inherent religiousness, nor dismiss the sense of unity that exists when outsiders pose a threat. While it is true that Lumbees accept the idea of private property, as do many other modern Indians, they nevertheless part with their land only with great reluctance and usually out of extreme need. While it is true that they follow the teachings of Christianity, their religion is not just a philosophy to be practiced on Sunday, but rather an all-encompassing way of life. Finally, while it's true that many ethnic minorities are protective-minded, Indians, including the present- day Lumbees, are notoriously individualistic until some external danger overrides this characteristic and causes them to function as a unit, a phenomenon anthropologists refer to as "the massing effect." Thus, the Lumbees are Indian because of their history, their self-image, their status in society, and in many of their characteristics.

In conclusion, it seems incontestable that the Lumbee Indians are the product of an environment that produced a swamp-surrounded island of land, which in turn afforded isolation and protection and brought together in one community remnants both of the "Lost Colony" and several Indian tribes, of which the Hatteras and various Eastern Siouan peoples were the most prominent. While there are some who will find the conclusion of amalgamation unsatisfactory, it is the only conclusion possible in light of the facts, traditions of the people, and logic of the situation. The origins of the Lumbee Indians should no longer be viewed as lost.

Delano Cummings

Delano Cummings (Lumbee) was born August 9, 1945, near Pembroke, North Carolina. He graduated from Magnolia High School, near Pembroke, in 1963. Cummings recounts his three tours of duty in Vietnam with the Marine Corps in his autobiography, *Moon Dash Warrior* (1998). His second book, *River Dreams: Tales of a Lumbee Warrior* (2001), is a semifictional collection of stories, largely autobiographical, but highly imbued with the imaginative insights provided by dreams. Following his enlistment in the Marines, from 1965 to 1971, he attended Robeson Technical Institute (now Robeson Community College), and afterwards he worked as a refrigeration mechanic with a railroad company in Illinois and Virginia. He later worked in construction for several years until retiring in 1991 in order to devote himself full time to writing. Cummings lives in Lumberton, North Carolina, near the Lumber (also called the Lumbee) River, and is presently at work on a book about Indian participation in America's wars.

The Land of the Lumbee

Chapter 4 of River Dreams

I came home to the land of the Lumbee Indian. Things had changed a lot since I had left in 1963. There were no longer three separate schools, one for the black, one for the white, and one for the Indian. There were no longer three separate public bathrooms in town. There were no longer three separate water fountains to drink from. This was a good thing.

My people were living in two worlds and making the best of both. Some were still farmers and gatherers, making their living from the land, using modern machinery and working ten times as much land as my father and grandfathers did using the horse, mule, and plow of their day. Now most of my people had been to school, some with post-graduate college degrees. Some held high positions in the government, both county and state.

There were now Indian teachers, doctors, lawyers, and even Indian judges. There were Indian-owned restaurants, a bank, a newspaper, stores and all types of Indian-owned businesses, especially construction companies. Some of the young men traveled hundreds of miles all across the United States into the big cities, helping to build the sky-tall buildings. They were steelworkers, dry-wall workers, roofers, painters, and so on, and they were very good at what they did. If a large construction project is going on in just about any part of the United States and in many places overseas, there is a good chance you will find some of our young Indian men helping with the building. They make good money, and most come back to the land of the Indian on their days off or when the job is finished.

We have warriors who choose to stay in the military and help protect our country. Some hold high rank in the military today.

Most of all, the children of today are in school, learning from books. In the early days, before and during my father's time, most of the Indian children in the land of the Lumbees had to work the land helping their fathers who were trying to scratch out a living from Mother Earth. Some learned to read and write even then, and through the years became schoolteachers. They knew the value of an education and passed their learning on to the children

There is a university now that started out in 1887 as a normal school for Indians, then became a state-supported college, and today is a part of the University of North Carolina system, and is known as the University of North Carolina at Pembroke. There are now Indian studies in the schools; the university has a special course on the American Indian. We are studying and learning about our heritage.

We have powwows, and the elders tell stories of the old days. Years earlier the stories we learned from mothers and fathers, our grandfathers and grandmothers, were the only way we had to record our history. There was no written record among the people, and what got recorded by outsiders was written from their point of view, and they could not see it from the Indian's eyes.

Until a few years ago the government encouraged the Indian people to reject their Indian heritage. Now young people of all races want to learn the old ways of the Indian. Some even choose to live as our forefathers did and want to clean up Mother Earth.

We, the Lumbee, are a tribe of non-reservation Indians numbering between 45,000 and 50,000. We have been recognized by the state of North Carolina as a tribe since 1885. We are the ninth largest tribe in the United States. Most of us make our homes near the Lumbee River close to the town of Pembroke in Robeson County, North Carolina. Here the land is flat and the long-leaf pine grows tall. For as long as anyone can remember anyone saying, we have always been along the river, fishing, hunting, and farming the land.

The government has changed our name several times in the past 300 years. We now take our name from the great river that flows through our land, the river we call the Lumbee—itself officially named the Lumber River in 1809, because logs and timber were rafted down its waters into South Carolina and on to the coast.

There are about 50 swamps that drain into our part of this river, and because of the decaying trees that dissolve dark tannin into the water, the river runs black. But it flows strong and is not polluted or unclean. There are over 100 miles of the Lumbee River in Robeson County that snake through the land of the Lumbee Indian. It is the most crooked of Carolina rivers.

The government, through the United States Department of Interior, has designated a part of our river as a "National Wild and Scenic River."

This great river has a very strong undertow. It may look calm on the surface, but the current can be raging underneath. The Lumbee River has taken the lives of countless numbers of people, sometimes wiping out entire families at one time.

Only a few years ago the river took five members of the same family, each one trying to save the other. It took one of my cousins several years ago and has taken the lives of several family friends over the years. The river has many secrets.

My father told me stories of people who lost their lives to the river during his time. He told me to always be careful, and to respect the river. He told me how his father—and also his father before him—lived from the river, how his father and uncles were sent to the river and told not to come back until they had enough game or fish for the whole clan to eat.

When I was a baby my father put me on his back, just as his father had done him, and swam the river up and down and across, to give me the feel of the river and the water spirits.

The river tried to take me when I was 12 years old. While swimming below the iron bridge downriver from the prison camp, I got caught in the current, and it carried me straight down the middle of the river. I was swimming as hard as I could just to keep my head up, but I could feel the current underneath pulling me down. I was trying to swim towards the riverbank, but was so exhausted, and the pull of the river was so strong, I could only go with the current.

I looked back and could not even see where I had been swimming or any of the other boys who had been swimming with me. I was dizzy, and then my head went under, causing me to drink some of the river water. The river felt like it had two big hands that were holding onto me, pulling me down.

I wanted to give up. And I was ready to quit when something inside my head, a voice I did not recognize at the time, said, *Fight. Don't give up. Keep your head up and fight.*

All at once the river grew calm, its huge hands turned me loose, and I found myself near the bank where the water was low enough for me to stand. I crawled up on the riverbank and lay under the cypress trees there for a long time, thinking about what had happened to me, and about what had almost happened to me.

The river must have decided not to take me that day.

Some have called our river "drowning creek" because of all the lives it has taken. But it is a part of our heritage, and everyone who has walked its banks, or fished, swum, or taken a boat down its waters carries a part of the river spirit with them wherever they go.

There have been many great stories told around the campfires about the Lumbee River. Our river, the Lumbee, has strong-running black waters, and it has many secrets known only to itself.

The Wall

Chapter Thirteen of River Dreams

There is a wall in Washington, D.C., made of shiny, black stone slabs. It is the Vietnam Veterans Memorial, dedicated to the Vietnam Veterans who died in Vietnam, warriors who gave their lives fighting for their country in a dirty Asian war. There is something about that black granite wall going down into the ground with almost 60,000 names of fallen warriors on it. Some of them were my friends. I was with some of them when they were killed fighting for their country in that land so far away from their homes. I helped load their shot and torn bodies onto helicopters to be taken out of that hellhole. Some I watched over as the spirit left their bodies. I knew the names of many of them, but some I did not. Most were just young men who wanted to go home to their families—but not that way.

I have been to the Wall to look for my name several times over the last few years. It should be there along with the others.

I have found the name of a warrior who taught me how to stay alive in a war. He was killed. I have found the name of a warrior who took my place in battle. He was killed. I have found the name of a warrior who was my leader in combat. He was killed. I have found the name of a warrior who saved my life more than once in battle. He disappeared into the jungles of Vietnam, and his name is on the Wall. These are only some of the names I have found on this Wall.

I have found their names and can feel their spirits when I go there. There is something inspiring about going into that dark hole and seeing all those names—even people who know nothing about Vietnam say there is something there, that they can feel it.

My wife went with me to the Wall a few years back, and when she passed by the panel that had the name of one of my special friends on it she told me she felt strange. I had told her nothing, but then I showed her the name of the friend who had saved my life in Vietnam. He is on panel 13E, line 42 on the Wall.

When I go the Wall I go very early in the morning. I can watch the sun come up from the east then, and a few times I have had the Wall to myself. At those times I can talk to my fallen friends. I tell them they may have been the lucky ones and I ask them to look out for me when I cross into the Spirit World.

They had the dedication for the Vietnam Veterans Memorial on Veterans Day 1982. At that time I was working and living 20 miles away, right across the Potomac River in Virginia. But at that time I would not or could not go there. I could only ride in my car down Constitution Avenue by the White House in all the traffic and look over at all the people by the Wall and wonder.

At that time I was still running from my war, running from my Indian heritage, running from my spirit voice, running from myself.

It was ten years later and I was living 400 miles away before I could go to the Vietnam Veterans Memorial, and then it took the Veterans Hospital and a lot of coaching from other Vietnam veterans I had met along the way to get me to go.

At the Wall I have seen other veteran warriors, some of them like me feeling uneasy about being alive. Some have their families with them; some wear suits; some wear jungle utilities and bush hats; some have beards and long hair; some look like everyone else. But one look into the eyes and I can tell if they were there and have seen the things that can happen in a war. They are warriors and will always be warriors. Like me most will have a hard time living in this world among everyday people, because once you have experienced war and have killed your enemy you have killed a part of yourself.

Sometimes I see people leaving things at the Wall, and I see people crying there. What makes a person cry?

What makes a strong woman cry? My mother, who gave birth to eight children, has lived a good but sometimes a hard life. When she was 12 years old her mother died, leaving six small children. My mother took her mother's place, taking care of her brothers and sisters and working in the fields helping her father work the land. When she was 18 years old she married my father, who also worked the land that the Great Creator put here for us.

During the time she had us children and worked the land right beside my father, both of them sometimes working from daylight right into the night trying to scratch out a living from the earth—living between the modern world and the old ways of the Indian. My mother was and still is very proud and is a woman who very seldom shows her feelings.

The day President John F. Kennedy was killed I was out behind our house cutting firewood for the night when I heard my mother call for me to come. "Hurry up!" she shouted. I ran as fast as I could. As I got closer I could see she was crying. That was not like her. Something bad had to have happened. "What's wrong?" I asked.

"Someone killed the President! Someone shot President Kennedy! Run, get your father!" she said.

My father was feeding his horses. As I turned to run to him I saw tears running down my mother's cheeks. What had happened had made a strong woman cry.

What makes a man cry? It was April 1968. We were nine recon Marines sitting on an isolated outpost on top of a hill deep in the jungles of Vietnam. This was the team called Moon Dash. This was my team.

The hill was surrounded by thick jungle and other hills. We had fighting holes and wire around the top of the hill. All sides dropped almost straight down. We were put there by helicopter to watch with telescope the valley floor below us. We were watching for North Vietnamese soldiers moving through the valley. When we spotted our enemy through the valley we would call our rear command and they would fire artillery or send out jet bombers to destroy this enemy.

The mountain-top outpost was impossible for our enemy to get to, even though they had tried a few days earlier. They had climbed straight up and attacked the hill, but failed to get to the top. Some of their dead still lay below us.

The day before I had taken two men and some rope and had climbed about 100 feet down and found three dead enemy soldiers who had been killed trying to take the hill. We searched the bodies but found nothing on them. It looked like their friends had taken all their gear and left the bodies there, knowing they could not carry them away.

With the rope and the help of one another we climbed back up to the top of the hill. But that night and the next day I had that smell in my head and on my hands, the smell of dead bodies that had been lying in the sun two or three days. It was terrible, and I could not get rid of it.

It was late afternoon when the radioman got a report from our rear command and yelled out to the rest of us that Martin Luther King, Jr., had been shot. A few minutes later he yelled out that Martin Luther King, Jr., was dead.

We had one black American Marine with us. He was a big and strong man who was on the quiet side and did not bother anyone. He was a good Marine. Everyone in our recon team got along fine with one another, even saving one another's life at times while fighting our enemy.

When the word came that Martin Luther King, Jr., was dead, one of the other Marines—without thinking—said, "That's good. King was a communist, anyway."

When the black Marine heard this he got mad. He was ready to fight. Since I was the recon patrol leader I went to talk to him. He had tears in his eyes. "Sergeant Cummings, he should not have said that," he said.

I told him I knew, that it had been a stupid thing for the other Marine to say, that he had not thought before he spoke. We walked to the far end of the hill where we could talk.

"This is a bad thing," I began. I had a lump in my throat. "I'm also hurt. Martin Luther King did a lot for all the people. I'm Indian and what he was doing was helping my people also. Things have already changed because of this great man."

He shook his head. "I know," he said.

This warrior was hurting, so I left him so he could be alone. As I was leaving I saw this big strong American Marine look out over the valley floor and the jungles of Vietnam and then put his hands over his face and cry. When I looked back once more I could see tears rolling down his face and dropping from his chin. What happened that day had made a strong man cry.

Later the Marine apologized for what he had said. He told the black Marine he was sorry that Martin Luther King was dead, and they shook hands and remained friends throughout that long, dangerous year in the jungles of Vietnam.

I cried when my father died. I went out into the cornfield so I could cry alone. After a while I told myself to go to the family. "You are a man," I said. "You are Indian. Enough crying."

Now I don't cry. I don't know exactly why. One of the head doctors at the Veterans Hospital told me I needed to cry and that I needed to stop isolating myself from the world. I told him I like to isolate—that may be the Indian in me—and right now I don't want to cry. And that was that.

Watching men and women crying at the Wall, I think crying is all right.

Linda Boyden

Linda Boyden (Lumbee-Cherokee) was born in Attleboro, Massachusetts, but her parents came from the Appalachians. She is an enrolled member of the United Lumbee Tribe of North Carolina and America. Her book, *The Blue Roses*, was published in 2002, and has won several awards: the Lee & Low Books New Voices Award, the 2003 Paterson Prize for Books for Young People, and it garnered for the author the Writer of the Year for Children's Books Award from the Wordcraft Circle of Native Writers and Storytellers. She is the coeditor of *Cemetery Plots: Stories Beneath the Stones* (2006). Her poems have appeared in *Woven in the Wind: Women Write about Friendship in the Sagebrush West*, *Through the Eye of the Deer*, and *Maui Muses, Volume II*. She is presently living with her husband and children in Redding, California, where she conducts storytelling sessions within the local libraries and schools. Boyden is a member of Wordcraft Circle of Native Writers and Storytellers and maintains a webpage devoted to the art of storytelling.

Cedar Songs, Left Behind

She stayed behind, the mother of my grandfathers,
Not by choice, his or hers: theirs.
Singled out, she was, by soldiers.
Spared, they said, by yaller hair, blue eyes.
Spoilt tho' she was, still no kind of fate
For a white woman, this trail.
This Removal.

In the guile of their final night,
In the lull of the dark, they slept,
The mother of my grandfathers and her man,
Her red earth man
His skin in rich opposition to her pale,
They lay entwined until he woke.

Stirred by the cadence of boot-heel crunch on gravel,
The thick man-scent rising in the air,
Whiskeysmokesweatwool
He woke.
My grandfather's father

"Cedar Songs, Left Behind," copyright © 2004 by Linda Boyden. Published with permission of the author.

Crossed to the rough-hewn mantle for his flute,
The smoothed cedar flute,
Which under my living fingers
Delivers still the songs.
The haunting cedar songs.
Gifts left behind by the Tree People
In the branch
He carved so long ago.

The mother of my grandfathers taught her son,
And her grandson, the songs he played that night.
In time, he taught his granddaughter,
Child of pale hair and red earth skin.
Told her, too, the story.

Played me awake that night, she said.
Placed my fingers one by one on his;
Played into them the cedar songs, one by one,
Until the soldiers came.

As they broke down the door,
As they dragged him away,
I faltered once, she said, *but did not stop.*

I released the cedar songs
Instead of tears
As they pushed my man from the dawn.
From my arms.
I played for him the songs;
For the son born after;
For the grandson of my old age . . .

Now as grandmother
I tell her words.
I, the girl blessed with
Grandmother's name and hair,
Grandmother's red earth skin,
I play
The sweet cedar songs,
The haunting holy gifts
Of the trees
He left behind.

Will Moreau Goins

Will Moreau Goins (Cherokee–Lumbee / Tuscarora / Cheraw) was born in Washington, D.C. He holds a bachelor's degree from The George Washington University (1983) and his master's (1989) and doctorate from Pennsylvania State University (1994). Goins is a descendant of the "unconquered" Eastern Band of Cherokee Indians of upstate South Carolina and the Lumbee / Tuscarora / Cheraw Indians in the southeastern portion of North Carolina. For many years, he was the director of the National Native Network of Talent and the First Americans Theater in Washington (Free Spirit Players). He is a stage and film / video actor, director, film consultant, and ceremonial singer and dancer, in addition to his work as an educator and administrator. Since 1994, Goins has been the chief executive officer of Eastern Cherokee Southern Iroquois and United Tribes of South Carolina (ECSIUT). In 2002, his anthology, *The People Speak: A Collection of Writings by South Carolina Native Americans in Poetry, Prose, Essays, and Interviews*, was published. He is also the coauthor of a play, *Feathers in the Wind* (1984) and the musical version of it, *Feathers* (1989). Will Moreau Goins is also a freelance correspondent, and his journalism has appeared in such publications as *Indian Youth Magazine*, *Eagle Wing Press*, *Tribal Scroll*, *The USET Calumet*, *The Washington Times*, *Washington View Magazine*, and *News From Indian Country*. He lives in Columbia, South Carolina.

All American Boy, A Native Son

I am a Native
I am Carolina Blue
I am Crystal Blue
I am Turquoise Blue
I am an "All American Boy"

You're not "All American," they say
You're tan, you've brown hair, you look different
"You're urban, you're not a real Indian, Indians live on the plains!"

Many times while I was growing up, I wished for blonde hair
That a bit of white blood in my veins would surface
That I could be Me and yet look . . . Their way

Urban Indians really have it rough, especially the children
"You left your people for economic survival,"
How awful . . . You're a traitor
What about kids who had nothing to do with the move?
What about the parents' wish for their children?
What about economic survival? Trying to make a better life

The kids still grow up, doesn't matter where
Trying to maintain sanity
Trying to know what they have missed
Trying to fit into both homes, both worlds, many worlds

Each day is a new battle of . . .
"Who are you? What are you?"
I ask: "Why don't we ask each other?"
Then an "Indian brother" comes up, playing their game
"Why are you NOT traditional?" "Do you have a number?"
Yeah, like cattle. ARE YOU BRANDED?
Do you have a pedigree? like a dog or a horse, Thoroughbred
I am not a dog, horse, I am a human.

The usual question is
"Are you from South of the border?"

Loretta Leach

Loretta Leach (Wassamasaw) was born February 11, 1950, near Varnertown, South Carolina. She continues to live in the area, a traditional Wassamasaw Indian community, where she is a grandmother and a respected elder and tribal historian. Leach is a widow and the president of a construction company.

Varnertown in the 1950s

When I was a child, I was told not to ask about my heritage. My parents would say that they did not know. People around us would say we were too dark to be white and too light skinned to be black. So what were we? Because my mother would not talk about it, I never understood my heritage. So, when my children were born I put them down as white. My parents had said it was too hard to be Indian because you would be cast out of the community. You could not claim black, because you might be lynched. Best not to claim anything at all. Just to be safe.

My father's mother was the first to break the silence. She spoke to someone who came through the community asking about our race. She told them that her mother had told her she was an Indian. It wasn't until years later that we found out what she had said. She was the only one who stood up for her race. My dad was embarrassed because he was put down as Mulatto on his birth certificate. Thereafter, he would always claim white, and never admit to his heritage. He thought that everyone looked down on him, even his brothers.

Varnertown in the 1950s was a bad place for you if you claimed anything other than white. So that is why we went along with the flow and claimed to be white, as well. My grandmother's voice telling our story back in 1938 has helped me embrace my heritage more fully. If it was not for her, I may still be claiming "white" today.

I want her words to echo in the community today and for Varnertown to grow and regain its culture. There is no longer a reason to be ashamed of who you are.

III

Deep South

Georgia, Florida, Alabama, and Mississippi

Louis Owens

Louis Owens (Choctaw-Cherokee) was regarded as a major Native American author when he passed away on July 25, 2002, in Albuquerque, New Mexico. Born on July 18, 1948, in Lompoc, California, he attended universities in California, receiving his Ph.D. from the University of California–Santa Cruz in 1979. As well as achieving renown as a Native American novelist and critic for such books as *Wolfsong* (1991), *The Sharpest Sight* (1992), *Other Destinies* (1992), *Bone Game* (1996), *Nightland* (1996), *Mixedblood Messages* (1998), *Dark River* (1999), and *I Hear the Train* (2001), Owens established himself as one of the foremost critics of the work of John Steinbeck in the United States. He taught at the University of New Mexico from 1983 to 1995, and thereafter was employed by the University of California at Davis, but he continued to maintain a home in Albuquerque. Although Owens had ties through his father with the Choctaw and Cherokee Nations of Oklahoma, his mother was of Mississippi Choctaw heritage. Recently, two critical studies of Owens's writings have appeared: Christopher A. LaLonde's *Grave Concerns, Trickster Turns* (2002) and Jacquelyn Kilpatrick's *Louis Owens: Literary Reflections on His Life and Work* (2004).

Yazoo Dusk

1. COLUMBUS BAILEY

"You got to fish ever damn day." That walker hound started up again outside, probably smelling last night's coon tracks by the chickens. The old man rubbed two or three white chin hairs and looked up at me under the bill of that Redskins cap. Like it always had since I was a kid, my brain started running like a scared rabbit, heading out toward the river and then doubling back to the woods and thinking about climbing one of those big oaks. But it wasn't any use, just like it hadn't ever been any use, and I let those black eyes catch me.

"It ain't a lot I know," he said. I studied the mason jar of shine he had surrounded by those big, bony hands. "But one thing I can tell you is you got to fish ever god damned day."

Uncle Col Bailey had come as close to doing it as anybody I ever heard of, though these days Uncle Col only fished in his own head, ever since he'd

"Yazoo Dusk" (chapter from an unpublished and untitled novel). Collected in *I Hear the Train: Reflections, Inventions, Refractions* (Norman: University of Oklahoma Press, 2001). Copyright © 2000 by Louis Owens. Reprinted with permission of the University of Oklahoma Press and the author.

started hearing fish scream. I'd heard stories about him as a boy being out there on the river when the sun came up and out there when the sun went down. Columbus Bailey was a famous fisherman all over the Yazoo country, up to Yazoo City and down as far as Vicksburg. Everybody said it was because he could think like a fish. He used to talk to them, too, I heard. Once over in Louisiana, in Catahoula Parish where my grandma was born, I had a man ask me if I knew Col Bailey the fisherman. I don't know why I told that man no I hadn't never heard of him, though I was more or less named for him, if you believe one story. Cole Bailey's my name, and my dad told me he come as close to Uncle Col's name as he could without spelling out the whole name of that Italian Spanish burglar, but truth is my dad likes a good story. Uncle Col is my great uncle on the Choctaw and Cajun and Irish side, you see, and I'd made the mistake this summer day of coming all the way to Mississippi to ask Uncle Col's advice on love. If I'd thought about it at all, I'd have remembered that with Uncle Col it's best to ask a little question, because the old man's answers was always a hundred times bigger than any question, maybe a thousand.

I'd started junior college out in California a year before, because my cousin, second cousin, sort of, whose name is Cole also, Cole McCurtain, talked me into it, said go on out to California and work at that mushroom farm he used to work at before he became a professor and then go to junior college. I could've gone to junior college right here in Mississippi, of course, but Cole McCurtain thought it'd be good for me to see something else, and he'd liked California pretty well I guess. The first thing that happened, naturally, was I fell in love and suffered more than I ever thought a person could. Cole McCurtain didn't help a bit when I called him to tell him how bad it was, just grinned over the phone. Adela Camacho was as beautiful as a winter sunrise on the river, when all that new light comes down through the black bones of trees and lays gold on the slow water and you don't hear nothing except maybe a lone dog out there deep in the woods and the air is that kind of sweet cold that makes you dizzy. Skin as smooth and brown as maple syrup, eyes black as the old man's but big and deep and a smile you couldn't forget in a million years. And that way of looking back just when you think she's gone.

"So my nephew come all the way from California to ask me about love." The old man got up slow, unfolding his long body carefully, the way you open a new-sharpened jackknife. Lifting the cap off, he ran a hand through what was left of his white hair so I could see his brown fingers right against the same brown skin on his head. He settled the cap back, adjusting the thing two or three times to get it just right, the way he always did, while going over to the stove. Being summer and well after daylight, it was already getting warm in his little cabin, but Uncle Col was always cold, always had been, so he opened up the stove and began shoving some more sticks in and stirring the coals around.

"How old is this girl?" He'd closed the stove door and spun around so fast I'd half jumped. "Sit down, boy." He jerked his head toward the other chair, a high-backed wooden thing he'd got from a white woman across the river. Twenty years old and I was still "boy."

"Not so young," I said, thinking if he knew she was eighteen he'd start laughing and not stop like he did sometimes.

He pulled a frying pan off a shelf and set it on the stove, and I realized why he'd poked the fire up. When he reached for the slab of bacon on the same shelf and started cutting, I felt a jab of hunger. I could already smell bacon cooking even before it was in the pan.

"You could make some coffee." With his back to me, he nodded sideways toward the crate shelf with the coffee pot and can of Folgers in it.

"Love." He sliced the bacon thick with a filleting knife, and laid eight slices delicately in the iron skillet.

As I reached for the door pull to go outside, I heard him mutter the same word, and then a brittle kind of chuckling followed me out the door. That hound pup came up wriggling and slapping my legs with his bony tail, and I saw a couple of yellow chicken feathers on his snout. I knew he hadn't killed any chickens because Uncle Col would have known a chicken-killing dog before the first thought of chicken dinner ever crossed the animal's mind. The pup must have been snuffling coon scent by the pen and snuffled the feathers onto his jowls.

I pumped a few times to get the rust taste out and then filled the pot and headed back inside. It was true that I'd driven four days in a fifty-seven Chevy to talk to the old man. I was desperate, crazy in love and ignorant. I'd been stupid enough to propose marriage the fourth time we were together, sitting out in the Pismo dunes with a bottle of wine and a box of fried chicken. When she laughed, I felt like my heart had one of those cracks you get in a windshield, the kind that start out small but unless something's done just keeps going right across until the whole thing comes apart in your face. Six months later, I knew I had to do something. I couldn't live without her, I knew that. One day she'd say she might love me, she didn't know, and then the next she'd act like she hardly knew me. And when she took me to her parents' house I felt like a spaceman setting there with everybody talking Spanish and her sisters giggling behind their hands at me. But that's another story.

Back inside, the old man was turning the bacon with a fork and scratching his flat belly under the overalls with the other hand. I set the pot on the stove and dumped in two fistfuls of coffee, standing so close I could smell smoke and lye soap and age on him. By the time I'd woke up, he'd already been to the river and took a bath like he did every day. Most of his life, he'd check his trot line and re-set it before his bath, but he didn't do that any more.

"Ever day." He forked the bacon onto a tin plate and broke six eggs into the deep grease so that they became brown and lacey the second they hit.

Over the years, I'd noticed that Uncle Col was different from most Indians I knew, even mixedbloods like him. For one thing, most Indian elders didn't swear so much. But the old man had a hard time getting a sentence out without at least a damn in it. For another thing, he was kind of a loner. I'd never known him to go down to Philadelphia where a lot of the Choctaws were, and he didn't even cross the river to where some of his own family was scattered. When Cole McCurtain was back here that time, I never even knew it because Cole was down there with Luther Cole, and him and Uncle Col hadn't talked in years. All these names kind of run together. Indian names is like that sometimes.

Columbus Bailey didn't go nowhere to see people, but people come to see him. He had things they wanted. The old man was *alikchi*. He knew the kinds of medicines people needed. Right now I needed for him to tell me how to make Adela Camacho fall head over heels all the way to the bottom in love with me and marry me. I know she didn't think much of me working at the mushroom farm, but why do you think I'm going to college I told her.

He didn't talk again until we were setting at the bare wood plank table with bacon and eggs and boiling hot black coffee. He'd put the moonshine up on the shelf next to the bacon and with some kind of magic produced a pan of cornbread not more than a day old. He was sopping cornbread in egg and bacon grease and looking doubtfully at his coffee.

"Luther Cole was my friend," he said finally, still not looking up.

I got interested immediately, hooked by the fact the old man hadn't added any swear words to the statement. Luther Cole had lived down the river about five miles in a little cabin. I'd only seen the old Choctaw man a couple of times, and each time I'd been scared to death. There was an old woman with him both times, tall and beautiful with hair silver as a new dollar. Shiny dark skin, and a big smile. The old couple had seemed like ghosts to me.

2. LUTHER COLE

Dusk lay close in the woods along the river. The way it does toward the end of summer just before the sun goes down and the trees lift night up like an old blanket until everything's black. When there aren't any stars and maybe only a new moon. Night in those coon woods gets so thick a man can walk right into himself in the dark. Luther Cole lay under a muscadine thicket, the heavy vines drooping all around him and over him heavy as hanging ropes and the big purple fruit, kind of sweet and rotten-smelling, sixteen years old and watching the girl on the front porch.

Slivers of gray edging toward black in the pecan tree and darker still where the woods sloped down to the river in vine and brush, tree-thickened and rancid with August. Luther Cole saw the owl swoop up from the woods to land in the tree, near-white belly and broad pale wings so soft he felt smothered by the sound where he lay beneath them vines. Damp summer rose hot in leaves and rotten earth through the sleeveless flannel shirt and spread across flat, adolescent stomach and chest, itching and creeping inside his shirt and over-alls. Start of crickets and frogs down toward the water and a poorwill begin-ning, too, its double voice out over the water the way it had been all of the boy's life. But the boy's eyes were on the *owl, ishkitini,* again. He realized he'd stopped breathing only when he began once more, sucking the thick Yazoo air in like he was drowning, thinking about moccasins and copperheads, too, and stranger violence.

When the owl disappeared through the high gable window of the big house, Luther Cole lay for a few moments and then unbent from the ground, brush-ing leaves out of the straight black hair that hung past his shoulders. Damn the girl, he thought, and that old grandmother who wouldn't stay dead like she ought to. Fourteen years old and he knew he'd already been in love all his whole life and more, with the Yazoo just a hundred yards down the hill telling him violence would indeed lay hold of every goddamned thing the moment he moved. Hadn't it already taken hold of everybody he came from all the way back to Red Shirt and more?

Running a hand down overalled stomach and muddy knees, he moved out of the woods, pushing aside the muscadines, and angled cautiously across to the pecan tree, watching the darkened window. At the tree he embraced the straight trunk and climbed like an inchworm to the first heavy limb, where he pulled himself up with thin, hard arms to stand and reach his scrawny body upward again and climb until he was at the big branch near the window and he began edging outward, gripping higher limbs with his hands and balancing like a circus clown, bare toes grabbing smooth bark.

A few feet from the open window he stopped and peered inward, determi-nation stronger than fear of the old woman. The *alikchi* had been sending dreams all over the damned place. He'd found himself tumbling down at the bottom of the river, head over heels in a strong current. knowing he was supposed to understand but failing and angry when he couldn't. And the girl wouldn't help because the *alikchi* was her grandmother.

A foot began to itch, and he lifted the other foot to scratch just as the owl appeared in the window, cream-white and enormous, the yellow eyes locked on him so that he dizzied and fell.

*   *   *

"Serves you right for spying on me."

Onatima Blue Wood stood looking down at him in her yellow nightgown, arms folded across her chest, a thick black braid over each shoulder, and a scowl on her extraordinarily beautiful face and in her green eyes. Dark cusps hung beneath sharp cheekbones and shadowed her fine lips.

"She didn't mean to make you fall. We didn't know you were where you shouldn't be, spying on other people's business." She cocked her head and continued to look down at him where he lay folded awkwardly on the grass.

"And don't pretend you're hurt when you're not, Luther Cole. I've seen you fall twice as bad as that a hundred times and never get hurt."

Unmoving, Luther stared up at her thinking that maybe this time he was truly dead and finally she'd be sorry. The dark had spread out from the woods to cover the sky like a blanket full of holes, and around Onatima's head a new constellation was spinning, *fichik luak, lukoli, shubota*. Something like that. *Issuba*, the ones pointing northward. *Tohwikeli*. The old language was spinning in his head, too.

"Your head is on fire," he said, wishing he knew the old language to speak to her.

"Enough hog talk, Luther Cole. Now get up off the ground before my father hears us and runs you off again." She stepped back, never uncrossing her arms from her sixteen-year-old chest, and shook her head.

Luther gathered the pieces of himself and stood up carefully, feeling joints coming back into alignment.

"It's a good thing I grabbed them branches on my way down. Else that old lady would've killed me this time."

"Nonsense. Grandmother would never hurt one of my friends."

A dog began barking in the kennel behind the house, and instantly ten others joined in, all wanting to be out nosing things in the night. They heard an upstairs window open and the old man yell. The dogs stopped, and then Luther was aware of the hounds sulking and the silence that spread over the whole countryside at the sound of the man's voice. The shadow of the big barn reached out at them, and he realized that the moon was there. How long had he lain in the woods watching, he wondered.

"You have no reason to watch me and worry about me, Luther. You know I can take care of myself." She reached out to brush debris off his shoulder and her hand continued to his hair, gently raking twigs out. "You should see yourself."

"One of your friends?" He shook himself and finished raking twigs and leaves from his tangled hair. "I could've been killed by that witch. Why's she coming around so much all of a sudden?"

"You know why. Now go on home before my father comes out here. I wish I'd never ever kissed you, Luther Cole."

"But you did. And not just once, neither. You said we'd be married."

The girl shook her head and then wrapped her arms around her shoulders. "Child's talk, you know that. You're still a boy, Luther Cole."

"And you're growed up all of a sudden. It's because of him, Granger."

She shook her head once more. "I told him to go away. It's because of nobody, and you're going to school, too."

"I ain't going to no school, especially not way up there."

"Any school. Don't say double negatives. You know better."

"I'll kill that white man."

"I told him to go away and he will. Now you have to go, too. We aren't children any longer, Luther. My father might have you whipped if he finds you out here again. You know he said he would."

"You think I'm scared of that? You think that Granger'll go away just because you say so? Didn't you say it before?"

"My father encourages him. Now go home, Luther."

She stepped forward and touched both of his shoulders with her hands and kissed him on the forehead, stepping back again before he could react. "I'm not a child any more, Luther. We can't play in the woods any more. Everything's different."

"Nothing's different. I'll come back tomorrow. You stay home from church. Say you have a gut ache like you used to and stay home when they go. I'll come."

She shook her head. "Not tomorrow. I can't. You don't understand at all. You have to go to that school. Goodbye, Luther Cole."

"I'll kill that white man."

Onatima turned away. "Go home and sleep, Luther. Granma won't let it happen."

The girl went away, gliding barefooted through the grass around the back of the house without any sound or motion in the air so that abruptly he found himself alone.

3. ONATIMA BLUE WOOD

If you think it's easy being an Indian girl, you're crazy. People think because my father's rich, or richer than most in these parts anyway, that it's all easy. Last night the moon climbed up behind the pecan tree, climbing up out of the woods the way I've seen a coon go up, smooth and slow, until it sat right there on the highest branches and waited for something. I understood because I've been waiting for something all my life. People always look at me. Like they expect something, something that a girl who wasn't half Indian wouldn't do. And school, that's a real barrel of fun. Ever since I was little, if I read "See Dick run" the teachers acted like a prize mule had sat up and recited the Lord's Prayer. Like an Indian wasn't supposed to read, like my mother, who was born in Scotland actually, and whose name I can't say any longer since she passed on, hadn't taught me to read when I was not even three and a half years old and I wasn't writing whole sentences by the time I was four, which is more than a lot of grown up white folks around here can do. As if it was an accomplishment for a half-Indian girl to read about stupid Dick running when I'd read all of the Brothers Grimm and Hans Christian Andersen by second grade.

Those teachers never knew anything about the real stories, the ones my grandmother, my *apokni*, told me when she came to live with us after Mother's death. And the other things, *alikchi* medicine. She taught me those words, too, and I listened as hard as I could but still only heard a little bit. Deep woods stories, olden time true stories. Chahta things, *fahpo* things, what Granma called *aiukli*. Stories I could not even let my father know I heard, because Father was modern, a fullblood stepping away from Indian stories into this thing called America. Two worlds, two kinds of stories. But those little people in the fairy tales, we knew them, my granma and me. They were *bohpuli* senders and throwers, hide-behinds. Be secret, she said, tell no one, even Father, her own son, and especially teachers. The first time she came after they buried her, to keep the teaching alive. I was frightened for only a moment until I understood. I read *Moby-Dick* at thirteen years of age, and understood every ephemeral shadow of that teller's story. Ishmael, outcast like me and Luther Cole. Wanderer, friend to Indians. Ha. And Burns's wee cowering timorous beastie from my mother. Having both worlds, I thought, would put me ahead of them all. But that Luther, pulling his head into the Indian world like a snapping turtle into one of those ridged shells, didn't seem to worry about being behind one little bit. Girls mature sooner, Granma said. Those Jobe and Owens girls didn't seem to, however.

I lay there in my whitest nightgown, after mothers and grandmothers had gone away, and let the moonlight bathe me in its radiance. I glowed, a princess, a rare and radiant maiden whom the angels named Onatima. My skin was made of light, and I felt like I could just float right out the window. Luther had been here, hiding in the woods and making animal calls that any fool who wasn't deaf and retarded would know wasn't any animal that ever lived. Like an old-time Indian, Luther Cole didn't approve of the ways of white people. "Apple" he called my own father, an Indian who was not just red but red-brown on the outside and white like all rich people on the inside. He would take me away, across the river to that life his kind of Chahta lived, not understanding at all the way these two worlds had steel hooks pulling from both sides until I thought I would be left just bloody muscle and broken bone all the while thinking, remembering, waiting. All those years from when we'd both run and fall and laugh like babies, knowing Luther had marked me for his world against my father's desire but, and this so strange, precisely within the wishes of my mother who told stories of Highland clans and warriors so in keeping with Granma's Choctaw stories. Massacred MacDonalds. Highland ghosts. Pushed toward an Indian world by my red haired, freckled, indescribably beautiful mother and denied the same world by my fullblood, dark-as-stone father. Is it any wonder I am a misfit, a castaway, a Gypsy, an Ishmael? Not ignoring what is good I, too, am quick to perceive an evil, or something like that. Like him a lover of words. English words because I don't speak the old language at all. Promised while still a child by my father to Granger with his stable of horses and that school in the North that taught him not a fraction of what I learned from two women in my father's house against his knowing and his will. Which is the way women work nowadays. Unlike the olden times when, Granma told me, Choctaw women were the ones to make decisions. The ones at the center.

Luther Cole has my heart and will take it away to that raw plank cabin on the other side of the river, but Granger Collins shall have my woman's body, alas. All the world ordains as much. And I should be grateful that a white man of standing would marry a halfbreed, they say. Not for Onatima Blue Wood to leave a big white house and barns and stables and cross a brown river to twelve square feet of darkness. They say. Granma says, Wait. She comes now at night and says the story will be a long and twisted one. She says this is not the real story. All time is one, she says, and I must bide it as well as Luther Cole, who is, she says, the one who will learn. Whom I will teach.

Down there by the river, where I walk sometimes, the water is brown and heavy, moving so intently that I know there is no end to it. Never, I think, have Chahta people been far from such water, and I know I cannot leave it. Granger talks of other places, Saint Louis. Chicago, New York, but he might as well be talking about the bottom of an ocean I've never even seen. Away from this river I shall die. Luther Cole can go off to school and come back, for he carries the river inside him, but this brown water is not inside me. It surrounds me, gives me breath. I'll stay and outlast them all, Granger, my father, all. I will not change my name nor cut my hair for him or anyone.

4. LUTHER COLE

Luther Cole lay under the muscadine thicket, the heavy vines drooping heavy as hanging ropes. Sixteen years old, and watching the girl on the front porch the way he'd been watching her for the past hour. Something was up, and it didn't involve the fool sitting on the porch with her.

"Chiggers for sure," the boy whispered aloud, thinking how downright stupid it was to be lying in the damp rot of leaves and decayed bark and bird-eaten fruit pulp but unable to lift himself from the earth and tell his body to go elsewhere. The same way he'd been unable to ward off the girl all these years.

On the wide porch, Onatima shone in light from a lamp inside the house, and he could see the fine taut brown cheeks and smiling lips and smooth forehead and long, long black hair that he knew she refused to wear coiled the way she should but insisted on letting fall straight and shining dark to the seat of the chair. Uncut all these years. The white dress rose in a crimped collar halfway up her neck, with buttons down the front and long sleeves that lapped over her hands. He could see her straight shoulders in the wicker chair, the fan in her right hand, and the white man who sat in the other wicker chair facing her. He hated and pitied the man, knowing who he was and why he was and how he was and so much more than he'd ever wanted to know about any man. Rich white folks were like that, living *big* and wide across everybody's lives. like they owned the full moon and the whole sky of stars and everyone who walked or ran way down below moon and sky. Rich Indians, like the girl's father, were different. They kept their lives quiet, moving slowly, careful to cast no shadows across others' paths or doorways, a way of life both ancient and learned sometimes painfully. Pitied the man because the man didn't know the truth about the girl and himself, or anyone maybe. *Hatak yushpakamma,* bewitched.

Onatima Blue Wood was the girl's name, and her father was the richest Choctaw on that part of the Yazoo, her mother a white woman who'd come to teach the poor Indians like Luther Cole and married one of them. Like Luther

Cole, the girl was a mixedblood, a halfbreed. But she was different because of the big white house that pushed that porch out toward the river, the barns and stables full of blooded horses, the white dress, the old Choctaw man inside the house wearing a suit and vest and, when he wanted to, a fine white hat and driving a buggy and paying black men and women to do his work.

Luther studied the man in the lamplight. Granger Collins, a name that made him want to cut the suit coat off the man with a rusty can lid. At least fifteen years older than the girl who, Luther knew exactly, had turned sixteen just three weeks before. A fool.

Lying deep in the moldering leaves and stench of Yazoo mud and all the tangled darkness of the Choctaw people who had lived and died on that land for a thousand years, Luther Cole was not his father and mother, for he had never known either, nor his brothers and sisters whom he had never known, nor his Choctaw and French blood relations from across the Mississippi in Louisiana, of whom he had heard only whispers and speculations that forked like rabbit trails only to run out in river brush; nor was he the sixteen year old boy who had been in love with Onatima since before either had breathed the wet air of the Yazoo Trace or imbibed the old stories. But he was, steeped in blood and bone, much more than he knew or the white man could know or the girl would desire to know. More than the screech owl bothering the newly risen night not far off, causing the small hairs to stand on the boy's neck or the hounds baying dinner in one of the barns behind the big house. Or the slow slap of the river on its mud bank to his back or all the lives that had graced and perished the land before and after what they called the removal.

The white man was still on the porch, the girl had not run off yet with that gambler, followed by the bitter old shadow of her fullblood father. And Luther Cole had not yet been sent up to Haskell.

5. TELLER

Poking around in the woods. Swallow tail coat and plug hat, those black suit pants worn to shine and the white shirt now possum gray, his beard full of moss and twigs, and not finding, much at all. I can see the committee, all the way back here from the Territory, looking for Chahta people. *Chahta isht atia. Chahta yakni. Chahta okla. Chahta hatak. Chahta anumpa.* So many words now, throats dry and cracking. And the people staying right back there in the woods, watching the strangers with familiar sounding names, some of them like the bearded one, more white than Choctaw, searching for what they said was relatives.

They been gone so long, you see, more than two generations out there in

Indian Territory, that we almost forgot them. Some had relatives, but it's a long way out there, and the trail just disappeared. I remember when it happened, all the people herded up like hogs drove out of the woods into pens and put on boats and wagons, coming in from all over, thousands of them, little kids hiding behind those deep brown eyes, scared, lost, hanging on to folks. Men trying to look like they knew, but knowing no more than their own children. And the women really knowing the way women always know when home is gone and what they're standing on isn't the same and keeps shifting and they have to somehow keep touching everything and body so there's a whole somewhere. There was the rich ones, like Pitchlynn. And some stayed in Mississippi, but most was poor and most started walking westward, going the way the stories told us we'd come from so long ago. People clung to that, they were going back where they started in time immemorial walking with the brothers, Chahta and Chikasa, following the leaning pole to this home.

"If you are Choctaw, you are entitled to land out in the Territory where most of the people are now." That's what the committee said, speaking patiently the way they might of spoke to a child. "You just have to come out there and you'll have land now. It's called allotment. Our land will be given to each one of us, each family, and you are entitled. If you are Choctaw."

If they were Choctaw, as if white men from somewhere north could just come and tell people who they were. The people watched, that Yazoo mud on their feet. Those other Choctaws had been taken away seventy and eighty years before by the government, leaving a handful who wouldn't go, or couldn't. Torn away, like a piece of flesh caught on a briar and just ripped from the body, except this time it was the body itself ripped away, leaving that bloody piece behind. There was some that turned back from that awful walk, straggling home to tell of dying children and old folks, births in frozen mud beside trail and road. White farmers charging ten times the price for any kind of food. A picture of a daybreak that showed a hundred horses standing dead, frozen in mud up to their withers. A hundred Indian horses coming out of the night like that frozen, all facing back the way they'd come. "I druther die right here, right this minute," the coming back people said. So the ones left behind knew the truth of what they called Removal. And there was some that come back from the Territory now and then, and some that left Mississippi and went out there, some that slipped back and forth during the war when so many Indian people fought and got cut to pieces for something that didn't mean a thing to them.

So we knew about the other place where our relatives went, knew they built up a Choctaw Republic out there with schools and all until that war killed everything. But we didn't know our relatives any more until the committees came back to get us. "It's the law," they explained. "We got to offer every Choctaw some of that land. One hundred and sixty acres for head of household . . ."

They didn't seem Choctaw no more. We didn't go.

That was the year Luther Cole was born across the Yazoo in a cabin, into a Choctaw world of so much magic that it already had possessed Onatima Blue Wood for more than a year in the big white house with black servants and blooded horses in a stable.

Honorée Fanonne Jeffers

A native southerner, **Honorée Fanonne Jeffers** (Cherokee) now lives on the prairie where she teaches at the University of Oklahoma. She is the author of three books of poetry, *The Gospel of Barbeque* (2000), chosen by Lucille Clifton for the 1999 Stan and Tom Wick Prize for Poetry, *Outlandish Blues* (2003), and *Red Clay Suite* (2007). Her poems have appeared in several journals, including *American Poetry Review, Callaloo, Iowa Review, The Kenyon Review, Ploughshares,* and *Prairie Schooner*. Since childhood, Jeffers has heard stories about her mother's Cherokee great-great grandmother, Mandy or Amanda, who stayed in Georgia with her black husband after the Cherokees' removal. Jeffers tries to tell her grandmother's history through poetry and story.

Hawk Hoof Tea

My mother lost an eye to a butcher knife
when she was only five or six.
I've told this story before, but as I age, the story becomes
a lesson, how, if a family had not been poor
and black, a child might have been able
to see on both sides of her face.
As a daughter,
I feel my mother's phantom grief,

But she tells her story very matter of fact, and she ends
the tale with pride. She was the best student
when she re-entered school after two absent years.
The best student and only one eye.
You have to hear that story first before
you can realize the day the measles crept
into a house of children, that crowded space.
The presence of Sickness, antagonist.

and again, the threat of absence.
Mama could have lost her remaining sight
because she lived in isolated Georgia woods

and no doctor or money and her skin was not white
and her mother and father were hapless.
Then,
there arrived Great-Grandpa Henry,
the son of a full Cherokee
woman whose own story got lost,
but what we do know is Henry
walked in the door and cured my Mama
and her brothers and sisters.
This story is a spiritual awakening in me,
sure enough.
Who wouldn't want to claim a great medicine
woman and her son as blood, make him a king

beyond a small act?—That's what writers do,
but did Henry seem to Mama some sort of copper
royalty, especially deep and profound?
No, she says. Henry was a cranky old man,
long-lived, over a hundred years,
and he frowned whatever the season.
And how about his saving her and the others,
his causing a miracle in that place? Well,

Henry just did what he had to do
out of love or impatience with dying.
He boiled down a hawk hoof into a tea,
but who knew if that was really the cure,
or even what hawk hoof might be?
A bird's talon, a flower, a root?
whatever it was, he made her drink a teacup full—
it tasted nasty, too.

Oklahoma Naming

I cried a while when I moved here
and saw trees so short and few,
prairie altogether flat,
and the earth near scarlet like my Georgia

earth but that was where kinship ended.
And then, the land started hurting

me like an amputated part of my body.
I had the dreams again

where my dead father appeared
with unusual cruelties.
I cannot believe anything
is what I learned from visions,

and then, when I became grateful
for deception, a new insistence
some long-gone Indian grandmother
who came to me and I spoke

her words and knew they were true.
And then, when she left me, I laughed
at my foolishness. I have relatives
out here—though I can't prove it—

cousins many times removed
with last names that tell something useful.
How many enemies our ancestors have killed.
what kind of song a wounded animal makes.

Sometimes I wonder what would
be my name if I had to choose again.
My father's daughter might be called,
Woman Who Still Loves and Cannot Say Why.

My grandmother's child,
Woman Who Pretends Her Visions Are Lies.

Drucilla Mims Wall

Drucilla Mims Wall (Alabama Creek) resides in St. Louis, Missouri. Her poems have appeared in the anthologies *Times of Sorrow/Times of Grace: Writing by Women of the Great Plains/High Plains* and *Sunflower Anthology* and in the journals *The Cream City Review*, *Red River Review*, *Kalliope*, *Plainsong*, and *Pearl*. Wall's fiction and essays have been published in *Eighteenth Century Life*, *American Jones Building & Maintenance #3*, and *True West: Authenticity in the American West*. She is legally blind.

Dirty Hands at the Gateway to the West

My steel trowel slices a Holland bulb.
That hateful sound of waste.
Maybe it will bloom away,
blending with the native species.
Lance-leafed coreopsis, bluestem,
prairie cordgrass, butterfly weed
wait in pots from wild-ones.com—
the authentic prairie sampler.

I place them as shown on cable TV,
then dig spots for nodding onion,
thimbleweed, wild indigo, and switchgrass.
They will flourish as guaranteed, I trust.
Butterflies will come disport themselves
and tease the cats. Song birds will approve.
Will tricky rabbits know the flowers are native?
Are they native rabbits? Do the moles
destroying the lawn know tall fescue
is an exotic invader? Do moles know?

Yesterday, we took our children
and their friends downtown.
We walked to the Mississippi
and stood on the western shore.
The river lapped its concrete banks

and our son's friend Dana shouted,
"How many corporate executives
does it take to screw up a river?"
Matthew got one foot soaked
and the girls shouted, as only younger
sisters can, "Your shoe is polluted.
Get away, get away." Traffic whooshed
over the Martin Luther King Bridge;
recorded jazz whined from a paddle boat
docked next to the floating McDonalds.
Could we please eat there, they wondered.

The Mississippi flipped its waves,
exhaling fresh water smells
like lost ancestral tongues
under the bright steel Gateway Arch,
and we felt happy in our drumming
hearts that beat with the jack hammers,
buses, parks department lawn movers,
and soft river waves of our dwindled world.

In the shadow of the Arch, I leaned down
and touched the wet brownness showing
clearly, after all, how clean my hands
wavered under water. Could it be
dioxins caressed my palms? Sparkling
juices from submerged cars and corpses?
Or was I baptized at the threshold,
the gateway to the West?

In the immense ladies room
of the Westward Expansion Museum
deep in the bunker under the Arch,
I blinked into the mirror and hesitated
at the row of blinding white sinks.
I should wash the river from my hands,
should ride in the egg-shaped pod
to the apex of perfect metal for the view.
Everyone was waiting by the fountain
that hurled bright blue dye up and back

to its square pond. The kids were tossing
pennies, a wish with every splash.
Beyond them a stuffed grizzly posed,
a red stage coach hugged a wall, both real.
At the outermost circle of the spiral displays,
a life-size bronze of Thomas Jefferson
gestured toward a teepee set with genuine
artifacts and polyurethane Indians.

I turned from the sink to rejoin them,
the Mississippi still stuck to my hands,
rivulets of blue veins swelling in the heat.

Grandfather's Lost Farm

Standing up like a man in Beaumont, Texas,
at the cookin'-with-gas stove, Saturday
kitchen, no bugs in no more wood piles,
three frypans hopping mad with beans, rice,
eggs, shaker of Cajun red to hand, and ready
to slap on the table—was never a problem.

Drinking was never a problem.
"Not that kind of Indian," you'd joke,
when you weren't saying you're white, "
just tanned from plowin' and pickin'
and having no luck at all." Never
heard of you drunk. Wasn't like that.

The problem was more like never
saying, "Mornin' Son," before Daddy
left for school. "You havin' toast with
your eggs? Any homework, Hotshot?"
without the acid from the dirt on that
Alabama farm splitting into the eyes
looking up from the table.

Your Granny promised you that land,
relic of the cheated past, promised that
red earth you wrestled mules to plow,
child muscles lashed to reins and cursing
the heat. Promised you until she lied you

two years older and into the army, then sold
it all. "Jes coverin' Uncle Dee's gamblin',"
she said like nothing. Left you sweating
dirt furrows through the barracks sheets.
Sweating chickens, cotton mouth rivers,
shotgun leaning by a flaking kitchen door.

You grew three inches, saw seven nations,
and cussing seven languages, stayed the hell
away. Waited seven years to show your son.
Black flocks of gawking crows screamed
you the last two miles of gravel road.
That night you scared Daddy to peeing
the bed, telling him crows was what happened
to ancestors who killed their own: crows
cawing hungry forever in the damned trees.

Just shouting, "Stay clear of Granny,
Hotshot," so she could hear it, even old
and deaf, "just an old Indian woman,
give you a good lick of that cane,
you get in her way," was your only revenge.

Reading lead Linotype upside down
and backwards was never a problem,
setting the *Beaumont Daily News*,
proud to be the one with the paycheck.
They needed some sent home regular:
crop shares thin; Porter lost his truck route;
Iretha's coughing blood; Haddie's talking to Jesus.
Can you send some store-bought soap?

Driving over to the police
to pick up Hotshot was not a problem.
Not a surprise. Just a matter of time
before Daddy got arrested for something.
He's not too big to cut a switch.
Maybe a night in jail. "What the hell
is wrong with you? Dumbass library books?
Last time I checked they give them out free.
Never amount to chickenshit that way.
I thought it'd least be grand theft auto."

The problem is, Grandfather,
I am standing up in Omaha.
Out here, the cicadas are almost finished;
central air rushes on against summer.
Out here, I couldn't name a fish in the river,
never owned a shotgun, and the keyboard
creaks more than the crickets.
I'm cooking electric, no flame on the pot.
Out here, it's just the two tomato plants.
Some crank reached over the alley fence,
broke the heads off the sunflowers,
only stalks now tall as the garage.
The problem is that I crouch by the porch,
hidden in cardinal bush and cedar.
It's getting dark, and a red squirrel
brushes past, neighbors laugh
two yards away, start a mower,
and bees flash the old stomp tune.
How is it, Grandfather, when I stand up,
the acid of that Alabama farm
boils in my mouth?

Chip Livingston

Chip Livingston (Florida Creek) was born in Fort Walton Beach, Florida, on July 6, 1967. He attended the University of Colorado, where he studied with the renowned Chickasaw writer Linda Hogan. His novel, *Naming Ceremony*, won the Native Writers' Circle of the Americas First Book Award for Prose in 2000. After working as a journalist for a while in the Virgin Islands, Livingston returned to the University of Colorado for additional graduate work. He is presently living in New York City and has recently completed a book-length poetry manuscript entitled "What Calls You Home." His poems have appeared in such publications as *Ploughshares*, *Apalachee Review*, the *New York Quarterly*, *Barrow Street*, *Cave Hill Literary Annual*, *Brooklyn Review,* and *Stories from the Blue Moon Café*. His fiction has appeared in *Red Ink* and *Storytellers*.

Pond

Caroline Lake turned her head and the sheet of flat black hair caused a breeze to flush Pond's face. There is power in hair like that, he thought, and continued to follow her through the crowd at Podo's. She laughed easily and spoke quick hello's to friends before sitting next to another thin Indian girl at the bar.

"Hey, Caroline. Looks like you got yourself a shadow," Theresa said.

Caroline rolled her eyes and nodded her head. "Yeah, I got a dark cloud all right."

"He's kinda cute, aye. You know him?"

"Yeah, I know him. He's my cousin or something, visiting from somewhere. My dad found him in New Mexico."

"Cousin cousin?"

"Yeah, cousin cousin for once, right. Not by blood though. He's adopted."

"What tribe?"

"Miccosukee."

"From Florida? How'd he get so far from home?"

"Powwow highway, girl. He's staying with us. You interested?"

"A girl's gotta keep her options open."

"Yeah, I know." Caroline turned to her shadow. "Hey, Pond. I want to introduce you to my friend Theresa here."

Pond found himself in Oklahoma after meeting up with his Uncle Remo and Aunt Grace at a powwow in New Mexico. He spent his summer on the powwow highway trying to discover his roots. Trying to find some Indianness. Trying to be traditional. His parents were Seminole, but like so many other Indian people in the Southeast, had lost many of their traditions, lived in apartment complexes, and only wore beads or shell necklaces at powwows. He got to talking to an Indian couple in Albuquerque who introduced him to Remo, his mother's brother, and his Creek wife Grace. "Not too many Florida Seminoles get out this way," Remo had said and invited him back to Oklahoma where they lived in Okmulgee.

Pond knew he would have to return to Florida in a few weeks, only had a little money left for a Greyhound ticket home, but he was overjoyed with his newly found relatives. They had a daughter his age, too. Named Caroline.

Theresa bought Pond a beer and made room for him to sit down between her and Caroline. "How'd you get a name like Pond, anyway?" she asked.

Pond blushed. He liked the attention, but didn't like talking. The truth was he didn't even know how he got the name, Pond, he'd just always had it. He never asked his mother about it; somehow he knew it wasn't going to be funny, knew it came with sadness, with shame.

"Oh, you don't really want to hear about that," he said. "What about your name? How'd you get a name like Theresa?"

"My mother named me after the patron saint of aviators and foreign missionaries. She's a Catholic."

"And you? You religious, too?" Pond asked.

"Nah. The nuns taught it out of me."

Pond decided to tell Theresa one of the versions of his naming. The one he'd told the white kids years ago in elementary school.

"Well, I guess that's kind of how I got my name, too," Pond said. "I mean it being religious and all. You see, I was adopted. Not really adopted but found, like Jesus, floating in a river. Except the way I was found wasn't really in no river, but in a swamp, in the Everglades."

"Really," Theresa said, ignoring the mistake about Jesus.

Caroline got up to dance with another girlfriend in the bar. Indian men watched her, waited to make their moves, waited to see if she would go back to the strange man she'd come in with.

Seeing that she was interested, Pond continued. "Yeah, my mother found me floating in a wicker basket, well, not wicker, but Styrofoam. I was in one of those beer coolers, insulated with sugar cane shavings. It was winter, just like with Jesus. I guess my real mother was something like Mary and had to send me down the river for something."

Theresa wanted to right the story he was telling. He was getting it all wrong about Jesus. But she was intrigued by Pond's story, about being found in the Everglades. She'd heard about the Miccosukees and Seminoles who lived in the river of grass.

"So my other mother," Pond said, "the one who found me; she took me home and raised me like I was her own."

"That's really interesting," Theresa said. "Kind of lucky."

"Yeah, interesting," Pond repeated. "And after she got me home, there appeared this eclipse in the sky, and these three warriors who were out hunting saw it and followed it to my mother's old house in the swamp."

Theresa smiled.

"And they brought my mother gifts, you know. Eagle feathers, cedar, tobacco."

Theresa laughed, and Pond joined her. Theresa caught Caroline's eye, where she swayed to Patsy Cline, and winked at her. Caroline rolled her eyes and circled her finger around her ear to say Crazy. When the song finished, Theresa watched Caroline make her way to the jukebox, put a dollar in. When she turned around to the two-step, an Apache they knew pulled Caroline back to the dancefloor.

"So how old are you, Pond?" Theresa asked.

'Nineteen," he said. "Maybe twenty."

"You don't know?" she asked.

"No. Since I was found in the river, I'm not sure. I celebrate it on Christmas day, though. Just like Jesus."

Theresa laughed, but she wasn't sure it was funny.

When Pond first arrived in Oklahoma with Remo and Grace, Caroline was immediately suspicious. Caroline was always suspicious when a cousin showed up. He wasn't the first Indian to visit under the guise of staying a few days or a few weeks. She had been suckered into believing the first one, of believing in him. Of believing him a way out. She wanted to move to a city, any city, and the travelers who passed in and out of her house were thought to be possible tickets to somewhere.

But this guy Pond wanted to be traditional. Or at least he was trying to learn. He was respectful, and this impressed Caroline's parents and the elders around town. Pond didn't get drunk, and listened, actually liked sitting down with the old ones and listening to their stories. The morning after Pond arrived Caroline's father said to her, "Why can't you be more like your cousin?"

"He's a good boy," her mother added.

Caroline held her tongue for once. She didn't know any good boys. Caroline didn't want to know any. She tried to ignore Pond. A one-way train to nowhere. He was the type to move to the reservation instead of away from it. Caroline couldn't imagine.

One day while Pond was helping her father shoe a horse, Caroline's mother asked her in the kitchen, "Why don't you like Pond?"

"What's to like?"

"He's considerate, respectful." Grace stirred a pot on the stove.

"Like I said, what's to like?" Caroline sat at the table, drinking black coffee.

"He's your cousin."

"He's not my cousin. He might not even be Indian. How do I know he's my cousin?"

"Well, you should be nicer to him. Get to know him. He's a good boy."

"He's a loser, Mom. You just want to save his soul. One more Baptist conversion and you'll be a shoo-in for Heaven."

"Well," Grace said, turning away from the stove. "Take him out to meet your friends. Introduce him to young people."

"You know that story you're telling," Theresa said. "It isn't true."

Pond was surprised and wounded by her attack. "How do you know it isn't true?"

Theresa tried a different approach. "I'm sorry, Pond. I'm not saying your story isn't true." She corrected herself, said she didn't want to hurt his feelings. "Just the part about Jesus isn't. Jesus wasn't found in a river. He was born in a manger in Jerusalem. You've got it confused with the story of Moses."

"Oh," Pond said. "Oh, yeah."

"Yeah." Theresa nodded her head, and smiled. "You didn't go to Catholic school, did you?"

"No," Pond answered. "Ponce de Leon Elementary. Jackson Junior High. Columbus High School . . . for a while."

"Well, I went to Catholic school," Theresa said. "And that story you're telling is about Moses, not Jesus. At least, most of it."

"Moses, huh?"

"Yeah. You ever hear of Moses?"

"I had an uncle named Moses."

"Maybe you're telling his story then," Theresa laughed.

"Yeah, maybe," Pond said, and he laughed too.

"You want another beer?"

"Naw," Pond said. "Drinking causes me to tell the truth."

"You want to go walk around, then. See my folks' farm?"

"Is it far from Caroline's?"

"No, it's just a walk from her house. And I can show you a short cut."

Pond stayed on the bar stool while Theresa went and told Caroline she was taking Pond out to the farm. Caroline said she should wait a bit, she had played a song for Theresa. She said there were things Theresa didn't know about Pond, things she should know before she went off with him. Caroline walked back over to the bar with her, ordered two beers. Theresa sat and shared hers with Pond, who took a few reluctant sips.

"What have y'all been talking about?" Caroline asked.

"Pond was telling me how he got his name. He's very funny," she said.

"Pond Scum? That's what it means," Caroline said. "Look at his eyes."

Pond looked down at the bar. Theresa lifted his chin.

"They're green," Caroline said.

"They're beautiful," Theresa said.

"They're the color of pond scum," Caroline said.

"Well, I think they're nice. I think he's nice. We're going now."

"Suit yourself," Caroline said. "Oh wait, here's your song."

As Theresa and Pond walked toward the door, Joan Osborne sang from the jukebox. Caroline joined in the chorus and Theresa could hear her drunken soprano as she opened the door to leave. "*Oh, Saint Theresa, leaving so soon. Oh, Saint Theresa, higher than the moon.*"

Theresa drove her mother's old LTD the few silent miles to her house. She parked and got out of the car, but Pond remained in his seat until she went around and opened his door.

"Don't let Caroline bother you," she said. "She's just drunk. She gets mean when she's drunk."

But Pond was bothered by Caroline. He couldn't shake it. He didn't understand why she didn't like him. He had just met her— had never done anything to her. He didn't even really know her. But he let Theresa pull him from the car and followed her to the corral, where a couple of horses paced and whinnied.

"You ride?" she asked.

"I've ridden," he said. "But I don't feel like riding now."

"I don't either," she said. "I was just asking."

She climbed up the wood fence and sat on the top rail. Pond followed her, and they watched the horses, who, noticing they weren't offering sugar or apples, kept their distance. Theresa slipped her hand into Pond's.

"Thanks for being so nice to me," he said.

"Thanks for being a nice guy," she laughed. "It obviously doesn't run in your family, aye. How much longer you going to be in Oklahoma?"

"A few more days," Pond said.

"And then?"

"Back to Florida. Probably join the Army Reserves," he said. "Find a job. Not much else to do."

"Plenty to do before you leave, though," Theresa said. She smiled at him.

Sitting on the Greyhound bus at six-thirty in the morning, as it rolled out of the station and headed east toward home, Pond pulled Theresa's envelope from his backpack. As he did, another folded paper, one he hadn't noticed before, fell to the floor between his seat and the seat in front of him. He picked up the letter, unfolded it, and although he had never seen her handwriting, he knew it was from Caroline before he read the name at the bottom of the page.

Dear Pond, it began. The paper was torn sloppily from a spiral notebook. *I just thought you should know the real story behind your name. Theresa told me the one you told her and I know it isn't true. My mother told me the truth about you and how you were supposedly "found." First of all, you weren't found at all. All that crap about the Everglades is something you either dreamed up or something my aunt told you to hide the truth. Apparently, your real mother was a total loser. Not some saint or holy mother like you pretend. She didn't send you down some polluted river to protect you from something tragic, but rather it was just that—tragic. She was a nasty alcoholic who took you to a pawnshop to get rid of you. She wasn't trying to protect you. She was trying to get some money so she could buy another bottle of whiskey. My uncle, your adopted father, was there at the time and overheard the shop owner saying he couldn't take a baby for pawn.*

The woman, apparently a prostitute, screamed at him and demanded he take you, demanded ten dollars at first, and then she said she'd take five. My uncle followed her outside the shop after the owner threatened to call the police. He felt sorry for you, I guess, or for your mother, and gave the woman the ten dollars he had gotten for his own mother's beads. He took you home to his wife and raised you like you were their own. Apparently my aunt couldn't have any of her own children and it worked out real nice for everybody. But as you can guess by your eyes, you ain't all Indian. Who knows what kind of blood you got mixed up in you? And further more, you're not my cousin, so should you come back this way (and I hope you don't), don't be telling my friends that you're related to me, because you ain't. Not by blood, and every Indian knows his blood. Who knows if you're even Indian at all, so maybe you should stop pretending. Stop going to powwows, and just get on with your life. Find a life! Maybe you should do back to the swamps where you came from, Pawned. Cause that's your true name. Pawned, not Pond. And you can be sure that I will tell Theresa this too.

Not your cousin, (got it?)
Caroline

Pond crumpled the paper into a ball. He started to throw it out the window, but the window didn't open and he wasn't going to litter, so he stuffed it back into the pocket of his backpack. He started to open and read Theresa's letter, but before he did, Pond tore it into tiny pieces, letting them fall to the rubber floor-mat below him. Tears formed in his eyes, but he fought against them, damming them behind his clenched lids. He tried to ball himself up like Caroline's letter, as if he could make himself smaller in some way, less conspicuous, and he leaned against the window of the bus. His head rattled against the tinted glass, and the Greyhound's wheels moaned a slow mourning song. It was *Ninety-nine Bottles of Beer on the Wall.*

Deidra Suwanee Dees

Deidra Suwanee Dees (Poarch Muscogee [Creek]) was born in Mobile, Alabama, and now lives in Atmore, Alabama. She holds a doctorate in cross-cultural education from the Harvard Graduate School of Education, a bachelor's degree from the University of South Alabama, and a master's from Cornell University. Dees is a former director of education for the Poarch Muscogee Nation and is presently an instructor at Pensacola Junior College. Her poems have appeared in such journals as *Red Ink, Zhibiigewinan, Struggle*, and *Lucidity*. A collection of her poems, *Vision Lines*, came out in 2004, and she has a new work, "Indian Ice," for which she is seeking a publisher.

Fading Sight

deep
lines

in her face
she braces herself on her

cane.
one loose shoelace
she stands
hunched over in the rain

aged.
wind-burned skin

she's
trying to look both ways

mud
splashed

on her stocking shin
by a taxi

howling through haze
fading
sight.

she's not looking for any
great feat

pursuing the light

she struggles trying to
cross the
street.

gods of nature

i watched the golden moon drip,
drip, drip
until she fell into Dog River,

moss-laden oaks
watched the shiny moon smile
as she hid among the ripples,

an old south
wind blew a tiny note of rhythm
to her playful mischief;

i watched the gods of nature
dance before the stars just
like they danced before my

grandmothers in this same spot
a thousand years before

Indian Ice

Indian drums
evoke my spirit

when they are silent
everything that's right
turns back into Indian ice

Trenches of Poison

the earth
said to the nation that
burrowed

trenches of poison
into her belly,

"if i die,
you die too"

My name is Deidra, and I'm a Muscogee

after enduring extremely painful years
with a cruel
and abusive mother

after suffering through many
grades in school
with
rich white kids
who never allowed me to be included

after grasping and holding the
instructed premise that
muscogees were debased and void
of any veracity

i have finally learned to like myself
i like myself today more that i ever have
before

Poor Indian Boy

Dedicated to my father, Otis Cullen Dees (1911–1984)

When school was over at our one-room schoolhouse, I grabbed Berdie's hand, and we headed for home. We ran and we ran, trying to get past the white boys, because they all laugh at us. The white boys say we're no good 'cause we're Indians.

Robert Davis said he was gonna take me behind the schoolhouse tomorrow and scalp me. I told the teacher when Billy Ray said the same thing last week, but she's white too, so she didn't do nothin' 'bout it of course. I don't think she likes me neither.

As I ran past John Goosby's house, he yelled so everybody can hear, "Otis Dees is a poor Indian redskin!" I just told Berdie to try and keep up with me, and I ran faster than I thought I could.

When we got home, Berdie and me got a drink of cold water in a big giant dipper from the well. Then we fed the chickens and the cow. Mama told me to ring two chickens for supper, but Berdie-had-to-cook-'em! Mama was too sickly to get out of bed. I think she might be gonna have a baby or some kind of grownup stuff like that.

Daddy broke his hip last spring 'cause the mule bucked the plow when he was tryin' to plant cotton. Now I gotta do all the work on the farm. I just wish I can get paid for it. But I'm old enough to know that Indians ain't got no money.

I wanna learn some schoolin', but I just can't catch up to fifth graders. I wish I can read as fast as them. My oldest sister, Ruby, always says I should be thankful for gettin' to go to school. Sometimes I get tired of hearin' her say it, but I don't pay her no never mind. The government didn't pass the law so Indians can go to school until Ruby was getting in fourth grade. She must of caught up, 'cause she's thinkin' 'bout being a teacher now.

Daddy looks like he's more sickly than I ever saw him. He told me Mama had two babies last night, but Dr. Reeves had to come back and get 'em cause they both died. Daddy said it was kindly strange that while he was sleepin' in front of the fireplace, a round fireball of gas woke him up and shot up from between his toes and went up the chimney and that was the same time the babies died.

Mama's still kindly sick, but she's goin' visitin' Aunt Queenie in the big city down there in Mobile. She's my big aunt (the biggest person I ever seen). I hear they got beaches with white sand down there, where water comes in and out to your feet and the water gets really big.

I earned twenty-five cents picking cotton last week from old man Gladshaw. I was savin' it up to get a second-hand football, but Mama asked if she can borrow it for her trip. So, I gave it to her.

I'm glad my cousins, Jesse and Wesley, are Indians too, 'cause I wouldn't have nobody to play stick ball with. Me and Berdie went over to Jesse and Wesley's and we played all day long. On accident, I hit Jesse in the head with the stick ball, and I know his Mama's gonna whup me when she sees his black eye.

Jack Kindle, who lives behind us, said one of the boys down the road got an indoor outhouse. I don't figure I'd want one of those, due to the bad smell. Ain't nothing wrong with our outhouse. Only thing is, it's a long ways to walk at night when it's cold and I don't like usin' no slop jar.

Joey Cramer and some six graders let me play marbles with 'em this morning at school. The reason why is they wanted my marbles, but I won their marbles. I don't expect they'll be asking me to play again.

When I came in from school today, Daddy told me Mama died . . . in Atmore . . . comin' back from Aunt Queenie's. The doctor told him it was pneumonia. They said Mama got sick on the train and never got no better. She died right there in the train car.

I'm scared.

I'm glad I lent her my twenty-five cents. I don't mind now that I'll never get it back.

Right after Daddy told me 'bout Mama, company came up in the front yard and me and Berdie ran under the house to hide. We don't know all the people what come, but they said they was our relatives. I never seen so many Indians in all my life. Later, we had to come out, 'cause Daddy made us. Through the cracks in the floor, he seen us hidin'.

Johnny Blackshire's Mama cooked some fish and said I can come over and eat dinner with 'em last Sunday. I wondered why, 'cause they ain't Indians. They had the best fried okra—kinda like Mama used to make, but better. Johnny's mama even gave us a Coca-cola in a see-through bottle. We can't afford 'em. Daddy says they ain't no good for you, no way.

Daddy asked me if the fish was from the ocean, the saltwater kind. One time Daddy went to town and saw a peddler who had some saltwater fish on sale. It was all the fish you can eat for just ten cents. Daddy said it would of been a good deal, but he couldn't eat none of that fish on account of it being salty.

A white man from the county seat came out to the house and told us we gotta get new birth certificates on account of the fire that burned the courthouse down in September. He said all the papers inside burnt clean up. But Daddy says birth papers ain't important to Indians. That's something the white man made up just to find out how many of us there is. So we didn't pay him no never mind.

There's some colored boys that live across Dees Creek behind us, and they came across the creek today. I hid in the bushes so as I can get a good look at 'em. The teacher told us not to get near 'em cause, she says if they touch you your skin will turn black. I took a good close look at them boys and there weren't a one of 'em black—they was all kindly brownish color.

When I came in from huntin' today at almost dark, there was two horses hitched to two wagons in the front yard and one automobile. We ain't never had no automobile in our yard before. One of the wagons was like a covered wagon, like the wild, wild west kind. Like the kind cow boys says the Indians shot up with arrows for no blame reason. They're just ignernt and they don't know. But the cowboys, stealing our land and taking our food, and changing us poor Indian trash, sounds like a good enough reason to me to shoot 'em all slap up!

When I went inside to see what all was going on, Ruby met me at the door and told me Daddy had died. I know Daddy was very sickly for a long time, just like Mama. Berdie was in a awful way. Dr. Reeves was there to get him ready for the funeral. Daddy was laying on his and Mama's bed. I'm fourteen and I'm supposed to be a man about it, but I swear, I had to get away from that house and go in the woods an' just let loose. I especially didn't want to let Berdie see me cryin', Indians ain't allowed to cry.

They built a new school house, 'cause the old one burned down last summer. The new one's got lots of rooms and it's built out of red bricks. It's even got two stories.

Now that I'm in high school, the boys don't pick on me half as bad. I think it's 'cause I grew bigger than all of 'em. They quit fightin' me 'cause I started winnin'.

I'm playing high school football for the Blackshire Yellow Jackets. I got my first football letter at the end of the season. All the boys call me Square Dees 'cause they say I can knock a square hole in the line of defense.

Me and Berdie really miss Daddy. I wish he could of been there so he could of seen me play football with all the skinny white boys. The ones what used to call me names and make fun of me for no reason, no reason at all, except 'cause I was born a poor Indian boy.

Janet McAdams

Janet McAdams (Alabama Creek), of mixed Creek, Scottish, and Irish ancestry, grew up in Alabama. She received her bachelor's degree and master's in fine arts in creative writing from the University of Alabama, and a Ph.D. in comparative literature from Emory University. McAdams taught Native American literature and creative writing at the University of Oklahoma from 1997 to 2001. Her poetry collection, *The Island of Lost Luggage* (2000), won the First Book Award for Poetry from the Native Writers' Circle of the Americas and also the American Book Award in 2001. Her second collection, *Feral,* was published by Salt Publishing in 2007. Her poems have appeared in *North America Review*, *Poetry, TriQuarterly, Kenyon Review*, and other journals and anthologies. Her reviews and criticism have been in *American Indian Quarterly*, *The Women's Review of Books, Studies in American Indian Literatures*, and the edited collections, *Women Poets of the Americas* and *Speak to Me Words: Essays on Native American Poetry.* She has recently completed a novel about the experiences of mixed-blood people in the Southeast and is writing a critical study of contemporary indigenous American poetry. In 2002, McAdams was named a Mentor of the Year by the Wordcraft Circle of Native Writers and Storytellers. In 2005, she founded Earthworks, a book series for Salt Publishing focusing on new works by indigenous authors. McAdams teaches creative writing and Native American literature at Kenyon College, where she is the Robert P. Hubbard Professor of Poetry.

From *Betty Creek:*
Writing the Indigenous Deep South

It rains today. The first of a week of rough mountain storms, a rage of water and wind, distant thunder and lightning. Pine trees crash in the forest around me, trees already half-dead from an infestation of pine beetle that began a few years ago. It is too wet to walk today, but I walk anyway, push away the rhododendron, wish that waterproofing my boots wasn't one of those tasks I continually put off. I am in a rare place: a 600-acre artists' retreat in Rabun County, Georgia. Rabun County is mostly National Forest land. I am surrounded by a green world largely uninhabited by human beings. As I walk I am aware of the road to the north, the main house up the road, but I see no one though I walk for several hours. If I were willing to do a little bushwhacking on this wet day, I could escape every trace of humanity. This is the fifth week of my seven-week retreat in these north Georgia mountains, Cherokee land—this *used to be* Cherokee land, people tell me—where I try to sort out the life story of Anna Packard, the Creek mixedblood heroine of the novel I'm writing.

Like mine, Anna's roots are in Alabama, not Georgia. Disenfranchised from her own tribalism by the same historical forces that nearly obliterated indigenous America, Anna's Creek mother leads the life of many urban Indians, a nuclear family, a city (Atlanta), a life of not quite passing. The South was hit hard by the genocidal practices of European invaders and settlers. When I teach about the indigenous South, I point out on the map of present-day Native America the large white space in the heart of what is now Alabama, Georgia, the Florida panhandle, noting how the nations were pushed not only west, but north and south, in the Removals of the 1830s. There are a handful of reservations in the Deep South, as well as state-recognized tribes and bands. Anna's family, though, represents the other faction of the indigenous Southeast, those families and individuals acutely aware of their Native ancestry but disconnected from a tribal community.

This disconnection is one of the many things Anna and I share, along with Alabama, Georgia, and Central America, but Anna is not me. Although the novel was originally sparked by my experiences living for a year in El Salvador during its civil war, Anna went her own way months ago, pages and pages ago. Whatever path I might plot for her forks or twists, leading sometimes into a thicket so dense I'm not sure how to find my way out and sometimes into a clearing, ringed by brush but open to the sky. Other characters in the novel are equally resistant to being told what to do. Someone in a writing group once suggested I make Anna "more Indian." "Have her eat some sofke or something," he said. But Anna resisted, and her grandmother went on packing her the same lunch to take to school: bologna on white bread, an apple cut into four quarters (probably a Golden Delicious), a moonpie or Little Debbie.

The retreat's resident artists—we are writers, painters, sculptors, composers —gather for dinner at the main house and someone asks if it's true that I'm "part Indian." "How much?" she wants to know, assuring me that the more Indian I am the better. Other residents nod, watching as she scrutinizes my face, ignoring my white skin, assessing my cheekbones, my dark hair and eyes as definitely Indian. The group talks about bear hunting. Georgia is one of the few states with an open season on bears. A short season, thankfully, and the bears, knowing the acreage of the retreat is protected land, huddle down in these woods during the two weeks that hunters and their radio-collared hounds try to tree them and shoot them down. A young bear runs across the drive just before dinner. We are reminded to wear our orange safety vests, to report any signs of hunting we see on the retreat land. Someone mentions a Cherokee guy down the road who takes white guys on bear hunts. The carcasses hang, skinned and bloody, like lumpy human bodies, from the porch of the Cherokee hunter. Guide, the white customers likely call him, when they return home with their prizes, their authentic Indian experience.

My studio sits just off Betty Creek Road and not too far from Betty's Creek, named after Little Betty, a Cherokee woman who evaded the Removal by moving deeper into the mountains. There is some talk of Betty Whitecloud one night. Many of the residents are from other parts of the country; while they've heard of the Trail of Tears, they don't really understand that a Cherokee woman could not have simply stayed in north Georgia after the 1830s, not without difficulty, or concessions, or both. What happened to her? I wonder aloud. Did she stay? Was she taken to Oklahoma? Or did she die along the way? No one seems to know.

Later, I google Betty Whitecloud only to find some confusion between "Betty Whitecloud," who lived along the creek in the 1920s, and "Little Betty," a Cherokee widow who petitioned for the 640 acres she was entitled to under the 1817 Treaty, a treaty that guaranteed the Cherokees the right to stay on their land in Georgia. A treaty even more short-lived than the many, many abrogated treaties between the Indian nations and the United States. According to the Dillard Family Association, Little Betty was the widowed matriarch of a large family. When white settlers encroached, she moved further up the creek that bears her name. Did she stay? Are her descendants living on in the Southeast? I can't help but hope so.

An Alabama Cherokee friend tells me she is "Cherokee, Creek, German, and English," but that "Southern is a layer over all of that." She's not suggesting a hierarchy here, but pointing to something I, too, know well. That Southern mixedbloods don't exist at intersections of identity categories; "Southern" isn't something that taints an otherwise authentic Creek- or Cherokee-ness. One is indigenous *through* one's Southernness. This construct, though, can't necessarily be invented. Because in the Deep South so much Indian land remains occupied by settler descendants, indigeneity is marked by a peculiarly simultaneous disenfranchisement and acceptance. Among many Southern mixedbloods, an Indian grandparent or great-grandparent is worth noting, but it is a marker of specialness not otherness, an ornament, not a different body.

My own parents affirm their Indian blood but think of themselves as white people with Creek and Cherokee ancestors. An aunt responds with horror when the topic comes up, having been taught by some past minister that miscegenation is strictly forbidden in the Bible. My mother considers me her "Indian daughter" and has identified me that way to others. In this, they are not unusual. Mixedblood families in the South approach their Indian ancestry in all kinds of ways. My Alabama Cherokee friend, whose life work as a psychologist has focused on the experiences of Native children, comes from such a family. Her brother has served as chief of a state-recognized band in Alabama, but several of her siblings could sit next to my aunt. No, they say, we are not Indian. We are white.

And the indigenous Deep South shares with the non-Native South its peculiarities, the tragic, comic world of the grotesque depicted by Faulkner and O'Connor. Once, while I lived in Atlanta, I talked two friends into accompanying me to a "re-enactment of a Creek village"—perhaps I hoped that I would meet some long lost cousins. I found a village of the small square houses Creek people lived in before the Removal. Interesting to stand inside one, thinking about sleeping there, dreaming over the ancestors who would've been buried beneath the floor. Yet outside one of the houses was a half-excavated grave, a skeleton topped with long, fuzzy black hair lying in it. Horrified, I complained to a staff member, who reassured us that it wasn't a real skeleton. It and its accompanying long black Halloween wig were from Toys 'R Us.

"I'm part-Creek and it doesn't bother me," the staff member told us. "In fact," she added, in a baffling nonsequitur, "we're all a little bit Indian." To be fair, one of my friends has a distant Powhatan ancestor, but the other can only be descended from that secret Indian tribe living in the Czech Republic these last 100 years or so. I am wary of the word "authentic" and the way notions of authenticity drive imperialistic nostalgia, how they divide the disempowered from each other, yet there are moments when the weight of the inauthentic pulls down the very air around you, thick, intangible, undeniable. Moments when you could just as easily weep or laugh or turn away.

Like the rest of Native America, the Deep South contends with Disneyfication, the foam rubber tomahawks and face paint of Atlanta Braves games, the simultaneous erasure of living Indian people and the celebration of comic book versions of them. While the emphasis among academics and activists in Indian country these days tends toward recognition and rearticulation of Indians as sovereign citizens and not hyphenated Americans, this Disneyfication, particularly in its internalized form, is still troublingly powerful in the Deep South. Powerful for many reasons, among them the post-Removal habit of hiding, since, until the passage of the 1924 Indian Citizenship Act, it was illegal to be Indian in most of the Deep South. In addition, the South's shameful and highly documented anti-black racism obscures the presence and history of other cultures, Native Americans and more recently, immigrant cultures. The South's historical racial white/red/black hierarchy exacerbates the problem for black Indians. For Deep South Native and mixedblood people, hyphenation might be a step up. Hardly ideal, but it beats representation as a bewigged plastic skeleton in a fake grave.

In this soup of paradox and simulacra, how to discover and transmit the important stories? It isn't that I don't write about and from the South in every piece of writing I produce, poetry, fiction, class lectures, letters and emails, this essay. But the world that poetry makes is a slant one, where there is metaphor instead of map, image in place of sentence. The heart of a poem appears to me indirectly, the way some stars can be best seen by looking slightly away from them, stars that may have burned out years ago. Sometimes we understand our stories as they rush around and through us, but more often they unfold in the telling, or with distance, the way in sharing a dream at the breakfast table, a dream that had seemed merely an extravagant and fanciful story upon awaking, it meanings reveal themselves with shocking clarity.

The indigenous South is not a subject I have taken on with much directness in my poems. In "A Map of the Twentieth Century," a sequential poem in my first collection, I consider the very Southern phenomenon of my grandfather, who had one Creek grandfather and one who, according to family lore, kept his Klan robes hidden under the mattress. (Those who tell this story are adamant that the robe never left its hiding place, but whether this is factual or white Southern apologism it's impossible to know.) "Three generations later we are pale as sand," I wrote. We and our pale history, for the poem is less about my grandfather than the failure of history to tell us who we are exactly, than the grief over the "past we own [existing only] on stone and white paper."

My second collection, *Feral*, is a book about wildness, about what gets tamed and what cannot be tamed, only destroyed. I first called the collection "The Children of Animals," believing that one key to our destruction is something crucial that white culture has forgotten, this simple fact: that we are animals, children to them, siblings, kin, and they to us. But a friend renamed the collection *Feral*. This book is wild and fierce, he told me. Now a wolf races across the cover. In "Earth, My Body Is Trying to Remember," the long anti-epic that concludes the book, a people undertake a long journey toward what they believe to be their homeland, toward land that remembers them, land they are trying to remember.

Our deepest metaphors are the furniture, language, oxygen of that other world, the "unacknowledged" world. It is a life's work to understand them. It is the lifework of a poet to write them down. If autobiography is that which seeks to transmit the facts of one's life story to others, then I have never written an autobiographical poem. I had to find a different form to write about these issues that bear so greatly on my life, yet continue to elude me as a poet. Fiction remains for me a more secular process. I write down Anna's story at least in part to try to understand the lives of Southeastern indigenes, and to try to make sense of the currents even, of material history, of stories that can be mapped and remapped, followed and perhaps understood, if only a little.

Meanwhile, back at the retreat, yet another resident wants to know: How much? He asks me, *How much?*—the question that seems to obsess so much of non-Native America. I keep thinking about Little Betty and *her* retreat with her children, farther up the creek, deeper into the mountains, in the hope that Andrew Jackson's soldiers won't find them. I hold up my least finger—about this much, I tell my fellow resident—or colonist—since places like this one are, after all, also known as artists' colonies. He nods, satisfied. Or maybe a little more, I continue, shaking my left leg in his direction, realizing too late it's the leg with the crisscross of scars across the skin over the patella and the hip that pops when I attempt something too fancy in yoga class. An interesting choice, to designate the land called "Indigenous" on the map of my body. If this were an afterschool special, I suppose I could thump my chest, just over the heart and say, "Here! This part." But this is real life, which is inexact, messy, and I am not sure how irony will play here, in this milieu where Indianness is simultaneously sentimentalized and ignored, in this place that *used to be* Cherokee land.

This place that is, that always will be, Indian land.

Whippoorwill

It's May and you're so dead
the Astroturf is sharp with age and twice-
replaced or more across the graves where you
and Miss Audrey are said to lie, as she
was said to lie, the boy

nothing like you, though Number III
so like they had to call him Hank.
We swap the camera back and forth. I snap
my sister kissing your carved face, she takes
me curled by the marble boots, by

marble hat. But that was years ago
Montgomery, the year my Birmingham
sister left to live down there.
Up here, Ohio's half-year fog of winter
settles white as the niceness, as the voices

that nice all around my plate of root
vegetables, unseasoned, and noodles
piled on potatoes, mashed,
white gravy over all, white
these five half-years of winter.

You can never get out of Ohio alive.
Some say you were headed here, some say
Knoxville, where tonight the bands are tuning up,
ready to play the New Year's concert
you never played, lone

lonely bird. Your Cherokee face
thin, voice tinny like an old machine,
the heart too tired to try.
The bands played on for hours—

What lies they tell themselves to call this love.
What lies they tell to take you on, lone
lonely bird, the heart wasn't pine but muscle, sick
and sick of it, of all of it, the liver fat
from bottle after bottle.

The bands are on for hours, the music
fierce, the audience too young to know
how soon they'll start to lose too much.
I leave before it's over.

How hard that bird will call to them.
I buy a Hank Williams Memorial Concert blue
bandanna. I pack my car
and drive north for hours,
looking back. Then never looking back.

Patricia White McClanahan

Patricia White McClanahan (Cherokee-Creek), a clinical psychologist in Montgomery, Alabama, also writes and publishes poetry. After living and working for several years with the Behavioral Health Center of the Eastern Band of Cherokee Indians in North Carolina, she returned to her home state of Alabama. McClanahan holds a bachelor's degree (cum laude) from the University of Alabama and her master's and doctorate degrees from Emory University. She is the coeditor, with Candice Fleming and Michelle Christensen, of *How to Help Children and Parents with Common Problems* (1999). While at Cherokee, she wrote articles and / or responses for a weekly Behavioral Health Center column in *The Cherokee One Feather*. As a poet and short story writer, her work has received honorable mention in the journal, *The Black Warrior Review*. McClanahan has been a claims representative and manager for the Social Security Administration, office manager, legal secretary, receptionist, disc jockey, flower shop manager, volunteer crisis counselor, and a psychologist. She serves on numerous boards relating to women's and Native American affairs in the areas of health, education, psychology, and literature.

life-mares

What good are dreamcatchers to those who fear sleep?
     in cities where concrete smothers Mother Earth?
her gasps for breath are skidrow wheezings
alcoholic haze blinds eyes searching for trees
cracked tongues no longer thirst for waters clear
. . . all souls afraid to sleep
dreamcatchers aren't needed here

souls asleep . . .
spirits rest only in havens
safe from enemies, life predators
in places to fear only one's personal demons
in places where rage's deepest fears may find us

     cities have no caves, no Mother's womb of safety

chaosdiscordcacaphonyblaringechoesdrunkenhornsdisharmony
of a thousand souls screaming life-mares
. . . all seeking oblivion

night is their time of vigilance
for sleeping brings dreams
    dreams will kill lives cities breed

dreams must die
dreamcatchers will destroy Metropolis
in our dreams . . .

    grass will cover sidewalks

    highways become trails

    timesand wash highrises into buttes

    mesas rise where lay concrete mountains

    underground parking as caves
    subway caverns of the underworld

    automobiles ridden as ponies freed

    busses our longhouses where we sit at the feet of Elders
        hear the Teachings spoken once more

dreams . . .

daylight shatters dreams
slapping reality against our face
freezing our stare into concrete/steel/blue lines/neon—lifemares
a taste of whisky drowns the smoke of dreamfires . . . sage sweetgrass cedar
dreamcatchers not needed here!

dreams . . .

dreams of Red Road/Beauty Way/Rainbow Bridge/Medicine Wheels

                taunt us

waking/sleeping cities
life-mares
        galloping across our souls

Poems Which Came to Me

    Many things in life are confusing to me. Often the understanding which resolves that confusion comes in the form of a poem. The words have typically been spinning around in my head for a while—sometimes years—and are influenced by the lives and words of other people as much as my own. The poem, "Warrior," came during my first year of graduate school after I realized from students that our stories about our academic experiences were similar. Regardless of whether the Ph.D. was attained twenty-five years ago or last year, the pattern was the same. Thus, "Warrior" could just as easily be titled "Indian education."

Those academic experiences included rudeness from people on campus which still surprises me. Some people's responses to our introduction was, "You don't look like an Indian." Others were just as rude in saying, "I *knew* you were an Indian when I saw you." The poem, "it's just a face," came from my efforts to understand what I know is in my face and the ancestors who gave it to me. It doesn't matter what anybody else sees or doesn't see when they look at me, I know who I am.

Maurice Kenny arrived in Atlanta on a book-signing tour as my "Indian education" was occurring. The community invited Maurice to a potluck dinner at the now-defunct Atlanta Indian Center where we shared lots of coffee, food, and stories. As we exchanged addresses, the paper we used was a flimsy, white paper plate. It seemed inevitable that Maurice, Ron Colombe, and I would write about the evening. "Passion of the plate #1" derived from the paper plate on which we exchanged addresses and the fact that it was the first poem written about our circle that night.

As Indian peoples, we struggle with the images and the reality of our histories and our present lives. I have become a psychologist because I believe that more healing occurs through the practice of psychology than contemporary medical practices. And we need healing of many things, only one of which is chemical dependency. After years of attempting and failing to understand what *aesthetic* or *spiritual appeal* alcohol and other drugs have for us, I concluded that I could help people to heal from the need for them without that understanding. If the time came when I needed to understand how such toxic chemicals call our spirit, the understanding then would come. It took several nights of being awakened at 3:00 A.M. before I realized that it wasn't simply the stress of graduate school which awakened me, but that I needed to get up and listen to the night. The understanding of how alcohol and other drugs call to our spirit came in the words of "life-mares."

The racism which now thrives among Indian peoples has been described as one of the legacies of colonization. Its depth and long-term effects may be as damaging to our communities as that of alcohol and other drugs as it is strictly by our own volition that we choose to deny our kin. My efforts to understand the racism among Indian peoples culminated with a poem when one friend publicly and maliciously accused another of not being a "real Indian." The hurt and anger which I saw during that interaction and the choices we, as Indian peoples, have to address it are described in "Some Call It Xenophobia." Whenever I read the poem, I always find myself beating the lectern in tune to the ceremonial drums I heard when the poem came to me.

Some elders say that Indian women have kept the circle intact while Indian men have not fulfilled their roles of warrior who protect women and children. And that much healing is needed for those men and for the women who have held their place in the circle. But what has life been like for those women? As I looked at my own life, I remembered stories shared by other women who had found their way to wholeness of Being via a sometimes twisting, jagged path. "Still-life in Motion" describes a woman's journey to a place of well being.

There are events in the history of America which are devastating to remember today. The massacre at Wounded Knee, South Dakota, in late December 1890, is one of those events. Yet, we must always remember them so that we do not dishonor those who came before us as we prepare the way for those to come after us. My first visit to the Wounded Knee Memorial was more painful than I'd expected. The wails of generations who've suffered for simply being Indian continue to echo among us. The poem "Wounded Knee," came to me as we drove away from the cemetery, and continues to come each time I read it now. I know it will be finished when it no longer needs to be remembered so clearly.

Cynthia Gaillard

Cynthia Gaillard (Chickasaw-Choctaw-Cherokee-Seminole), an Emmy Award-winning television producer, has worked in public broadcasting for over twenty-five years. Producing historical documentaries about amazing artists and amazing women are her life's passions. Although Gaillard was born and raised in the Southwest, summers were spent with her grandparents and extended family in northern Mississippi where she learned to skin catfish and make banana pudding, two skills she deeply cherishes. She received her B.S. in psychology at the University of New Mexico and she is completing her M.F.A. in creative nonfiction at the Ohio State University. Her poetry has been published in *Outlook Magazine* (a GLBT publication distributed throughout Ohio), *Poets Against The War* (poetsagainstthewar.org) and she received an honorable mention in the 2005 Espy Awards for her nonfiction essay, "Rabbits in the Moon." Of Chickasaw, Choctaw, Cherokee, Seminole, French, and Irish descent, Gaillard resides in Columbus, Ohio, with her partner, two feisty cats, and her loving dog, Skye.

Shards

I hear the voices in the sage, in the grasses, along the washes with shards of pots tumbling down through the canyons. The voices are in the forgotten places where children have learned to hide, listening for ghosts and stories of their own souls emerging.

I am not Indian, my Grandfather says.

Herman Half Breed. I imagine that's what the white men called my grandfather, shouted it from Model T's as he whipped his mare away from the muddy ruts. Herman looks at me from a photograph, his dark skin, black hair, black eyes, his brother next to him the same shade of shame.

Herman Half Breed went to a Ku Klux Klan meeting in Tippah County, Mississippi. He bribed a friend with a paycheck and whiskey to sponsor him into the tribe. Laughter hits the ceiling like thunder claps.

Grandfather is proud of his grandchildren, their white skin that never tans.

Great-grandmother speaks now. She wants her sharp knife. She yells for her son Herman; git me my sharp knife, boy; there is a neighbor with foul language at my door.

Her father was murdered. He was an Indian shot over twelve dollars and fifty cents owed to some white man from town. A blast of gunpowder in the chest escorted great-great-grandfather to the grave as the Whippoorwills called their mates. A white man can shoot injuns when he has cause, great-grandmother says, spittle forming at the edges of her mouth.

His name was Two-Moons.

Two-Moons became Thomas. The bank gave John Thomas a loan for a farm. John Thomas earned money for a mule. A white man murdered John Thomas because he owed twelve dollars and fifty cents for a pig. The grave of John Thomas is lost to us, somewhere in Union County, Mississippi; anonymous in two worlds. Great-grandmother knows, though. She is there now, stripping away kudzu with her sharp knife.

My father makes knives, puts the metal puzzle together, sands the shaft, sharpens the edge. Dad's friend, Franklin, an Acoma man, gives him buckhorn sheds from the reservation, the horns become hilts; transformations.

I polish Dad's knives. The chalky porous buckhorn, bone that is not bone, once holding up the sky on the heads of tawny mule deer. Sanded, polished, preserved, the knives come to me in dreams, cut me open, expose my liver, slice it, push bloody morsels between my teeth.

A white mother and mixed father, my mouth moves in opposing directions. One incisor is shovel-shaped; the other teeth ignore it, biting into apples like quarrelling sisters.

Look at the little injun girl, my mother says, pushing the doll toward me. Mother has a doll waiting for me, a doll with buckskin and black hair, moccasins, a miniature tomahawk. Look at the little injun, my mother says. Look.

Sage smoke fills my house. The smell of mesas, of sand. November skies and yipping dogs. It is the smell of childhood, of sun and wandering. Small hands and thick legs, the child that I was wandered the desert, head down, eyes skimming the parched ground for signs that the ancients had been there. Some shards are the size of my fist, delicate black painted lines intersecting, suggesting what is absent. Some shards are like a fingernail, thick yet fragile, fingerprint fragments smudged on the clay slip. I remember that child, the innocent one, too young for family secrets, for unpleasant matters. I remember her, pockets full of shards, pulling me into the earth, an embrace.

John Woodrow Presley

John Woodrow Presley (Choctaw) was born in Trumann, Arkansas, in 1948. He earned his bachelor's degree from Arkansas State University (1970) and both his master's (1972) and doctorate (1975) from Southern Illinois University. He has done post-doctoral work at the University of Texas and at The Johns Hopkins University. Presley has published nine books on composition or reading, a book on the British writer Robert Graves's manuscripts and letters, dozens of articles, reviews, notes, and book chapters on modern poets, and hundreds of poems in journals ranging from *North Dakota Quarterly* and *Southern Humanities Review* to *American Indian Culture and Research Journal*, *InPrint*, *Writer to Writer*, and *Troubadour*. A collection of his poems, *How Like a Life*, was published in 1986. He has been a college administrator since 1974, in Georgia, Pennsylvania, New York, and Illinois. Presley is currently serving as provost (and professor of English) at Illinois State University. He continues to write and revise his poetry, and is editing, for reissue, Robert Graves's *The Nazarene Gospels Restored*.

Landscape: White on White

in winter
the geese make vees
no clouds muffle their cries

a barnyard fowl with clipped wings
sees them and longs to rise

a hunter brings his gun to bear

in the house a boy lies weeping

and the barnyard fowl walks
back to his shelter

Prologues and Disasters

1. THE FATHER

This must be the rough assedest country
God ever made. In Mississippi this time

of year there wouldn't be this rotten smell,
everything would be growin' already.
I bust my ass after the war to get
one of their cheap loans, even go to school to farm,
and wind up mortgaged forever
to fifty acres knee-deep in water twice a year.
Weather's so lousy once you get seed in the ground
and fight off weeds and bugs most of a year
it rains all September, and the cotton rots.

2. THE SON

The spring ones are always the best.
When the water comes up in the winter
it's too cold to play in, but, spring,
you can sit on the porch and put down your feet.
Nobody watches you because it's shallow
but the fish and snakes that are tired of swimmin'
will try to get in the house if you don't watch.
Once when I was nearly asleep a snake
fell out of a bulge in the wallpaper.
When you sit on the porch you pretend it's a boat
cause the little waves make the porch move.

3. GLADIOLI

The trees shake, windows shudder,
radio weaves wind and death. Calmed,
I sleep, and wake to a dawn like any other:
a red east, a white morning star.
In the woods, I am stopped by
loosened houses tilted against trees
leaning leafless over gardens stripped of green.
Blossom and bud shine at the sun, thousands about,
drifting on mud-rack: bright, ruined hill.

4. COTTON

Sprouted they split the soil.
Near the house, children
pull at these cracks, find a white sprout,
a neck pressed on nothing. Early summer

and the rows grow, green and orderly.
White blooms will purple with the sun,
drop in August, spin a fierce dance
before the stalks stand black in September.
Autumn has hazed, and you have thickened with seed
hanging delicate toward delta soil.

A Lover's Lesson: The Immigrant Cemetery at Lepanto

In this valley, stone lies broken,
foreign characters spilled into grass.

Here, a name once lived in upper air,
speaking in ancestral tongues.

(Even here, in his wet sleep,
where the casual visitor's heel
draws water to its imprint, dear,
we must hold ourselves apart.)

                    Machines move
wormlike in the fields; sons have gone,
and will go. Names are silence but once moved.

Larry Richard

Larry Richard (Choctaw-Abenaki), although a member of the MOWA Band of Choctaw Indians of Alabama, was born in Texas and has lived most of his life in Louisiana. While serving in the U.S. Navy, 1965 to 1969, he spent three tours in Vietnam during the war. He received most of his post–high school education through the United States Armed Forces Institute. Richard has worked for both the Houma and Chitimacha tribal governments and is deeply involved in research of Louisiana tribal history. It was his association and relationship with Chief Nick Stouff of the Chitimacha Tribe that led to the writing of his book, *Eagle Feathers and Tartans* (1996), an examination of the influence of Scottish culture on Southeastern Indians. He lives in Church Point, Louisiana.

A Young Horseback
—*Delvina Marie Daigle Richard*
February 8, 1911–May 23, 1997

Gray and bent, in a wheelchair,
Alone beside the bare septic walls of the nursing home.
To a passerby, talking to herself it seems,
But none other can see through her eyes an unfolding scene.

Atop "Dolly," her "wild and gallant steed"
An old mouth her father didn't any longer use or need,
Riding through the wild flowers and tall prairie grass.
Sun sinking, slowly turning the Attakapas to the color of brass.

The young girl halts, cocks her ears to hear.
It's PaPa, calling her home,
Mother, brother and sisters are waiting there.

As the horseback turns and wheels
She emits a delighted squeal.
Her face, one large smile,
You see, she hasn't seen them for quite awhile.

Then the old grandmother sighs and sags in the wheelchair,
Her face one large smile surrounded by silvering hair.
Her spirit no longer there.

Meanwhile, the young girl, Delvina, and old Dolly
Thunder on home,
Her braids flying behind, only touching air.

Jennifer Lisa Vest

Jennifer Lisa Vest is a mixed-blood (Florida Seminole–black) poet and philosopher from Chicago. She teaches philosophy and women's studies as an assistant professor in the Philosophy Department at the University of Central Florida at Orlando. She obtained her Ph.D. from the Ethnic Studies Department at the University of California at Berkeley, with a dissertation on Indigenous Native American and African philosophies. Vest is currently finishing a book on academic Native American philosophy. Her poetry has been published in the anthologies *The Fire This Time*, *Ache* (pronounced *Ah-shay*), and *Tongues*, and in such journals as *Testimonies*, *Fast Talk High Volume*, *Out of Many One*, and *Face America*. Her chapbook, *Names*, was published by Indigenous Speak in Berkeley in 1997, and since then she has produced three poetry CDs (*Ancestor Count: Purple People Poems*, *Camping at a Distance: Indigenous Recountings*, and *Wonder Woman*). She has also been a member of the San Francisco Poetry Slam team. More recently, Vest has begun to combine the two genres into a new field she calls "philopoetics." CDs of her poetry can be obtained on her website, MxdMessages.com.

Traditional

They told her
Her clothing
Was not traditional enough
For Grand Entry
They whispered
Looked at her sideways
Asked her
What kind of Indian
Was she anyway?
And was she on the rolls?

They told her her hair
Was too curley
And not traditional enough
For Grand Entry
Her skin too dark
Suitable only for intertribal

Indians don't have blue eyes, they said
Indians don't have black skin, they said

And she could dance
You should have seen her!
And she could talk story!
You should have heard her!
And she knew medicine
You should have felt her!

But she wasn't traditional enough
For those urban Indians

So when those powwow Indians looked at me sideways
And started asking too many questions
She said come here little girl
Take this shawl, come and dance
And she taught me
How to be traditional.

Bones

They called us
The scientists called us
They said
Come get these bones

It's the law now
They passed a law now
They have to return
All those Indian bones

Into a cold cellar
They led us
To a box among many boxes
Many boxes of bones

He was busy
The archeologist
He had work to do
Here it is he said
Handed us a box of bones

Here is it he said
Take it and go

We wanted to sing a song
But that room that man
It was so cold
We needed to sing a song
To burn some sage
We looked to the mountain
We looked for where to go

Without a ceremony
The right story
Some cedar some sweetgrass
We couldn't take
Those bones home

Moses Jumper, Jr.

Moses Jumper, Jr., (Seminole) was born January 4, 1950, in Hollywood, Florida. He is the son of Betty Mae Jumper. His poetry collection, *Echoes in the Wind*, was published in 1990. With Ben Sonder, he coauthored *Osceola: Patriot and Warrior* (1993), a biography for young readers. Jumper is director of athletic programs for all the Seminole reservations and communities throughout Florida. He is currently living in Clewiston, Florida.

Harmony

The mystic cooing, I heard it
as I walked among the cypress
and willow tree.
At first thought it was
my mind playing tricks on me.

But as the Breeze of the Gentle Wind
flowed through the glades
and softly touched my face,
I knew I was on Hallowed ground
and it was right for me
to be in this place.

Soon, the Hammock flowed with the phrases
of the Habitants' melody.
Each singing their songs of wit,
humor and mystery.

And for an instant,
I became a part of them
as they became a part of me.
Perhaps, if only for a moment, Harmony . . .

Simplicity

The small tunnel which the rabbit uses for escape
and travel,
The small imprints of the killdeer in the soft white

sand near the pond,

The fragileness of the newborn doves and how the mother puts on an act to lure away approaching enemies,

The unity of the small minnows as they protect themselves by staying near the shoreline of the stream,

The clear whistling sound the scorpion makes to let one know he's near,

The shagginess of the owl's nest and the neatness of the hummingbird's,

The long, graceful jumps of the sleek, green frog,

The short, choppy hops of the lumpy toad,

The agileness and grace of the otter,

The awkward wing flapping of the crane,

The camouflage nest of the mobile alligator and the will to reach the water of her young,

The winding tunnels, that lead to nowhere, of the sly red fox,

The abundance of life in the wet season and the stench of death in the dry.

The persistence of the mother hawk to nudge her young to make that flight,

I saw all these things, and many more, and I knew they were right.

Betty Mae Jumper

Betty Mae Jumper (Seminole) served as tribal chair of the Seminole Tribe of Florida from 1967 to 1971. She was born April 27, 1923, in Indiantown, Florida, on Lake Okeechobee, but grew up on the Dania Indian Reservation, near Hollywood, Florida. Because Native Americans could not attend Florida's schools when she was a child, Jumper was sent away to attend school on the Cherokee Indian Reservation in North Carolina, graduating in 1945. Afterwards, she trained as a practical nurse in Oklahoma, and when she returned to Florida, Jumper pioneered in establishing health care programs and services in all the Seminole communities and reservations. One of the clinics she helped established is now named the Betty Mae Jumper Health Complex. In 1950, Jumper founded a tribal newsletter called *The Seminole News* (now *The Seminole Tribune*). In 1970, while serving as tribal chair, she was honored by the National Congress of American Indians as Indian Woman of the Year. Long known for her storytelling ability, her collected oral stories, two of which are included in this anthology, appear in *Legends of the Seminoles* (1995). She coauthored her autobiography, *A Seminole Legend: The Life of Betty Mae Tiger Jumper* (2001), with Patsy West. She is trilingual, speaking Creek (Seminole), Miccosuki, and English.

Two Hunters

"I remember my mother telling this story. It was her way of teaching us 'Don't ever eat anything out of place.' In other words, if you find candy, don't eat it off the ground. A lot of these stories are to teach children something important to learn."

On the edge of the Everglades lived two men from the Village of Many Indians. These two men were hunters who went into the Glades for months at a time. Sometimes, when the hunting was good, they came back to the village within two weeks or less with lots of meat which they would smoke and dry. They hunted deer and birds and picked up as many water turtles as they could fit into their two canoes. They only hunted when they had to, when the meat supply had run out.

Early one spring, the two hunters talked about the Big Lake and how there would surely be lots of game around there at this time of year. "We will return

"Two Hunters" and "The Corn Lady" from *Legends of the Seminoles* (Sarasota, Fl.: Pineapple Press, 1994). Copyright © 1994 by Pineapple Press. Reprinted with permission of Moses Jumper, Jr.

in two weeks or less," they assured their families. "Now is a good time to hunt near the Big Lake."

They left in the morning and, on the second day, made camp near the Big Lake. On the way, the two hunters talked about how the hunting would be good, for they saw many animals around eating the green grass. After making camp, they settled down to sleep.

As the sun rose the next morning, they hurried out and immediately killed a deer. It took most of the day to clean the large deer. They dried and smoked the meat so it would keep until they returned home. Both men were filled with happiness and good feelings for they were sure there was plenty of game around and this trip away from the village would be short. They would return soon with lots of meat for their families.

They went to sleep early. When they awoke the next morning, they were surprised to see that it was raining very hard. The rain fell most of the day, so they stayed at the camp. In the late afternoon, the rain finally stopped and the sun came out. "It's too late now to hunt," said one hunter. "I think I'll take a walk along the lake."

The other hunter was feeling hungry, so he cooked some deer meat. Soon the hunter returned carrying two big fish. "Look what I found," he said, "beautiful bass, big and fat."

"Where did you get those fish?" asked the other hunter. "I didn't see you take anything to fish with when you left."

"No," the hunter explained. "I found them jumping on the ground near the lake, so I picked them up. I guess they must have come down with the rain!"

"Go and put them in the lake," said the other hunter, "and let us eat the meat I am cooking."

"Oh no," his friend replied. "These fish are too good to throw away. I'm going to clean and cook them right away." And he did.

After the meal, they sat around the fire and talked. They agreed to start early the next day and maybe kill two deer and fix them before nightfall. Soon it was time to go to sleep. All the night birds were singing away. Somewhere near, in a tree, an old owl was laughing and crying throughout the night.

In the middle of the night, the hunter who ate the fish called and called, "Come here! Come here!" His partner awakened and yelled out: "What's wrong?" He stood up and walked over to his friend's mosquito net. He stared in fright as his friend spoke: "I think I'm turning into a snake. You told me not to eat that fish but I didn't listen to you. Now look at me!"

The hunter started a fire to get a better look at his troubled friend. His legs had already turned into a snake tail!

"I want you to go home. Don't wait to see how I look. You can't help me now," said the man turning into the snake. "By daylight I will be completely turned into the shape of a snake. Go home and tell my wife and children what happened to me. Also tell my parents, sisters and brothers. Tell them when the moon is full to come and see me.

"Bring all my family to the lake. Remember the big log near the lake? I want you to hit it four times when the sun is right in the middle of the day. I want them to see me and I want to talk to them. Tell them not to be afraid. I won't hurt them. Now go! Get out of here and run home!"

The other hunter left without looking back, taking with him the meat they had prepared. On the second day he reached the Village of Many Indians and told his friend's family the bad news.

Then the day came for the hunter to take his friend's family to the lake. They arrived at the lake beneath the full moon and camped out, waiting nervously for the next day. Finally, when the sun reached the middle of the day, he led them to the big log and fulfilled his friend's request. He hit the log once, twice, three times, four times.

When he was finished, bubbles came up from the middle of the lake. Then up came the head of a large snake. The children were scared, but the older people told them to be quiet and listen to what the snake had to say. The snake floated to the top of the lake and slithered near the shore where his family stood.

Slowly, the snake moved toward them. "Come close," said the snake. "It's me. I wish to talk to you. Listen close to what I have to say, for after this I will never speak again."

When they had all moved close, the snake began to speak again: "I did wrong when I cleaned those fish, cooked them, and ate them. I knew better, but went against the forbidden law of our elders. I am paying for it now. When you leave, I want my family to never think bad about me. Think forward and go on with your life, for I will never be back. This lake is going to be my home. I will live in this water until I die. When you all go, never come back to this lake, for once you all leave, all my memories will be gone. I won't know you at all. I might be mean and I might hurt you. It is the life of a snake I'll be living. Just remember all the good things and forgive me."

The snake turned to his hunter friend: "I want you to please help my family and share meat with them. Teach my sons to be good hunters like you. Make sure they take care of their mother." The hunter friend promised he would.

"Now," said the snake, "I'm coming to the top. I want you to see all of me." And when he did, everyone could see that he was huge, longer than a large canoe. Then, suddenly, the snake went underwater. When he came back up, he was back where he started from, in the middle of the lake. The snake stuck his tail high out of the water and waved it at them. Then he went down deep, deep into the black waters of the Big Lake.

With sad feelings, his family turned and left the Big Lake, never to return again.

The Corn Lady

"This is the legend of how the corn came to the Tribe. I can remember my grandmother telling us this one at night by the campfire. Sometimes we were under the mosquito net ready for sleep. Other times we were eating sweet potatoes and roasted oranges. On a cold weather night, those hot oranges were real good."

There once was a family living at the edge of the Big Forest, a wonderful place with swamps full of meat and fish. The family had places to grow vegetables, pumpkins, potatoes, beans, and tomatoes. They also raised pigs and cows. These were happy people with no worries—they had everything!

The children could be seen running about everywhere, playing around and swimming in the ponds nearby. But sometimes, when the older children were playing really hard, they would forget to keep an eye on the younger children.

One day an older sister put her baby brother down to play with the little children while she played with the older ones. They played a long, long time and she forgot about her baby brother. When she finally went to check on him, he could not be found anywhere. She called and called and called his name but could not find him anywhere.

The big sister ran home to tell her mother. Soon, all of the women in the village were looking for him. They kept looking until sundown but were unable to find the baby. When the men of the village returned from their Big Forest hunting trip, they all looked for the child well into the night. But no baby was found.

A few days later, the men returned to hunting and fishing. The father of the baby sent for the wise medicine man. Since he lived quite a distance from the village, it took the medicine man two days to get to the village at the edge of the Big Forest. When he finally arrived, he asked everyone to sit down. He told them about the "unseen people" that lived on small islands deep in the swamps.

The medicine man believed that one of these "unseen people" had picked up the baby and run off with him. He told the village people that they could not find these "unseen people." But, the wise medicine man believed that the baby was still alive someplace in the Glades. The family was very sad at this news and gave up looking for the baby and all hopes of ever seeing him again.

Years went by. The missing boy's family still lived in the same village. The brothers and sisters had grown up and some were married. Then one day a strange thing happened out in the jungle in the heart of the Everglades on a little island. No one had ever been there before, nor had anyone ever seen the place.

On the island was a beautiful camp with three chickees: one for the campfire, one for sleeping and one for eating. An old witch lived there and she had a young boy living with her. Every day she would prepare corn sofkee and vegetables for the boy. He soon grew to be a strong teenager.

The old witch was so ugly that it made you wonder where she came from. But her love for the boy was great and she raised him well. She knew that someday she would have to tell him the truth about himself. This made her very sad because she knew this day was very near.

The boy noticed that the chickees were old and falling apart and often asked why he was not allowed to repair them. The witch would never give him a reason. The boy questioned where she got the corn she prepared for him but she would never tell him. All he knew was that there was always plenty of corn to eat.

The day came when the boy decided it was time for him to follow the old witch. She would always get up very early, check to make sure the boy was asleep, pick up her basket and walk toward the swamps. One day the boy pretended to be asleep until she had gone, and then he followed her. She walked quite a distance to a cool running stream where she stepped in and scrubbed her legs until they were very clean. A little further away, she sat on a log, dried her legs and started rubbing them from the knees to the ankles until beautiful yellow corn fell and filled her basket. She continued doing this until her basket was full.

On the way back, she stopped and filled up another basket with white sand. The boy was watching her all this time. He ran back in front of her and quickly jumped in his bed and pretended to be asleep when she returned. She built a fire and parched the corn in the sand in an iron pot. She then placed the corn in a log which was about seven feet long and 12 inches around. She pounded it up and down until it was ground into cornmeal.

When breakfast was ready, the old witch called the boy to come and eat. But he refused. The old witch went to where he lay and said, "You know, don't you?" The boy didn't answer and she asked again. Finally he told her that he had followed her that morning and saw everything.

"I knew this day would come," the old woman told the boy. She began to cry. "Yes, my son, you have given me much happiness all these years, but it is now time you returned to your people."

She then told him the story of how she had taken him years ago when he was just a baby. She gave him the name of his family and told him where they lived. She also told him it would take at least two and a half days to reach his home. She then gave him the necklace he was wearing at the time she stole him away.

"I am an old woman and my time is drawing near," she told him. "You must do as I say: Leave and don't turn or look back. Just keep going! Tonight when the sun goes down, you must go to bed and sleep. When you wake up past midnight, you must get up and get ready to go.

"Go east toward the sun, and go past two big forests on the other side of the Big Lake. This is where your people live and you will find them there. Now, sleep, my boy, you have a lot of walking to do. When you get up, pick up the fire and throw it all over the chickees and run.

"Follow the trail we have walked many times and go. Run! Run! Run! Don't cry! We have had many wonderful years together and I have enjoyed seeing you grow into a fine boy. Get yourself a pretty girl and marry among your own people."

Somehow, the boy knew she meant well for him. She had been good to him and taught him everything he knew, including how to hunt. Past midnight, the boy got up, sadness in his heart. But he did as the old woman had requested. He threw the fire on the chickees and started running. He ran until he was very tired and started walking. He walked all through the night.

At daybreak, he passed the first big forest and continued walking until that evening, nearing the second big forest. He was very tired and wanted to rest because he knew he was near his village. He wanted to be rested before he saw his people.

The boy found a large oak tree and climbed up about midway to a large branch that looked like a saddle. He could sleep here without falling out of the tree. He awoke at sunrise with the birds singing all around. Feeling hungry, he climbed down from the tree to look for berries to eat. After eating the berries he found fresh water to drink.

He continued walking until he reached the Big Lake the old woman told him about. The men from the village were on their way hunting and he quickly jumped out of sight as he didn't want to meet them yet. He knew the village was very near.

The boy continued until he saw many chickees. He climbed up in a large tree and watched the people until almost sundown. He wondered what he would say to the people about where he had lived for the past years. After a while he climbed down from the tree and started walking to the edge of the village.

The children saw him and started yelling, "New man. New man. Visitor."

The older men of the village came out to shake his hand and talk to him. When he told the old men about himself, the old men remembered the story of the little boy who was lost long, long ago.

The boy then gave an old man the necklace he was wearing when he disappeared. "Yes, yes!" cried the old man. "I know your family." They slowly walked to the other side of the village, where a man and woman sat talking.

The old man placed the necklace in the old woman's hand. She stared at the beadwork for a long time and then looked up to say she knew the work. The old man then told her that this was her son, returned from being lost a long time ago.

The story was told over and over to everyone that joined the happy family around the campfire. They listened all night long to the boy's stories. After many months, the village men decided to go and see where the boy was raised.

They left early one morning and were gone for about a week. When they returned, they told of finding the place where the boy was raised. Only now it was a patch of beautiful green corn that stretched all over the island. Soon, everyone went to see the corn, which was so yellow and pretty. The men gathered all the corn they could carry and took it back to the village with them. They saved the seeds and planted them year after year.

After the boy returned home and the corn was discovered, a Green Corn Dance was held every year to thank the Great Spirit for his blessing. And this is where the Indians got their first corn.

Arkansas, Louisiana, and East Texas

besmilr brigham

besmilr brigham (Choctaw) was born in Pace, Mississippi, on September 28, 1923. She earned a degree in journalism at Mary Hardin-Baylor College and pursued graduate studies at the the New School for Social Research. She published her first book of poetry, *Agony Dance: Death of the Dancing Dolls*, in 1969. Other books of poetry include *Heaved from the Earth* (1971) and *Death of the Wild* (1984), as well as a collection of short fiction, *To Live as a Bird* (1984). Her poems and stories appeared in many national journals, such as *Southern Review*, *Confrontation*, *Southwest Review*, *North American Review*, *Beloit Poetry Journal*, *West Coast Review*, and *Wisconsin Review*. For many years, brigham lived in Horatio, Arkansas, but at the time of her death, on September 29, 2000, she was living with her daughter and son-in-law in Las Cruces, New Mexico. *Run Through Rock*, a collection of her stories, was published posthumously in 2000. Her unique pen name is pronounced "bessmiller," a variation of her birth name. She wished that her pen name always be rendered in small letters.

From Painted Grave-houses

the rain sags, narrows the sappy boards
seeps a bog wash under holes
where the lone wolves crawl
they gnaw the riddled hot-swell meat

in a dead heather of plants
the sunk-in skeletons (that lay
skulls strung on a rope of bark
they lie on their backs
heads at last ease turned sidewards
regarding down

at their long trunks with their huge eyes
having left them

flat grave land
sifted up by water
a piled up heap of willow bark, the heart
seeped through

Heaved from the Earth

after the tornado, a dead moccasin
nailed to the pole
boards scattered across a pasture

lying fierce crosses
jagged in mud

had flung itself
nail and wood
the square-head animal
hurled also in air

or as it raced in weeds
water flowing, water falling
impaled
        both the snake and timber
went flying through with wind

coiled, made a coil (they do
immediately from danger or when hurt
and died in a coil
bit itself
in pain of its own defense the poison

                birds
                hurled into yard
                fences
                one with feet tangled gripping
                the open wire, a big Jay
struggling from the water
throwing its fanged head
high at the lightning, silent
in all that thunder

to die by its own mouth
pushing the fire thorns in

In Arkansas

we drive through the bottoms, old road
packed wash and dirt—
our lights off, the close trees
reach, spreading to our fenders, slowly
we break through the dark areas

watching
water settled rushes to near our car wheels;
we hear wolves howl, a panther
rush (sound in the tree tops, our noise
wakes the birds

wakes the dead woods with our passing

Quapaw graves. One is buried
low in our own land grove; we never
dug down to see—the thick rocks
spread flat to make his shape
a long arrow
shaft of the wind thrown deep
covered with earth, hollow with roots

we hear them calling against our lights,
when our house lights
stand out against the night like one
secure shelter; we make our eyes big open places
to see them.

we move with a knowledge before their ways
conscious as moving birds of their presence
not still—
we go very slowly and without speed knowing
the dead in the wood
with cold eyes their still graves measure us

William Jay Smith

William Jay Smith (Choctaw) is not only a highly respected writer of Native American heritage, he is also one of America's major contemporary poets. Smith was born on April 22, 1918, in Winnfield, Louisiana. The son of a career soldier, he grew up at Jefferson Barracks, near St. Louis, Missouri. He attended Washington University, Columbia University, and Oxford University (where he was a Rhodes Scholar). In a long and distinguished career, Smith has published approximately eighty books—poetry, children's books, nonfiction, and translations. Some of his poetry titles are *Celebration at Dark* (1950), *The Tin Can, and Other Poems* (1966), *The Traveler's Tree* (1980), *Collected Poems, 1939–1989* (1990), *The Cherokee Lottery* (2000), and *The Girl in Glass: Love Poems* (2002). His children's books include *Laughing Time* (1955), *What Do I See?* (1962), *Ho for a Hat!* (1964), *If I Had a Boat* (1966), *Grandmother Ostrich and Other Poems* (1969), and *Around My Room* (2000); nonfiction works include a volume of literary criticism, *The Spectra Hoax* (1961), *Army Brat: A Memoir* (1980), and translations of poets whose work originally appeared in French, Russian, Hungarian, and Swedish. He has twice been nominated for the National Book Award. From 1968 to 1970, Smith served as poetry consultant (the position now designated as U.S. Poet Laureate) to the Library of Congress, and he has been a member of the Academy of Arts and Letters since 1975. Currently retired and living in Cummington, Massachusetts, he is Professor Emeritus of English at Hollins College.

From *The Cherokee Lottery*

VI. THE CROSSING

> *"There were among them (a band of Choctaws) the wounded, the sick, new-born babies, and old men on the point of death. They had neither tents nor wagons, but only some provisions and the sight will never fade from my memory. Neither sob nor complaint rose from that silent assembly."*

> —Alexis de Tocqueville
> Mississippi, 1831

That winter the southern land had all the contours
of a giant beast in the throes of a convulsion,
its writhing body creased with deep, soft folds

"VI. The Crossing" and "XVI. The Burning of Malmaison" from *The Cherokee Lottery* (Willimantic, Conn.: Curbstone Press, 1998, 2000). Copyright © 1998, 2000 by Curbstone Press and William Jay Smith. Reprinted with permission of the author.

exuding waterfalls like tears and gasping for air;
and into its mouth over the wide rippling tongue
of the great brown river frothing at the edges,
I watched the rafts of the Choctaws
with their hunched and silent burden—
women with babies at their breasts,
old men holding on with withered arms,
small children at their knees—
with never a word of protest,
all borne quietly as if over the world's rim
into the throat of the beast.

XVI. THE BURNING OF MALMAISON

i

On a brisk cool evening when the wind
    had rinsed the sky and the pines
      smelled fresh from rain the night before

the mistress of the house and her sister
    welcomed two guests from the town to the gilded
      parlor of Malmaison,

the mansion built a hundred years earlier
    by Greenwood LeFlore, the son
      of a French-Canadian trapper at the garrison

of Mobile and his part-Choctaw wife. At the age
    of twenty-four he had become the Choctaw Chief
      and ten years later signed

the Treaty of Dancing Rabbit Creek, which ceded
    to the United States most of northern Mississippi
      and sent its Choctaw residents off to Oklahoma.

Greenwood—which in Choctaw *Itta-oke-chunka*
    means "tough hickory"—stayed behind to build
      at Teoc ("the place of the tall pines")

a mansion named for Empress Josephine, Napoleon's
    gift to her, and had filled it with
      rich furnishings from France.

The ladies sat on gilt-edged sofas of brocaded
    silk damask across from the marble mantelpiece
      with its gilded candelabra

and its clock of gold and ebony, below which blazed
    a log fire that took the chill off
    the evening, and whose flames

opened and closed on the mirrored walls
    like the fins of tropical fish
    criss-crossing the room's

great clear green pool and bringing an elegant
    freshness from beyond, a freshness
    broken by a sudden rumble

as of thunder on a distant mountain, followed
    by a heavy steady pounding
    of horses' hooves

that grew more deafening until the Corinthian
    columns seemed ready to crack open;
    and the ladies, terrified, could see

themselves held prisoner, the attackers
    bearing in from all sides—they were
    there already pounding from above—

and then a voice called out to them
    from a hallway, a faint crackling,
    a clearing of the throat,

someone trying to call out but cut off
    in the attempt . . . And then they rose
    and pulled the curtains back

to find the moon so bright upon the lawn
    they swore the headlights of a pack
    of circling cars had blinded them,

and turning back to reach the rifle
    hanging in the hall, they stepped
    into the very throat

from which the crackling came, great tongues
    of flame leapt forth while smoke
    poured down and timbers crashed

and they had met their all-consuming enemy head-on.

ii

On the lawn the ladies stood beside the pieces
  they had saved, the boule table,
  the long gilt mirror,

a love seat and six chairs, goblet, tureens, epergnes,
  and candelabra—a sorry bit, an evil
  offering of Malmaison's

French finery, and on top, Greenwood's
  sword and the silver-embroidered belt
  that Andrew Jackson had presented

to him when he was named Choctaw chief,
  and fastened to the scabbard the silver
  medal, a gift of Thomas Jefferson;

on one side the pipe of peace lay across
  a tomahawk and on the other were
  the words "Peace and Prosperity."

The flames swept up into the night,
  lifting the stars as they swirled even higher,
  the embers from a flaking log,

and the cupola, gigantic red-veined,
  fire-rimmed eyeball fixed on heaven
  crumpled up and sank

and through the hiss, the crackle, and the roar,
  the cracking and melting of the glass,
  the merging of hot porcelain

and timber, still the ladies heard the pounding
  of the horses' hooves, and the insistent
  thud of marching feet,

the exiled Choctaw voices that would never cease,
  a century of voices choking
  in the flame and smoke of Malmaison . . .

Since there was nothing more that they could
  rescue from the house, they sent black
  servants to the stable

to save the carriage that had taken Greenwood LeFlore
 to Washington and back, and there it was—
 the solid sterling

trimmings and its ivory-tacked silk damask
 upholstery gleaming in the light
 beside the boule table,

the mirrors, and the glass, and the ladies
 turned to it now, a refuge from the inferno
 swirling ever more intense around them,

and sobbing softly, then they took their places,
 waiting, it appeared, for the carriage wheels
 to lift them far above the flames

   iii

In March twenty years later, in the brambles that had
 overgrown the family cemetery, two Boy Scouts
 came upon the headstone that read:

   Greenwood LeFlore

   Born June 3, 1800
   Died August 31, 1865

   The last chief of the Choc-
   Taw Nation east of the
   Mississippi River

and seeing that the earth around it had been recently
 disturbed, alerted the family, who days
 later had diggers

go down to a depth of eight feet where they found
 only three pieces of yellow pine,
 broken but intact,

that had perhaps enclosed the grave,
 but the coffin, and, with it, the remains,
 the skull and bones

of the Choctaw chief, had disappeared.
 Beside the headstone in the orange clay
 the diggers unearthed a thin blue vein,

a remnant surely of the stars and stripes
      so dear to the Choctaw chief,
      who, when he was dying,

had asked his granddaughters to come
      and hold the flag above him,
      which they did, and they granted

him his dying wish, to have it wrapped
      around him in his grave, and of it now
      all that was left: this small blue stain.

Kennette Harrison

Kennette Harrison (Cherokee) lives in San Diego, California. Her book of poems, *Dowsing for Light*, was published in 1999 and won the Alabama State Poetry Society Award the following year. She was born in San Antonio, Texas, of Cherokee and Scottish-Irish ancestry, the Cherokee folks being of the group that emigrated westward apart from the government-sponsored removal, and has also lived in Oklahoma and Alabama. Harrison holds a master's degree in English and creative writing from the University of Central Oklahoma and has published in such journals as *Nimrod, Negative Capability, The Chattahoochee Review, The Black Warrior Review, Southern Humanities Review,* and *Cumberland Poetry Review*. She was a winner of the Spanish Moss and Silences Poetry Chapbook Award for "Kitchen Without Precedence."

Grandpa witched for water weekdays

and Sundays under the steeple pursued
some deep history of soul from his pulpit
then stepped down, laying on hands
knowing the heart's dry holes
piercing through them
a thousand oracles below their desert
trusting his divining rod, believing
the promise curve, quivering
and alive with discovery.

Mother, tired of drinking bitter
iron water from our well, sliced
a green sap branch from the gum tree
and criss-crossed our land
aproned, flour on her hands
unconvincing water witch.

I drink her sweet water
until withered by unbelief
I scoff, yet never cease reading stories

of a captain stanching blood
on the battlefield, of crystals
spun on a string twirling toward
a body's pain, of a mystic spinning
tales that Stonehenge is a place
of underground streams dowsed by ancients.

Spun into my present on a twist of doubt
and a strand of faith, I take a knife
to the sweet gum tree beside my house
and cut a young branch, Y-shaped.
Over the earth I walk with it
expectant, two hands and a dream.
What if music happens?

Leaving the Women to Plow

for great-great grandfather Will Connally, reluctant soldier of the Confederacy

I fall with my face toward the battle
drummed into earth by marching hymns
no longer willing to perpetuate the lie guns tell
and I imagine that when my horse wanders home
one year later, there will be mourning like the time
my playmate died of poisoning from eating jimsonweed.

My cheek rests on the soft prayer that clung
to my mother's lips, green and faithful as moss
and in the dreamtime when I am forgiving everyone
forgiving myself, I see my father's eye aimed
down the gun sight of the rifle he taught me to use
in self-defense, his pupil black as the barrel hole
mind loaded, heart cocked.

Something unsoldierly rises up in me, willing bull's eye
and my fingers comb wild grass like they combed tangles
from my wife's hair. I breathe hard through the aroma
of blood and soil in my nostrils, bite my wet lips
and fall back to a weedy time, before jimson.

Reunion

I name what I love
by its distance from me
soft names carved into marble
burning my eyes like pepper dust
sprinkled over the family stew in the iron kettle
every Independence Day, tasting sweet-salt
like the tomatoes Uncle Pearl grew, cool skins
stretched like birthday balloons
and Grandpa's leathery cheek I kissed
while he sat watching everything
his fingertips pressed together.

I breathe them all
the women's best aprons
spicy from cedar chests
their busy feet laying down the fine net
that held my world together,
cherry lattice pie of Aunt Sibyl
Aunt Mat, smelling of green beans
she cooked to brown
with bacon and new potatoes.

I see Aunt Grace afterward, smelling sweet
with her grandma bath powder, its velvet puff
and the ribboned, round box, apricot
her wet footprints stenciled dark blue
in the dusty linoleum after her bath
when I go back to the honeysuckle embrace
the room where her tub sits
on white porcelain lion's feet
and you can hear the night-singing mockingbird
serenade from beyond the porch where I sit
in moonlight, rocking, snapping beans
while they are still crisp and green.

The Connally Family Cemetery, Farm Road 27
Texas State Historical Site

The sun lights my father
where he kneels in the family cemetery

like an actor bound for destiny
plays him bright against the dark
backdrop of holly and bog myrtle
as he reaches to stroke
the pink granite headstone
of his most ancient ancestor.
Sunbeams play about his straw hat
until it glistens halo on his bent head.

My four-year-old granddaughter's hands
drift over carved letters
of our shared name, and I tell her
about my long-gone Grandpa
as she leans, hardly curious
against his cold, gray stone
under the shadow of loblolly pines
but she comes into my arms
when she asks about the tiny graves
Infant Phoebe, and no-name infant.

She asks why and why until I seek
the sunny space with my father
see him spiral up from kneeling
wild muscadine rising, his arms
tendrils looping around me
and his great-granddaughter
in the patch of light
and we walk together through shade
of cedar, oak, and hickory to a place
at the foot of his parents' graves.

The three generations of us stand
on the spot he says he wants to rest in
someday, and then we leave our departed
lock the gate, squint against the sun
walk our Cherokee walk across Peckerwood Flat
because of Cousin Richard's prize bull.

"Can we pick blackberries here?"
the youngest asks, already at ease
with the stare of the bull, and the sun.
"Along the fence line," Daddy says

"where no one mows them down
but you gotta look out for snakes
'cause it's that time of year."

Unaccountably moved to recklessness
the three of us plunge our hands
into the dark brambles
fill them with dusky berries
laugh at each other's blue lips
as we drive down Farm Road 27, forget
death and destiny, snakes and stones.
We taste the sun's ripe sweetness.
We relish it.

The Translucence of Flesh

The earthly luminance
around the borders of your father's face
like the light that pressed outward
from your firstborn
the gleam that left your eye
in bright abandonment

and now when he lies there
swaddled in white sheets
the radiant years shine
from his old bones.

See how the skin clings to them
pearlescent, tightly, like his hand
held your small one then
and yours holds his now.

Where is he going
with his smile
that makes you reverent
with his moonlight forehead

his blue agate eyes
his mountain range chest at dawn
his feet that have sown lightning
into the ground with each step.

Dale Marie Taylor

Dale Marie Taylor (Cherokee-Seneca) is an English professor at Galveston College in Galveston, Texas. She is of mixed Cherokee, Seneca, and African ancestry, of people who migrated westward to Texas from the Pulaski, Tennessee, area, separate from the major removals of the Southeastern tribes. In 1976, Taylor received a B.A. in English from Delaware State University, followed by an M.A. in journalism from Texas A&M University in 1983. She wrote newspaper reportage and columns for the *Dallas Morning News*, *Lufkin Daily News*, and *Austin American-Statesman* until returning to school and receiving an M.A. in literature from the University of Houston in 2003. Taylor completed her doctorate in literature, specializing in issues of hybridity, from Indiana University of Pennsylvania in 2007. Her poetry has been published on the internet and is now beginning to appear in journals.

We Wait

We stare at you through these brown eyes
the eyes of our children.
We wait. We are here and we wait, wishing
Wanting,
our sons and daughters survive.
The Cherokee statesman who bought with one horse
the black, Bushyhead, from the whites
wanted slaves. So I used my black shoulders, my back
for the bidding of these new masters
who seemed as much a slave as me,
pushed around by whites from land to land.
The shackles come off; the whip gone; the tongue
harness left on the plantation.
But the work lasts from sun up to sun down
Even while the men fight.

I joined these people, brown skinned and red
As they struggled, mixed feelings, to keep me in chains
Finally, my freedom came one cool night
As I lay under the clouds in a blanket I hid on the range
He crawled under there with me; large wonder

after all the beatings that I had any love left to give.
And he took as the others what he needed and left
me to wonder who it was in the darkness of night.
He came again and again till I knew
every curve of his body and face.
Soon there was no hiding the curly headed children who
came from my body and blood.

When the soldiers came, my daughters fled to the Tennessee hills;
my sons walked and died with me on the Trail of Tears.
Still some of my 11 children survive.
One of my girls worked for a white man in Tennessee
and he came to her too as her father did to me.
Her children are here looking at you now. The strongest
of them made strong by trust and love.
We stare at you in the mirror that you see, in the
mirror of your mind. We are there in you and in me.
Waiting, waiting to survive.

Warrior Woman

This does not look right.
My friends all think I'm crazy.
A mixed blood, black,
I dream this crazy dream, this vision.
A woman appears to me in my visions
dressed in white leather
beaded and painted with the
signs of her conquests
a bear speared for safety
a deer speared for food
many horses captured from
her enemies, taken for good
her hair long, shiny and black;
she sits on the back of a beautiful
black mare, nostrils flaring
mane gently blowing in the soft
breezy air. She's walking beside me
watching me, not saying a word
just watching and waiting should I need

her; her horse walks beside me
on the rocky terrain; she above me
on the trail; behind her tall pine trees
deep dark green. The hilly path
on which she walks matches
mine, but her gait is smooth and easy;
she sits tall and proud in her seat.
Warrior Woman.

Her golden brown skin matches mine
Sometimes I speak to her;

Why great ancestor spirit, do not
my people see you in me? The African,
Portuguese, Cherokee, Scot
She smiles again, saying nothing;
but stops and reaches a hand down to me.
I take her hand and climb onto the mare
we ride together through life's changes.
A lost child, a lost love, a lost friend;
we ride together drawing strength from
the thoughts of two knowing that love triumphs.

Terra Trevor

Terra Trevor (Cherokee-Delaware-Seneca) was born in California on April 11, 1950. She has published poetry in several journals and newspapers and is a member of Wordcraft Circle of Native Writers and Storytellers. Her poem, "Pushing Up the Sky," is featured in the anthology, *Children of the Dragon Fly: Native Voices on Child Custody and Education* (2001). Trevor is project coordinator with the Red Ribbon Bridge Project within the American Indian Health and Social Services Program in Santa Barbara, California. She is also a freelance journalist for *Adoptive Families Magazine* and *Adoption Today Magazine* and is the mother of both birth and adopted children.

Finding Family Stories

Great-Grandma sat in a rocking chair near the big white front door. It was summer and the door was open. My mother said:

"Play a tune for us Grandma." But Grandma didn't want to play the harmonica, didn't want to take out her teeth, not in front of so many people; the house was filled with relatives. Perhaps she sensed my disappointment—she told me a story about when she and Great-Grandpa were sharecroppers. I remember almost nothing of her sharecropping story, only "We were sharecroppers," stayed with me.

All her life Great-Grandma had been a Cherokee, but in 1954, the same year I was born, the government decided Grandma was Lumbee. Uncle Elmer signed up right away, but Grandma said that was just folks talking and it couldn't change anything.

Squinting at me, Great-Grandma said,

"Child, you got eyes green as water ferns. Doesn't matter, they're still Indian eyes." Her words made me feel all warm and cozy inside. My great-grandparents' home was the center of my universe. The aunties with their high rounded cheeks, laughed in loud whoops while fanning flies off sleeping babies. The uncles discussed politics, clinging to their rock-bottom opinions, while the cousins played together like a pack of wild pups.

By the time I was six my great-grandparents lived in an old single-story white frame house in California, with a rock behind each door and chickens in the backyard. But when my dad was growing up their home was an old circus tent.

"Grandma's stove was in the center," my father explained. "The stove pipe poked through a hole in the top of the tent." I was ten, brown-haired and freckled-faced, when dad told me this story.

Every Sunday, Great-Grandma made chicken and noodles on an old cook-stove in the kitchen—my dad remembers her making them in the circus tent—she made a huge pot. There were lots of black-haired cousins.

For the first time in thirty years, I found myself surrounded by all my uncles and aunties again. I became the pest I was at age ten and begged to hear the family stories when my cousins gathered around the table.

Aunt Lydia, my grandpa's younger sister, sat across from me, a hand-rolled cigarette hung from her mouth.

"We're family who all got raised with our great-grandparents nearby," she explained. Aunt Lydia spoke in a flat hill dialect, her impish smile without teeth brought a grin to my face.

"Your grandpa and me, we learnt from our great-grandma to dig Sweet Root from the ground. Yellowroot, Ladies Slipper; she knew all of them." My grandfather leaned forward.

"She sewed quilts and none of us kids ever wore moccasins," he said. Grandpa is fond of letting me know our family became respectable homesteaders in Oklahoma and he almost never talked about his great-grandmother. Once I saw a photo of her, she was square and brown, sturdy not pretty, with boot moccasins on her feet. Aunt Lydia said she sang in the evening and that she lived to be ninety-nine years, nine months and nine days.

"She died peaceable in her bedstead." Grandpa reported. His face was flushed, yet it was cool in the kitchen; an early October breeze came in through the propped-open screen door. Uncle Elmer, grandpa's older brother, pulled up a straight-back chair, sat down and began giving the lowdown on what he remembered. He peered over the rim of his glasses, his skin was dark from the sun, white-feathered behind his ears.

"My mother was from the forgotten tribe," Uncle Elmer explained and I asked what that meant.

"If you drive through the Carolinas towards Virginia, you'll go through where the big army base is and just back this side is the Lumbee tribe. My mother, it turns out, wasn't half white like everybody thought, she was half Lumbee." Hearing this, Grandpa almost went to his knees, he waved his arm, nearly knocking my coffee off the table and said that Uncle Elmer was a possum-headed idjit and that he remembered everything wrong.

I got up to go to the bathroom. Grandpa and Uncle Elmer's voices faded in and out. As a kid, I had a hard time between them. I looked at myself in the lighted mirror of the medicine cabinet. My cheekbones are level with the tops of my ears, I have tiny deep-set eyes and new gray hairs on my head are strong as little wires. I know I'm somewhere between one-eighth and one-quarter Indian. I should leave it at that and think about something else, but I fill hours trying to decide on an exact amount.

When I came back to the kitchen Aunt Lydia had a raccoon soaking in salt water, getting it ready for steaming. Her secret to barbecuing a raccoon, especially an old son of a gun, was to steam it tender first. While she dusted it with onion soup powder and ladled sauce on both sides, Aunt Lydia blew little puffs of smoke from the thin cigarette she had rolled.

"That's bad for your health," Uncle Elmer said in a way that didn't sound like he was joking. The cousins tried to change the subject, then it was quiet for a moment that soft autumn morning. Aunt Lydia let out a deep sigh.

"I don't need a big brother telling me what to do. I'm old and I'm tired of it." She walked out on to the porch, I followed. This was a side of Aunt Lydia I'd never seen before and I dared more.

"Grandpa and Uncle Elmer tell me conflicting stories," I confided. Aunt Lydia clutched at her cigarette like it might fly out of her hand, her lips moved gently.

"They's just too taken up with theirselves. Elmer's got the notion we'd be better if we were tribal members and your grandpa thinks we'd be better if we weren't Indian." At eighty, Aunt Lydia's skin was like clay, so smooth and maroon. She flapped her hand in front of her mouth hiding those bare gums. We stood quiet, side by side for a long time. The air was clear and the wind still.

Aunt Lydia lit another cigarette. "Trust your memories," she warned. "If you do, you'll find everything you want to know is already inside you."

And then Aunt Lydia surprised me. She talked about what was good medicine and bad. Her shoulders had bent as she grew older, but Aunt Lydia was straight as a young girl while she told me her stories. Her words came from far away and sounded like wind in the trees, like running water and for a few minutes I was lost. But I caught her last phrase and it guided me like a rope tied from the house to the barn in a blizzard. She said, "We're a family of mixed bloods and there's nothing wrong with what we are."

Jimmie Durham

Jimmie Durham (Cherokee) is well-known both as an activist in Native American sovereignty rights issues and as an artist, and for his poetry and journalism. Durham was born in Washington, Arkansas, in 1940. He received his B.F.A. from the Ecole des Beaux Arts, University of Geneva, in 1972. In 1974, he was a cofounder of the International Treaty Council and functioned as the organization's director from its inception until 1979. During this period, he assisted in establishing a special committee on indigenous affairs at the United Nations. His book of poems, *Columbus Day*, was published in 1983. Durham is the coeditor of *We Are Always Turning Around . . . On Purpose* (1986), an anthology of personal and aesthetic statements by six highly original Native American artists, and numerous other works which stress the relationship of art and political/social activism, most notably, a collection of essays, *A Certain Lack of Coherence: Writings on Art and Cultural Politics* (1993). As an artist, he specializes in mixed media productions, often utilizing animal skulls and bones, wood, leather, and paint. Since the late 1980s, Durham has lived abroad, first in Mexico, then Belgium, and now in Germany.

The Poor People

You should have seen them
When they plucked leaves
From sword plants
And assumed dueling stances.

All soon withered.

At that, it was better than when
They tried to use icicles—

Licked away by enemies, cousins,
And other relations.

Now the rich people have offered a
Choice of weapons for sale:

1. Aerosol bombs
2. Emigration permits
3. Leaves from coca plants

Whatever Happened to That One Guy, And, They Think It Might Lead to Something

1 (Up)

This time may be only a rough draft
Of some history to be written fine
As froghair by some folks who know
How to write or fight to the point.

Our daughters may be mothers of fighters
Who never dull or get distracted.

2 (Down)

The white folks love that speech by Chief Joseph
When he eloquently surrendered (trying to make
a deal) and said, "I will fight no more
Forever." But me,

I remember Neamathla, the Seminole chief who said,
"Now I am captured, but if I had the power
Tonight I would cut the throat of every
Whiteman in Florida."

(It could still be done without innocent
Blood being shed.)

3 (East)

As boys we never thought *our* blood
Would drip and pour like piss through pain and
Through our desperate useless fingers
As we had seen blood pour from
Some of the men.

But then Joe Cruz got his belly cut and stabbed
One day just as me and him was talking
About how it must be to make love with a woman.
(Now look, you *know* I would not have added
That bit if it hadn't happened just like that.

I am not writing this history, and if I was
I would not have written me at the scene
When Joe Cruz got killed because I was
Too young to watch Joe Cruz get killed.)

4 *(West)*

Joe Cruz cried. At first he gasped and
Sucked in his breath and held it. Then
He tried to breathe in quick little jerks,
But that hurt too and he had his hands
On his cut shirt and I could see guts and
Blood was pouring he started falling and
He started moaning and saying "Unh, unh, unh."
Then he tried to writhe on the ground but
That hurt too so then he started crying
But that hurt too and finally he passed out
And died.

5 *(North)*

Plans are sincerely made everytime.
Some folks sit around a table or walk along
Making plans. They are sometimes very afraid;
Afraid about the plans, because a part gets left out.
They think, "These plans are not going to work."
But, they think it might lead to something.

6 *(South)*

There are so many people missing, not just Joe
Cruz. We need them for our plans, but that guy
Named Angel got killed in a car wreck out of Santa Fe,
And all the others got wasted somewhere.
If we could unite everybody's
Wasted pain and all our dreams (Yes! Our *dreams*—
Of being able to live it through in dignity
With a little security. Our great dreams!)
To the thread of our plans, it might lead
To something.
But whatever happened to that one guy?
I don't even remember his name.

7 (Inside)

Obviously, we have not thought of everything.
I want this poem to have seven parts.
The seven directions of the universe are:
Up, down, east, west, north, south, and inside
One's self. That is why there is no clear
Ending in the seventh part, here.

Statement Presented to the U.S. House of Representatives' Merchant Marine and Fisheries Committee Hearings on the Re-Authorization of the Endangered Species Act, June 20, 1978

In 1980 the U.S. government closed a dam on the Little Tennessee River, thereby flooding off the principal city of the Cherokee Nation. Thus ended a ten-year fight that we had fought to save that holy place. Maybe you remember reading about that little fish, the Snail Darter, that was an endangered species in the river? He lost. We lost. Even Ross Swimmer lost. Even Jimmy Carter lost. We were winning the fight, until our "chief" turned against us in a secret deal with Howard Baker, Senator from Tennessee. Carter also made a deal with Howard Baker, and that was the end of Echota.

Here is a speech I made to a congressional committee about Echota and the dam. It was quoted and reprinted widely, and we thought we were winning. Sentiment was on our side, but action was needed.

Tsi Yunwiyah. I am a Cherokee. In the language of my people, Ani Yuniwi-yah, or Cherokee as we are called, there is a word for land: Eloheh. This same word also means history, culture, and religion. We cannot separate our place on the earth from our lives on the earth nor from our vision and our meaning as a people. We are taught from childhood that the animals and even the trees and plants that we share a place with are our brothers and sisters.

So when we speak of land, we are not speaking of property, territory, or even a piece of ground upon which our houses sit and our crops are grown. We are speaking of something truly sacred.

Is there a people anywhere in the world that does not revere its homeland? Is there a human being who does not revere his or her homeland, and even if he or she may not return? We say that reverence is a great human characteristic. We say that reverence for ancestral lands, no matter how insignificant in our own daily affairs or how far from our own homes, is vitally important to the whole of humanity.

The Cherokee people lived for thousands of years in what is now Tennessee, Georgia, and Carolina. In our own history, we teach that we were created there, which is truer than anthropological truth because it was there that we were given our vision as the Cherokee people. But President Jackson illegally drove us out of that land, from Echota, the center of our world.

There is no Cherokee alive who does not remember that Trail of Tears, who does not remember and revere that sacred land and Echota.

Today the Tennessee Valley Authority plans to flood the sacred valley that held our two principal cities, Echota and Tenasi, after which the state is named. The Tellico Project would destroy an area of great religious importance, many settlement sites, cemeteries, rich farmlands, forests, and the river itself. This is an unneeded dam which can, at the whimsy of TVA, wipe out thousands of years of history of a great and currently oppressed people. To do so will be an insult not only to the Cherokee, but to all the people in the U.S. and to all humanity. Yes, I am proud enough to state that the history and vision of my people are important to humanity.

I want to speak to my children and my grandchildren about Echota, and I want them to be able to go there and listen to their ancestors. The anthropologists have dug up some bones and some pottery at Echota and TVA tells us that we can visit those bones at a museum.

But the spirits of our ancestors are not in a museum. They live in the Pine and Hickory and Walnut trees and in those free-running creeks and rivers.

I will never live at Echota, any more than a Greek in New Jersey will ever live at the Parthenon, but the hearts of our people say it must *be* there.

The fact that there is no stone monuments or large ruins at Echota is itself a monument. Our reverence for the land and its life maintained it in an unspoiled state for those thousands of years. Maybe someone will think I am being too emotional, but there must come a time when the American government and the American people can be emotional about the destruction of land and of sacred things.

The flooding of our old valley has been stopped temporarily because of a little fish that lives there and nowhere else. I have seen Griffin Bell, *The New York Times*, and a national television network make fun of this little fish and I would like to ask why it is considered so humorously insignificant. Because it is little, or because it is a fish?

It is this incredible arrogance towards other life that has caused such destruction in this country. Who is Griffin Bell or the U.S. government to play God and judge the life or death of an entire species of fellow-being which was put here by the same power that put us here? Who has the right to destroy a species of life, and what can assuming that right mean?

Let me be emotional: To me that fish is not just an abstract "endangered species," although it is that. It is a Cherokee fish and I am its brother. Somehow, it has acted to save my holy land, so I have a strong gratitude for that fish.

The Cherokee people in Tennessee, Oklahoma, the Carolinas, Georgia, and wherever we might be, are of one voice and of one mind that this dam, this degradation, be stopped. We want our universe, or Eloheh, with all of its fish and all of its life to continue. And we are sure that this *cannot* be against the interests and wishes of the American People.

> Jimmie Durham, Director
> International Indian Treaty Council

Kimberly G. Roppolo

Kimberly G. Roppolo (Cherokee-Choctaw-Creek) was born in Baytown, Texas, in 1968. Her ancestors include tribal people who emigrated to Texas separately from the federally imposed removals to Indian Territory. She received her B.A., M.A., and Ph.D. degrees from Baylor University. Roppolo taught for several years at McLennan Community College in Waco, Texas. After teaching for four years in the Native Studies Program at the University of Lethbridge, in Alberta, she accepted a position as a professor of English and Native American Studies at the University of Oklahoma. Her poems and essays have appeared in such journals as *Studies in American Indian Literatures*, *Paradoxa*, *American Indian Culture and Research Journal*, *News from Indian Country*, and the anthology *This Bridge We Call Home*. In 2001, Roppolo was selected as Wordcrafter of the Year by Wordcraft Circle of Native Writers and Storytellers. Her book-length manuscript, "Back to the Blanket: Reading, Writing, and Resistance for American Indian Literary Critics," won the 2004 First Book Award for Prose from the Native Writers' Circle of the Americas. She has also completed a poetry manuscript entitled "Breeds and Outlaws," for which she is currently seeking a publisher. Roppolo is the National Director of Wordcraft Circle of Native Writers and Storytellers.

A Song to Tell Robert Bly How We Do This in My Language

My 'skin kin the ants
begin again the dance
A-ga-sga—it is raining.

Antelope pokes a hole a world below,
the new sky cries,
People emerge—it is raining.

The soldiers crowd the shivering hungry;
in a pen intended for cows a child dies
from the eyes of the Aniyuniwiya—it is raining.

A man lifts his hands to the East,
the Grandmothers consult regarding blessings,
the dust returns from wind to earth—it is raining.

A white-washed church strains to reach the sun in Chiapas,
blood and brain stain its walls fresh from death,
the soil keeps drinking a five-hundred year old shot—it is raining.

The voices of my ancestors thin through brine
as they sing and flash in vast Atlantic,
a storm roars at sea, and I am born, not from shell, but their bones and
    dreams—it is raining.

Una Limpia por Chelleye

I remember that night
you threw away your pain
at the crossroads
of friendship
and this one particular journey,
bound to the new life
in el huevo de la limpia,
a microcosmic Aztec sacrifice,
exchanging itself for you
to a hungry God,
one more like your father's
than any
I've known on my path.

Our Cohuillateca cousins
have some complicated beliefs—
hard to bleed out
what's Jesús
and what's Quetzalcoatl
or if it's all
just the same
anyway.

Did you really give it away?
Or is it still nesting
up under your ribcage,
waiting to hatch

someday
and eat your heart?

Are you still feeding it,
keeping it warm,
your little one,
replacing the smiling-faced child
that your parents
only let live for two seconds
before you had to hide her,
began to hate her weakness,
her love?

Whom do you kiss
and call mijá
in the morning hermana?

Who is your God,
and what kind of Love
is this?

Song for All My Relatives South of the Red River

There was a time when the People had lost their ways.
When all they had almost two hundred years
Almost three hundred years
Almost four hundred years
Almost five hundred years
Was a name silent
Unvoiced even to God.

It was going to take a lot of medicine to get them back.
So we begged and borrowed all we could to strengthen up,
Genuflecting, Bible-banging,
or Holy-Rollin' our spirits up
Going Lakota way
Or Cheyenne way
Growing big enough to call them back.

Or did they call us?
Were we just getting strong enough

To hear it,
The tongues of that One Fire
The sound: sh-sh-sh-sh-sh-sh-sh and
The boom of men's voices in the call and response
The feet that keep the world going.

Or the call of El Corazón de Jesus
The Tuca
The water drum
The gourd rattle
Come down
From Tenochtitlan
Run away from Cortés' monstrous hordes to the Montañas con los
    Huicholes.

The sound of the ocean
The memory of turtles swimming in blue peace
Or of digging roots
And weaving our stories into the
Containers of our lives
Our families
Before Colombo or the Gold Seekers and Slavers

What is stronger?
A card? A piece of paper?
Or the Blood in our veins
The Truth en nos almas
Clan Lines wrapped endlessly around our hearts
From mother-to-mother-to-mother-to-mother
An Umbilical cord winding back to the Source of Life.

Texas Traces

The dry spring
the white men call China
still bubbling a world ago.
Tonkawa Grandmothers,
Comanche Grandmothers,
wash their children in its pool
and their splashes and baby sounds
are my aubade,

When De Vaca,
gone Native,
roamed these lands,
only Lake Caddo was born.
The Arms of God
cradled Earth's Children
and ran in their veins.
The place of each emergence
was Holy.

Now, Sugar Loaf Mountain,
where the first Tonkawa
came out of the clay
has been sliced away
by a land "owner"
tired of
"tourists."

There are Old Circles
out at Ft. Hood, though,
guarded by my old friend Randy,
"part" Cherokee,
part archaeologist,
mostly pothead,
but still a good guy.

My son finds bits and pieces—
birdpoints, speartips, "Huaco sinkers"—
when he hunts with his father,
but when the guy at DMV
asks him if we're "mixed,"
he says,
"She's Indian,"
pointing to me.

At the H.E.B.,
they think I'm either white
or Mexican
and decide upon the order of my service.

Good thing I'm not in Oklahoma.
I'd have to wait until last
if anyone of "authority"
guessed,
like the time when the Asian woman
in Oklahoma City
cheated me of a dollar of gas
and dared me with her guard dog
behind the counter
to complain.

Or the time in Seiling,
accompanied by a Cheyenne,
a Kiowa-Arapaho,
and an Italian with braids like a breed,
the black folks even treated us like trash.

But here, me and the Mexicans,
we know who we are.
Some of the traces are Cohuillatec.
like the graves of Ray's ancestors
in the mission courtyard
in San Antonio de Bexar,
down the street
from where he lives
in the same old barrio.
And the pictures of my great-grandparents
down near San Marcos,
with the census records
black and whiting their migration
don't lie,
though the textbooks
still say
all the Cherokees in Texas
died with Chief Bowles.

We still pray down here.
We respect those spirits,
not only of our ancestors,
but of the ancestors of those

forced north of the Red River
as well,
those old Kiowas.
Lipans,
Comanches,
Tonkawas,
Tehuacana,
Huaco,
those old ones on the coast,
by Annette's house
and my mom's,
those Karankawas
and others
whose names
the white man's story
has erased
from even our memory,
we still remember them.

That's just how it is down here.
It's just like that.

U-ne-ga

—For Leo Hernandez, Taxi Cab Poet extraordinaire, Puerta Vallarta, Jalisco, Mexico

Abuelita del pacifico, (Grandmother Pacific,)
tu eres muy hermosa y peligrosa.
(You are very beautiful and very dangerous.)
Yo te amo. (I love you.)
Madre del Mar, del Maiz, y de la Tierra.
(Sea Mother, Corn Mother, Earth Mother.)
Madre nuestra de Guadalupe, (Our Lady of Guadalupe,)
muchas gracias por tu ayuda, por tu gracia,
(thank you so much for your help, your grace,)
y por todo Puerto Vallarta. (and for all of Puerta Vallarta.)
Te doy gracias por esta gente, (I give you thanks for this People.)
mis parientes, (my relatives,)
y por toda mi familia, (and for all of my family,)

los Indios de Norteamerica. (the Indians of North America.)
Gracias por las huellas de mis Antepasados,
(Thank you for the footprints of my Ancestors,)
los Venados, (the Deer,)
que estan en la playa, (which are on the beach,)
el mercado, (in the market,)
en todas partes, (in all places,)
en mi corazón (in my heart)
y en mi alma. (in my soul.)
Vuelve, (Return,)
Madre nuestra, (Our Mother,)
danos tu luz (and give us Light)
y juntanos (and join us)
para que haya paz y unidad. (in Peace and Unity.)

Earl J. Barbry, Sr.

Earl J. Barbry, Sr., (Tunica-Biloxi) has served in tribal government and as tribal chairman of the Tunica-Biloxi Tribe since 1978. He lives in Marksville, Louisiana, and is a businessman and farmer. His grandfathers, Eli Barbry and Horace Pierite, were chiefs of the tribe. As tribal chairman, he has facilitated many outstanding changes in the quality of life of his people. Soon after the tribe gained federal recognition in 1981, Barbry was instrumental in initiating numerous projects that have vastly improved the tribe's housing, roadways, water and sewerage facilities, and tribal governing system. Under his leadership, the tribe also successfully undertook the construction of a Regional Indian Center and Museum and the Grand Casino Avoyelles, the tribal gaming complex. He has served terms as chairman of the board for both the Inter-Tribal Council of Louisiana and the United Southeastern Tribes (USET). Recently, under his leadership, the Tunica-Biloxi Tribe made a substantial monetary contribution to the State of Louisiana for the America's Wetlands restoration project.

Cherishing Our Past . . . Building for Our Future

Louisiana is a state that proudly boasts of its abundance of natural resources. However, the most important resource, its people, are often overlooked or taken for granted.

The various ethnic cultures of this state have contributed greatly to its development, and the customs and traditions of its natives have made Louisiana an enjoyable place in which to live and rear children. One combination that makes Louisiana unique is the manner in which we blend our traditions of the past into our present day lives, a factor which has been an asset in attracting people from different parts of the world to visit and settle here.

The Tunica-Biloxi Indians have played a major role in the founding and development of Louisiana, and without a doubt have been one of the state=s largest depositors in its vast treasure of history and culture. Since the year 1541, the Tunicas have had a lasting impact on the history of Louisiana. Unfortunately, this historical information has not been made available to the public.

We feel that the history of the Tunica-Biloxi people is far too valuable to be kept to ourselves. It is something that should be shared with everyone, therefore, we would like you to take the time to read this publication.

While we cherish our present status and the goals we steadfastly work toward for the future. Although they are set high, we feel this is essential in building for the future of not only our people, but also the state and country.

Since 1790, we have resided in Avoyelles Parish near the southern edge of the Marksville corporation limits on a 134 acre reservation. This is all that remains of the original Spanish land grant of three square leagues.

I grew up on this land and feel very much a part of it. Life was not easy for my family or for the other members of the tribe who were living here. Economic and living conditions were well below the norm.

The Tunica-Biloxi Tribe did not enjoy the status of federal recognition, therefore, there was no federal assistance available to the tribe. This would not come until many years later in September of 1981, after decades of dedicated hard work by my predecessors, all whom had a vital role in setting the stage of having it finally realized during the time of my administration as Tribal Chairman and those serving with me.

Although life was difficult for our family in those earlier days, we were happy and enjoyed our family setting. Little did I realize, at the time, that I would one day be the leader of my people. This is an honor and a privilege for me. There are moments of despair and discouragement, but the joy of our accomplishments far outweighs these; I enjoy the responsibility of helping to set the course of the future of the Tunica-Biloxi people.

During the latter part of the 1970s, we began to see some progress taking place on the reservation such as recreational facilities and the tribe's first Tribal Center. After federal recognition, improvement accelerated and we now have improved the streets throughout the reservation, sanitation facilities, housing, utilities, and a new Tribal Multipurpose Building out of which many needed services are provided to our people. These include health care, education, social services, programs for the elderly, job training, employment assistance, and various Bureau of Indian Affairs programs. I hope that in the near future we will also see the implementation of a Tribal Law Enforcement Program to deal with the everyday problems that any municipality might experience.

The Tunica-Biloxi Tribe, being a sovereign nation, has the ability to choose its own destiny as have other Indian nations. I personally feel that the term "sovereign Indian nation," is a bit misleading and is misunderstood by many. How can we really believe that we have and enjoy that sovereignty and status of autonomy as long as we are dependent on federal funding for our very existence? While we are grateful for this assistance, we must realize that we should strive to become self-sufficient. This is why our tribal government has been and is continuously seeking viable businesses to enter into, or some industry to locate on the reservation. We feel that this is the next step necessary toward reaching our goal of self-sufficiency. This will provide the employment and revenue for the tribe that is needed to provide those services for people that are currently being provided by the federal government. When we reach that goal and sever the federal government's apron strings, then we can truly say we are a sovereign nation.

Other projects that are in the planning stages are law enforcement, agriculture and beef production, a Regional Cultural and Learning Center, additional housing, and educational facilities. There remains also the need to provide services to other areas where many of our tribal members reside. In accordance with federal regulations, they cannot benefit from the tribe's programs as they do not live within a certain radius of the reservation.

I believe that with dedication and hard work, we can achieve all our goals. The final product will be a better tomorrow for our children, our most valuable resource and the leaders of the future.

Roger Emile Stouff

Roger Emile Stouff (Chitimacha) writes a column, "From the Other Side," for the newspaper, *The St. Mary & Franklin Banner-Tribune*, in Franklin, Louisiana. He is an avid boating enthusiast and fisherman and has written extensively about each of these activities. He is also a shrewd commentator on daily events— political, topical, and cultural. Stouff was born October 10, 1964, in Franklin, ten miles from the Chitimacha Indian Reservation, where he currently lives in a house built about 1840 by then-chief Alexander Darden, a direct ancestor. His grandfather, Emile Stouff, served for many years as the chief of the Chitimacha tribe, and his grandmother, Faye Stouff, is the author, with W. Bradley Twitty, of *Sacred Chitimacha Indian Beliefs* (1971), now being reprinted with illustrations by Margot Soule. Nick Stouff, his father, was the last traditional chief, serving as such briefly before the present-day tribal constitution and by-laws were drafted, after which he then served one term as the first chairman of the tribe. Roger Emile Stouff's columns are available on his website, native-waters.com, and his first book, *Native Waters: A Few Moments in a Small Wooden Boat*, was published in 2005. His book of short stories, *Chasing Thunderbirds*, appeared in 2007. He studied archaeology in college, but newspaper work prevailed, and he has been in the newspaper business since 1980.

Back End of the Canal

Chasing bream across the north shore of Grande Avoille Cove, to little avail, the boat drifted upon a wide but short canal cut into the bank. The loggers likely left it there, before 1930, when nearly all the old growth cypress in Louisiana was felled. Grande Avoille Cove was a pivotal point for the de-forestation of St. Mary Parish, and the many thousands of logs which were floated out of that small bay of Grand Lake staggers the imagination.

It was late in the day, and the sun was over my left shoulder as the boat brought me to the mouth of that canal, probably used to stash logs awaiting transport to the mills which once dotted the parish from one end to the other. It was covered by a thick canopy of new-growth cypress along with European and Asian invaders. Though I knew the canal was no more than 50 yards deep, I could only see darkness in its depths. I made a few half-hearted casts into the mouth of the canal with my four-weight, but the size eight black wooly booger went unmolested. The boat touched stem to a sunken log and waited there for me to push it free.

But the darkness at the end of that canal held my attention. Late in the day like this, when skies are clear, the Atchafalaya River basin turns golden and green, quiet, breezeless and still. Here and there, egrets rest on ancient, worm-ridden logs, peck at bugs in rotting stumps. A water moccasin coils within a patch of irises, and far, far behind me, I hear the splash of a largemouth. Down there, at the end of that dark canal, another world exists. A world of twilight, where the margins of the present and past, the dividers separating this world from the next and that which has come before, are feeble, thin. When this was a giant system of interconnected lakes, before the levee was built, and further back still when there was no one here but Chitimacha, this was a metropolis. White clamshell, evidence of a thriving culture from which I am descended, peeks unblinkingly like disturbed bones from layers of fallen cypress needles. Down at the end of that short canal, in the blackness, I can almost see the way it was. Lodged there against a log, the bow of the boat held firm, I can almost see all my relations since before there was time.

It looks like a tunnel, a cave, a passage. With a push of the paddle, the boat is freed, and I negotiate around the log, then point the bow into the canal. With the deft accuracy of a man searching for erudition, I fade from the sunlit world into the darkness of the ages. I can still see in here, and above me, the canopy of mingling limbs are like lovers, locked in death's embrace. Not a peek of light comes from above, but the glow of the cove is behind me now. The boat drifts a moment then settles quietly, almost in reverence. That part of me which stubbornly insists upon being a twenty-first century man removes the wooly booger from the leader of my line, replacing it with a black rubber spider. The part of me that exists in the here-and-now plays out a little slack and carefully sends a roll cast to the back corner of that dim canal's termination.

It is sad to me that people who lived their lives in the light of day, who frolicked and played and worked and hunted and fished under the full face of the sun, now lurk in shadows at the back end of shallow canals. That people who touched Creation by keeping an eternal flame burning at not far from here should be cloaked in darkness after the end of their final days. Most of all that I should drift into a world of distant forebears and feel I should roll cast to a corner of their resting-place to make sense of the world.

I glance behind me, and the waters of the cove are bright. Ahead of me, the foam spider is motionless, neglected. Past the end of the little canal, I peer into darkness and a shadow, a patch of darkness blacker than the rest, darts away behind the thicket. I think of *Neka sama*, the "new devil," who moved across these swamps from west to east each year, whistling and making a sound as if pounding on a hollow log with a tree branch. Does *Neka sama* still haunt the darkness at the end of that canal, afraid of the light and illumination of disbelief? A beast once so feared children were huddled close to the breast when the whistling and pounding was heard far off, now a prisoner. It may lurk in there, looking out at the bright cove beyond, hear and watch the speeding, noisy boats, smelling the noxious fumes of two-cycle engines. It may snarl softly at fishermen who pass by it, casting into the canal's mouth, uncertain why they are suddenly so uneasy and quicken their trolling motors to pass the canal.

When a people fade into the darkness at the back end of shallow canals, they take their monsters with them.

I move the spider to the opposite corner with a careful twitch sideways. The ripples of its fall expand outward, touching darkness. There are no fish here. The darkness is all I may catch, and the soft, fluid motions within it, final breaths drawn from behind curtains, like fingers tapping on a drum. I draw in the line and back the boat out slowly. The shadows recede from me, and the sunlight basks over the stern of the boat first, moves amidships, and finally floods me with warmth.

No breeze could penetrate the thicket behind that canal from the northwest. No wind could find its way through the dense growth. But it came nonetheless, pushing the boat just a little more, fondling my hair, tugging at my clothes. Then I was back on Grande Avoille Cove, and the air was still, that exhalation from the back end of the canal abbreviated and done. There were whispers on the breeze, inaudible but my perceptions were keen to them.

Perhaps that's why the black back ends of shallow canals on Grande Avoille Cove fascinate me so. I am no oracle, no seer. Just a wayward son who came home in the nick of time. Perhaps there's no one left who desires to see.

It is nearing sunset. I start the engine and idle out of Grande Avoille Cove slowly, the prop kicking up mud from the shallow bottom. Instead of turning east for home, I guide the boat west, down the rest of the borrow pit that was dug to build the levee. Less than a tenth of a mile and the pit opens up into Lake Fausse Point, *Sheti*, Lake of the Chitimachas. The surface is smooth as crystal, holding silent secrets. I throttle up a bit, not too fast, but circle the lake once, breathing in the dusk. I let the oranges and greens and saturated silvers sink deep within me. The depth finder shows me that I am moving through barely two feet of water; this lake once ran half a dozen feet deep in its shallow spots. But the levee has changed all that, filled it up with sediment, like darkness under a cypress canopy. I dare not slow down or I'll be idling out of the lake as well. On the other side of that levee is Grand Lake, and once all that separated it from Lake Fausse Point were two islands, Big Pass and Little Pass. The levee linked and absorbed these. Round Island lies to the north, across the levee, as does Buffalo Cove, perhaps the most beautiful spot in all the river basin.

My circumference of the lake complete, I return to the borrow pit channel and make my way home. I pass by Grande Avoille Cove on my way, and it seems translucent, fading. I think perhaps it might vanish during the night, only returning at dawn. Farther down, I turn south at the levee's lock system, installed to vent the overflow of water, should the Atchafalaya threaten to tear down the stinging violation of the levee. On south, under the bridge, I turn west again and find my way home. It's nearly dark. Back on Grande Avoille Cove, if it's still there, I imagine the canal is completely cloaked now. Perhaps the entire cove is covered by darkness. Are ancestors dancing there, wraiths on the surface of the water, lifting themselves through the trees and into the stars just twinkling on high?

We once occupied these waters and lands from east to west, from the gulf to the junction of the two great rivers, but now we are spread thin across time and space, hidden from the sun in the back ends of dark canals.

Edythe Simpson Hobson

Edythe Simpson Hobson (Arkansas Quapaw) was born along Wells Bayou near the Dark Corner community of rural Lincoln County, Arkansas, on May 20, 1918. When she was five years old, her family moved by mules and wagon thirty miles to Kelso, in Desha County, and, except for spending seven years as a girl in Indiana, she lived all her life near Kelso. Despite attending school only until the ninth grade, she completed her G.E.D. in the 1960s. Hobson became interested in family history and genealogy in the 1970s and went on to publish several articles on these subjects, as well as on Arkansas history, in local papers and journals. In the latter part of the 1970s, she wrote a novel, "An Inquest Every Sunday," but was unsuccessful in finding a publisher for it. In 2002, following some revision, the novel won the Native Writers' Circle of the Americas First Book Award competition in Prose. Her genealogical scholarship is proving to be extremely beneficial to the retribalization efforts of the Arkansas Band of Quapaw Indians. Mrs. Hobson passed away on July 11, 2005.

Twenty-seven Days on the Levee—1927
*Edythe Simpson Hobson**

The weather during the fall and winter of 1926 was unusual for southeast Arkansas. It rained almost continually; the first four months of 1927 were no different. The ground remained soaked and the streams overflowed.

Where we lived in Desha County, was on the Fehr place on Red Fork Bayou near the joining of the Arkansas and Mississippi rivers' levees. The levee was

"Twenty-seven Days on the Levee—1927" from *Arkansas Historical Quarterly* 39, no. 3 (Autumn 1980). Copyright © 1980 by *Arkansas Historical Quarterly*. Reprinted with permission of the author and *Arkansas Historical Quarterly*.
*Mrs. Hobson is a retired bookkeeper.
Author's note: Reams have been written about the great flood of 1927. Newspapers reported the vast devastation and distress of this, the greatest natural disaster ever to hit the state of Arkansas.

In *The '27 Flood in Desha County,* Volume 2, Number 2 (1976), of the publications of the Desha County Historical Society, pages 4 through 21, judge Jim Merritt more than adequately covers the statistics of the 1927 flood.

Since there is little need for repetition of these well-known facts, this article will be concerned with the actual experiences of my family, some relatives and friends who survived the flood by camping out on the levee.

As I was not quite nine when the flood came, my memories, though vivid, are difficult to put in chronological order. Therefore, I want to thank my older sister, Edna, for her help in this direction; also for remembering some things which, naturally, were unimportant to a nine-year-old.

some five or six hundred yards from the bayou at this point. J. U. Fehr owned and operated the farm and his widowed mother and youngest sister, Lydia, resided about three-fourths of a mile south. The levee and bayou were only about two hundred yards apart. A fairly large house, barn, feed lot with other outbuildings, and a big vegetable garden comprised the Fehr home place.

We were about three miles, by sometimes impassable roads, from Kelso, where the school was located. Since the weather had been so bad, we had attended school very little during the entire term.

My immediate family in 1927 was Papa, Louis Edward Simpson, aged thirty-five. He was called Ed. There was Mama, Belle (Hubbard) Simpson, aged thirty-three; my older sister, Edna, aged fifteen; myself, Edythe, almost nine; and Ermal, who had had her sixth birthday the past November.

We were, however, just one branch of the Clan Simpson. Papa had five brothers and sisters and his father, Louis Henry Simpson, an irascible old Irishman, was seventy-three and very much alive. Papa's gentle, yet highly intelligent mother had died in 1911, less than a month after my parents' marriage. Grandma Simpson, who was half French, half Indian, had managed the prosperous farm of 360 acres which they owned in Lincoln County. She was the hub around which the boisterous, irresponsible Louis Henry and their children revolved. With her death, all stability was gone and it did not take long for Grandpa to run through the proceeds of the farm and livestock, which he sold. His two oldest sons, Papa and Uncle Charlie, along with his son-in-law, Uncle Lonnie McIlvoy, all helped spend a part of the money. Papa's weakness was whiskey, Uncle Charlie's was primarily gambling, although he also drank a little. Uncle Lonnie could take any of the vices or leave them. He just liked fun.

Papa and Uncle Charlie were the first of the family to move to the rowdy little town of Kelso. They made the move in the winter of 1920–1921. Uncle Charlie opened a small grocery, and Papa was a commercial fisherman and trapper. He loved the outdoors.

Uncle Charlie married Victoria McIlvoy, sister of Uncle Lonnie, who married Papa's oldest sister Belle. Uncle Charlie and Aunt Vick had three children: Cecil, a year older than I; Jewell, not quite two years younger than I; and Charleen, born in 1922. By 1927, Uncle Lonnie and Aunt Belle had Eunice, born 1915; Lester, born 1917; and Varnell, born 1921. These cousins were like my own brothers and sisters and I adored Cecil. It galled me that they were all double cousins while I was just a first cousin to them.

Papa's youngest brother married in 1923 a widow some years his senior; she had two daughters, by a previous marriage, and they fitted nicely into the Simpson-McIlvoy clan. Their names were Willie and Inez Murray. Willie was sixteen; Inez, fourteen. Uncle John and Aunt Cynthia had a daughter, Nettie Mae, who was three in 1927. Uncle John, strangely enough, had none of the vices of his two elder brothers, but he was lazy, and to the Simpsons and McIlvoys that was the ultimate sin. Papa's other sisters married and we were never as close to them as we were to Uncle Charlie's and Aunt Belle's families.

The Simpsons, of Irish ancestry from Grandpa and French and Indian from Grandma, were a wild, fun-loving crew. Quick to anger, quick to forgive. The Indian blood did not allow for forgetting. They were like generous, mischievous children. The McIlvoys, primarily of Scottish descent, though some were not as generous, all were as happy and carefree as the Simpsons. My mother, whose forebears were among the earliest in the settling of America, had in her ancestry, English, Scotch, probably some Indian, and even a bit of Spanish. She descended from some of the oldest settlers of Crawford and Harrison counties, Indiana. Papa delighted in calling her a Yankee, sometimes in a most derogatory manner. Mama was northern born and bred, but until the day she died, her heart belonged to the South.

I think my generation of Simpsons came into the world dancing and fighting. It may be that Kelso, during the twenties, was such an isolated community that anything which offered a diversion was welcomed, and we children were merely following the example of our fathers. Boys and girls learned early to fight; sex made no difference, and girls learned that boys often could be beaten in a wrestling match. These matches usually wound up in an all-out fight.

The only certain means of egress and regress at Kelso was by way of the Missouri Pacific Railroad. In good weather various dirt roads led into and out of the town. These roads, for the most part, were old Indian traces which had been widened to accommodate wagons and automobiles. One rode a train to McGehee, Helena, or Memphis. The route to Arkansas City was a dubious road along the berm of the levee. Therefore, Kelso was a fairly lawless little town in the 1920s. Most killings were unpremeditated, the result of quick tempers, abetted by moonshine. Inquests were held in the back of Uncle Charlie's store, presided over by the justice of the peace, and usually ended in acquittals. Dances, inquests, and irregular church meetings were all enjoyed.

My family had been living at Kelso in the old Varden house until late 1926, when H. E. Perkins needed the house for my Uncle Lonnie, whom he had persuaded to leave Lincoln County to farm for him. We were glad to have more of our kin among us, and were happy when J. U. Fehr offered us a house on his farm. He was "sweet" on my pretty sister, Edna, and wanted to get her away from the competition of Kelso youths. J. U. was named by his Swiss-born father, Conrad, his name being Joseph Ulrich. Mrs. Fehr could never pronounce Ulrich; she called him Oledge. He became known far and wide as Orage Fehr. As for our move, Papa found it most convenient. He was a latter-day Daniel Boone, never happy for long away from his beloved swamps and Mississippi River.

As spring came in we began to hear disturbing news of melting snow and ice on its way to the Mississippi via northern tributaries. All rivers were at flood stage. In April men began patrolling the levees on horseback. Papa and Orage did this every night. It was feared that Mississippians would slip across and dynamite our levee in order to relieve pressure on theirs. Probably Mississippi people were afraid of the same thing happening on their side of the river.

On the night of April 21, Papa and Orage rode up and awakened us with the news that the levee had broken on the Arkansas River above Yancopin. We later learned it had broken at Medford and at Pendleton. We could hear the waters roaring like an approaching tornado. Mama helped Ermal dress, yelling at me to hurry, but I couldn't find the shoes which I had worn all winter, nor the new patent leather ones I had gotten for Easter. Ermal and Edna knew where theirs were, but I had never been one to keep up with my belongings. I never had any order or neatness and so I was half under my bed still searching for my shoes when everyone was ready to go to the Fehr home. Mama yanked me up and pushed me out the door and I whined and grumbled about my shoes every step of the way.

When we had awakened Mrs. Fehr and Lydia, Orage's baby sister, everyone began packing things to take to the levee. I suppose Ermal, Lydia, and I helped pack some of the Mason jars of fruits and vegetables in boxes and tubs, but I remember that Ermal and Lydia, aged eight, were sound asleep in chairs, while I sat the whole night through, looking out the window. I remember the eerie sight of Edna and Orage, with a lantern in his boat, making trip after trip hauling chickens to the levee. But before that, before the ground had more than an inch or so of water, Mama and Mrs. Fehr went out to the garden and pulled up all the onions, cabbages, and carrots. Papa and Orage hauled by hand all the trunks, bedsprings, and table and cane bottomed chairs. They even carried a big chest of drawers to the levee. Stock was driven to the levee and feed carried out by boat for both chickens and cattle and horses. Maybe there were also hogs, but I don't recall any on the levee.

At some point during the long night, Papa and Orage must have gone up to our house to get Papa's rowboat and salvage Mama's Singer sewing machine, because both boats were used to move Mrs. Fehr's boxes and tubs of food and bed linens. I later learned that our beds were past saving when they got the sewing machine.

About the last thing accomplished in the Fehr home was the breakfast that Mama and Mrs. Fehr prepared on the big wood stove. It must have been eaten on the levee about daylight, but I can't recall eating it. I know that the water was about a foot deep in the house as the women waded around cooking that meal.

As day was breaking, we left the boats and straggled sleepily to the top of the levee which was to be our home for the time being. Our first day on the levee is a little bit hazy in my mind. I know that Papa and Orage got everything carried to the top of the levee and put up a couple of tent flies which Orage was fortunate enough to own. I suppose we children slept most of the day, while the grown-ups worked. Of course, the cows had to be milked and that chore fell to Mama and Mrs. Fehr.

These inventive women took an axe and chopped a large opening about three feet wide and four feet long in the side of the levee, about three or four feet from the top. It was deep enough for a good fire under the sheet of iron which they placed over it, with the outside end left open. This served as our cookstove. Biscuits and cornbread were baked in a covered Dutch oven, with a five-gallon lard can placed upside down over it. Since it was impossible to keep Ermal and me away from the water, we were given hoes and rakes to pull any wood which floated by onto the side of the levee. These boards and limbs soon dried in the hot sun and made fine firewood. After all those months of rain, the days were hot and dry. This was lucky for us; tents are miserable homes in wet weather.

Lydia, Ermal, and I spent hours on the side of the levee, watching debris float by in the strong currents. Corn and cotton cribs and logs floated by in a never-ending parade. Sometimes these small buildings were caught in the trees which lined the bayou bank and Papa and Orage took Orage's motor boat and pulled them to the levee. They came in handy for firewood. Once or twice a chicken house or a part of one floated by with a few bedraggled chickens clinging to the roof. I recall quite vividly once seeing a short log float by with a small red rooster that seemed frozen with fear on one end and on the other end, sharing the log, was a large coiled rattlesnake.

As no one had thought of saving a calendar, exact dates could not be determined with accuracy. For the first two or three days Papa and Orage went out in their boats, checking on isolated families and gathering news of our relatives and friends at Kelso. Uncle Charlie and Uncle John Simpson as well as Uncle Lonnie McIlvoy and their families were all safe in boxcars on the railroad at Yancopin. A few Kelso families were in boxcars near Kelso. Many residents had gone to higher ground, out near Drew County; others had managed to get to Cleveland, Mississippi, before the flood. Walter Cook, who lived down the levee about half a mile from the Fehrs, remained on his plantation until the night of the flood. Then he drove his Buick to the top of the levee in front of his house and it was home for himself, his wife, and five children. They stayed there two or three days on the levee before someone took them to McGehee, by boat, naturally, and they stayed in the second story of the Cook Building (their own building) on Main Street in McGehee.

As news filtered in, we began to get some idea of the devastation of the flood, and it was mind-boggling to me, a child of nine. We heard of some people who were rescued from roof tops; that the sheriff and his deputies had to pistol whip some backwoods people who insisted on clinging to their shanties, refusing to be rescued. There were rumors of a few drownings of people unknown to us.

One of the first things Mama insisted on—all water must be boiled before we drank it. We used the clear water on the river side of the levee and she insisted that the outhouse be some distance from camp and on the outside, or landward side of the levee, down near the water. Papa, who drank from horse tracks if no other water was available, scoffed at Mama's Yankee finickiness, as he called it. Secretly, I agreed with him. It was common practice for me to fall on my stomach and drink from a ditch or bayou, rather than go to the trouble of priming a pitcher pump or going to the house for a drink when thirsty.

Orage and Papa built shelves about four feet high on three sides of a frame and topped the small area with canvas. Mama and Mrs. Fehr used this to set crocks of milk on, to protect it from dogs and children. They covered the crocks with cheesecloth to keep out flies. I don't remember chickens or hogs causing any trouble; they must have been kept up the levee some distance from camp. We had to chase a cow or horse away from camp on a few occasions. Cows had a tendency to rub against the pole frame of the rude milk shelter. The churn had been salvaged and we had plenty of milk and butter. Thanks to the Fehrs, we fared lots better than most.

Papa had a fondness for whiskey, much to Mama's disgust, and he had numerous friends among the moonshiners. I suspect he spent a good bit of time that first week helping them salvage their whiskey. At any rate, he seemed always to be able to obtain it when he wanted it. Most whiskey stills on the Arkansas and Mississippi rivers were located in the area between the levees and the rivers, known as the swamps or big woods. Since Papa fished the lakes as well as the Mississippi and trapped in the swamps, he knew all the moonshiners. He was generous to a fault, always giving fish and raccoons to his friends. In turn, I imagine his moonshine cost him very little.

None of us, except Papa, were acquainted with the dirty, unkempt family that came straggling down the levee to our camp about the third day. They claimed to have saved nothing and had been sleeping on the grass of the levee the past few nights. There were six in the family: the father; mother; a tall unshaven young man of around thirty, a son, we figured, though we never knew for sure; two grown girls who were rather fat; and a younger boy with a small pinched-looking pale face. He had small darting eyes and I immediately thought of a rat. He was twelve, we later learned, but was not much taller than Lydia, who was taller than I. His small frame was in sharp contrast to the rest of his family. He wore homemade pants and suspenders, and a little black hat sat atop his greasy brown hair. He was so scrawny and ugly that I pitied him. I learned soon enough that my pity was misplaced.

This family showed up about sunset and they ate as if they were starving. The little boy, Hosey, out-ate all of them. I heard Mrs. Fehr asking Mama, in an unbelieving tone, "Where in the world is he putting it?" Mama just shook her head and set about cooking another supper for the rest of us.

The family, Papa said, was named Wilson; I never learned any of the others' names; but none of us could ever forget the obnoxious Hosey. The old man and his wife talked incessantly; the two over-sized girls whispered and giggled behind their hands, while the bearded older son sat in sullen silence. Hosey prowled. He poked his pointed little nose into everything. Everyone was yawning as it was way past our usual bedtime. Papa suggested to Mama that she fix beds for them. Mama and Mrs. Fehr looked helplessly at each other. The Wilsons made token protests, but made no move to leave, and my hospitable father insisted they must spend the night.

A couple of the beds had two mattresses and these were removed and shoved partly under our tent fly. I don't recall the exact sleeping arrangements, but I do know we were so crowded that it was miserable. Hosey had a cursing, crying fit in the middle of the night, keeping everyone awake for an hour. It seemed that one of the fat girls had rolled over on him. His family petted him and I knew Mama's hands fairly itched to spank him. She hated cursing and this boy could put a muleskinner to shame.

None of the Wilsons bothered to wash their faces and hands before sitting down to breakfast next morning. They again ate like hogs, and when the last crumb was devoured, every one of them pulled their lower lips out and filled them with snuff. They spat all around the table, until Mrs. Fehr tartly asked them to go elsewhere to spit their snuff. Hosey spat on Lydia, Ermal, and me, and when I slapped him, the fight started. I could not whip him alone and Ermal and Lydia preferred crying to fighting. The result was that he tormented us all day. He pushed us down the levee, pulled our hair, kicked us, and hit us, until in a rage I would slap him and again get the worst of it. Still, the Wilsons made no effort to continue their journey.

To feed the fourteen of us, Mama and Mrs. Fehr opened jars of vegetables, peeled potatoes and onions and put them into a well-scrubbed washtub and cooked the tub of soup. They carried the hot tub of soup and set it on the ground near the table to cool, warning us to keep away from it. Then they began the task of cooking enough cornbread for the lot of us. I saw Hosey bent over the tub of cooling soup and gave a yell, for he was slurping it up like a pig. Needless to say, no one but the Wilsons ate any soup. The Simpsons and Fehrs ate cornbread and milk for the noon meal, called dinner, and for supper, as well. Our unwanted guests ate that entire tub of soup in just two meals.

About halfway through supper, Hosey's mother looked up from her soup bowl and asked where he was. No one had seen him since I had caught him gobbling soup again about an hour before. He had raised his head long enough to watch slyly as I put my toads in the tent pole hole for the night. The wallowed-out space around the center tent pole made a nice place to keep the toads which Ermal and I loved so well. I didn't tell any of them anything, however. I was disgusted with the entire crew, especially Hosey. All the Wilsons had to search for the little varmint. When ordered by his mother to see if Hosey was in the toilet, his favorite hiding place, the bearded son gazed longingly at his soup and sullenly obeyed his mother. Although none of us could bear the sight of the disgusting little boy, we all set aside our milk and bread and followed the family down the levee, on the river side. The tents had already been searched. The mother and sisters were yelling his name and crying, sure now that he had drowned.

One of Hosey's sisters spotted his little black hat lying near the edge of the water and the women howled louder. Then one saw some bubbles twelve or fifteen feet out and that made it certain for them that he had drowned. Papa and Orage tried in vain to assure them that the bubbles could be caused by any number of things; they paid no attention. Mr. Wilson blew his nose loudly and led his weeping wife, the little hat clutched against her breast, up the levee. We followed. Papa and Orage were talking of rowing out aways to see if they could find his body, if he had, indeed, drowned. I whispered to Ermal that I hoped he had drowned and she looked at me as if I were a monster, which I was, of course, but I was an honest little monster. As everyone reached the top of the levee, I wondered aloud where we could find clean water to drink, now that Hosey's dead body would be rotting in the clear water we always used. Papa grinned, but Mama told me to shut my big mouth.

When that Wilson family reached camp, they wiped their eyes and finished their supper. In fact, I think the older son was already eating when the rest of the family reached the table. They ate all the soup. Just as they were taking their dip of snuff, Hosey raised the side of the Fehr tent and crawled out, a sly grin on his pinched little face. He had been hiding behind the chest of drawers and was so skinny that he hadn't made the slightest bulge in the tent. His parents and fat sisters all took turns kissing and petting him. His brother gave a disgusted grunt and turned his back on the smirking boy. I told him he'd better be glad he didn't belong to Mama or he would be glad to eat standing up for a week or so. When his mother began fretting because he'd missed supper, I told of seeing him slurping from the soup tub while I was putting my toads to bed. He gave me an evil look, but his mother snatched up a pitcher of milk from our table and he drank it straight from the pitcher.

Ermal and I had always played with toads, turtles, beetles, and other bugs. So did our cousins. Lydia refused to touch a toad, claiming they caused warts, but I pointed out to her, that her hands were covered with warts, while we had only a few. Mrs. Fehr had given Ermal and me a few scraps of cloth and we tore strips of it to tie around our toads to identify them. These little toads, which we had found hiding under bedsprings and trunks, made wonderful pets. I had nine and Ermal had found six. Lydia sat and held her doll, shuddering as we fondled our toads. I longed to slip one down her collar, but I knew she'd kill it in her frenzied fear. I never cared much for dolls as they weren't alive. Dolls which Ermal and I had received during past Christmases had seldom lasted a week. If they had hair, I set up a barbershop, cutting as long as the hair lasted. Rubber dolls were unheard of, and dolls of the twenties were not washable. I soon tired of dressing and undressing them and invariably attempted to bathe them. Ermal's howls when I ruined her dolls caused me to get many a switching; therefore, I had no great fondness for dolls. Toads, I loved.

After gobbling the milk, Hosey grew petulant, pushing his mother and sisters away with horrible curses. Our mothers sent Lydia, Ermal, and me to bed. Orage and Edna took their usual nightly stroll and as they passed our tent, I heard him tell her that he'd see to it that the Wilsons left the next day, that he was borrowing a larger inboard from A. C. Zellner to go to Arkansas City for Red Cross supplies, and would deposit the Wilsons up the levee where they claimed to have friends. He called her "honey." I wished, meanly, that Mama could have heard that endearment. However, although eavesdropping was one of my nasty little habits, tattling was not. Edna had long since broken me of tale-bearing by a few sharp slaps on my jaws. I thought sleepily that it would be up to me to break Ermal of her tattling. This reminded me of the look on her face when I had told her I hoped Hosey had drowned, and I knew she would tell Mama on me. Mama was always fair, but she was strict.

Orage had already gone for Mr. Zellner's boat when I got up the next morning. The Wilson family were already taking their after-breakfast snuff. Mama, Mrs. Fehr, and Edna were washing dishes. Hosey was not in sight. After Ermal and I had eaten, we went back inside our tent to take our toads from their hole, but they were all gone. We searched under everything we could lift or move and finally concluded they had joined some other toads and had gone elsewhere. Just as we had given up, we heard the sound of a boat. It was Orage returning and we started down the side of the levee to look the big boat over. Hosey was sitting on the side of the levee, a triumphant expression on his grimy face. We soon knew the reason for his satisfaction.

Our poor little fat toads lay just below him on the side of the levee and they had all been stomped to death. Ermal and I wasted no time in mourning them; we tackled Hosey before he could get away and while Ermal pulled at his greasy hair, I used my fists, first on both his beady eyes, then his nose and mouth. Suddenly, he let out an unearthly scream, twisting his body so that I was thrown off his chest, on which I had been sitting astride as I punched his face. I looked around to find that the timid Lydia, who wouldn't touch a toad, had tossed her doll to the ground and had her rather long, protruding teeth fastened to one of Hosey's skinny shanks. I made a silent vow, at that moment, I'd never again bother a doll of Lydia's. At the same time, I realized the agony that bite was causing Hosey. I had been bitten a time or two by Lydia and knew the pain those teeth could inflict.

I suppose Hosey's mother and sisters rescued him from us. I remember his howls as he sat on the levee, looking at the blood oozing from the deep indentures made by Lydia's teeth. When he raised his head, I noted with satisfaction, his cut lip, his eyes, both of which would be blue-black and half-closed by tomorrow, and his pointed little nose, already beginning to swell. I looked at Ermal and we both grinned. She whispered to me that I was not to worry, she wouldn't tell Mama what I had said the night before. I was surprised to find Mama smiling at us, so were Edna and Mrs. Fehr, while Orage, still in the boat, was laughing so hard he was almost crying. Papa was hard to figure. He often threatened us with dire punishments, but never carried them out. He was openly pleased with his two youngest offspring for giving this twelve-year-old boy a shellacking; much more pleased than when one of us got

A's on our report cards. I think he liked us best when we acted like the rowdy tomboys we were.

Orage wasted no time in loading the Wilsons in the boat to take them to their original destination down river. And the Wilsons wasted no time in thanking us for their two nights' lodging and for all the food they had consumed. When they were rounding the bend in the levee, Papa said he didn't envy Orage having to ride downwind of the smelly bunch; how they were a crew of ungrateful moochers, and he would have said more, but Mama tartly reminded him that he was the one who had given them a big welcome, and to food and beds which were not his to give. She asked him where his own family would be now if it were not for the generosity of Orage and his mother. He got in his boat and went fishing.

By this time, we must have been on the levee a week. I know our house had washed away and had been battered apart against the big trees of the bayou. Mrs. Fehr's house had also been washed off its blocks and was lodged against the trees along the bayou, but it was not torn up as ours was. They could use it again after the flood.

When Orage returned from Arkansas City, he said the levee, which fronted the town, was just one long line of tent dwellers. He said the people were taking it all in good spirits and that the Red Cross had helped a lot. He laughed, when asked about the Wilsons, saying that they seemed to be about as welcome as an epidemic of smallpox. He would give the Lucca Landing settlement a wide berth when he next passed it.

The Red Cross had furnished tinned food, blankets, meal and flour and other food. Mrs. Fehr's supply of meal and flour had been almost depleted by the huge appetites of the Wilson family. Orage also got two tents. If I had ever before eaten pork and beans, I did not remember it, and I made a pig of myself, eating them at supper. After supper, I announced that when I married, I'd have pork and beans for every meal. We were all in much better spirits since the Wilsons were gone. It had been a busy day for Mama, Mrs. Fehr, and Edna. They had washed and dried all bed linens and blankets that had been used by the filthy Wilsons. They sunned mattresses and dried everything they washed by spreading it in the grass and clover on the side of the levee.

I think it was the next day that Orage and Papa went to Yancopin to see how our relatives were faring and to see if any of them wanted to come to us. They all came; a couple came back with Orage, the balance came in larger boats. What a reunion we had! Days were never long enough for us children; we whooped and hollered all day and as far into the night as we were allowed. We found more toads and not one of us would knowingly harm a toad. Lydia still refused to touch one. She sat on the sidelines, holding her doll, as we played with our toads or teased beetles. We tried in vain to find crawfish and turtles. Occasionally, we found a terrapin and teased it awhile, but we were afraid of them. We had been warned that if one bit you, it wouldn't let go until it thundered. We had dreadful fears of having to go for days with one of our fingers in a terrapin's teeth.

Aunt Belle and Uncle Lonnie McIlvoy were well-matched. He was a big husky man and she was tiny and pretty. They and their three children were a happy-go-lucky group. They enjoyed life more than any family I've ever known. They worked hard and played hard. I envied my McIlvoy cousins the lack of discipline they enjoyed. Aunt Belle seldom punished one of them, although they were as bad as the rest of us. The McIlvoys were more superstitious than any of us, yet all the Simpson-McIlvoy clan were superstitious. Aunt Cynthia, Uncle John's wife, was a first cousin to Uncle Lonnie and Aunt Vick; so she, too, was superstitious.

I recall the grown-ups sitting around campfires in the late April and early May nights, telling of weird, strange happenings. They often told of the ghostly happenings that revolved around an uncle of Uncle Lonnie, his sister, Aunt Vick, and Aunt Cynthia. According to all, this man, Uncle Bud Thorne, was ghost-ridden because he was an evil old man. Everyone, except Mama and the Fehrs, seemed to have witnessed psychic phenomena, at one time or another, while in the presence of Uncle Bud. I can recall how he looked, and the fear I felt when I saw him. He was old and very tall and gaunt, with a gray handlebar mustache over long tobacco-stained teeth. I must have seen him, since Edna and Aunt Belle have both assured me that my description fitted him.

Uncle Lonnie told of riding horseback with Uncle Bud from Dumas to the community of Dark Corner in Lincoln County where the Simpsons and McIlvoys lived at that time. He claimed to have heard a dragging sound as they passed a cemetery, but could see nothing. The old man predicted the occurrence of some dire event because he could see a coffin following their horses. Then Uncle Bud claimed a black dog, which Uncle Lonnie never saw, was following them home. When the old man slashed at it with a switch, Uncle Lonnie said he heard it yelp. That same night Uncle Bud's nephew, who was Aunt Cynthia's brother, was shot and killed in Dumas as a result of a quarrel.

Papa, not to be outdone, told of spending a night with Uncle Bud, and of being awakened by the sound of a baby crying on the floor near the bed. Aunt Belle said no one liked his spending the night in their homes because all manner of strange noises were likely to be heard. The coffee mill would start grinding, the sounds keeping everyone awake. As these eerie tales were recounted, we children would crowd closer, looking over our shoulders toward the dark water on either side of us. Lester usually wound up almost in the fire, his eyes wide with fear.

Some nights there was singing. No one played any musical instrument, but all loved to sing. Aunt Vick always sang "It's a Long Way to Tipperary." Everyone joined in. Papa's favorite was "Red River Valley." He had a fairly good voice for singing. We children always got into the spirit of things, but as we sang, we danced. Lydia, when she was persuaded to lay aside her doll and join us in our games and dancing, usually got hurt and started crying. We were rough and our play was likely as not to turn into a free-for-all fight. We took our lumps and jumped back into the fray.

Cecil, Uncle Charlie's and Aunt Vick's eldest, was quieter than any of us and only fought when forced to do so. Lester, a small bantam rooster, often dared Cecil to wrestle him and the contest always ended with Lester getting pinned to the ground and cursing Cecil; this, Cecil would not tolerate, and Lester received the shellacking he deserved. Inez Murray, Aunt Cynthia's second daughter, at fourteen, was above our childish rough-and-tumble games, yet she played some games with us. Her sister, Willie, at sixteen, was interested in boys and young men; Orage was the only one nearby and Edna had him hogtied. Edna wrestled with us sometimes when her beau was not around. She was often as not riding around with him in his motorboat.

With Red Cross provisions, since there were now so many of us, each family unit cooked and ate at its own camp. When Papa and Uncle John caught fish, there was a communal fish fry. Uncle Charlie had saved some of his stock of canned goods from his store. One of the other stores at Kelso, Cook Brothers store, had lost its entire stock to looters in the first day or two of the flood.

The days were never long enough for us kids. We had a ball. We were never bored or lonely. I know our parents worried about one of us drowning; at least Mama and Aunt Vick worried. They also worried about trying to rebuild and clean the mud-caked homes when the flood receded. Papa didn't worry; he had it all figured out. We would just continue living in tents until someone had a vacant house. Mama said little, yet she looked far from happy at the prospect of living indefinitely in a tent.

Aunt Vick loved to walk and one day she took me with her down the levee to visit Papa's youngest sister Kate, who was camping with her husband and his parents, the Burnetts. As we approached a sharp bend in the levee, we could see men working furiously, sandbagging the levee. The old Amos Bayou levee, built just prior to the Civil War, joined the Mississippi River levee at this point. The old levee had been washed into and the current was so swift as it hit the lower bend of the main levee, they were fearful of its being cut into. This was at Cook's Ramp. We watched awhile and walked on. The Walter Cook home, built on a slight rise just at the lower bend of the levee, was being hit hard by the rushing current. This must have been shortly after Aunt Vick and the rest had come from Yancopin, since the water was still rising. We watched as the current took out chunks of bricks from the foundation. Later, the white-frame plantation home was washed from its site, but was retrieved and used after the waters receded. The Burnetts fared very well. They were camped on the levee at Cook's Mound in a long shack built of salvaged planks.

As the weather grew hotter, most of the Simpson-McIlvoy nightly get-togethers were at first one tent or another and without the campfire. Kerosene lamps or lanterns were lighted and tent flaps rolled up in dry weather. I don't recall us having to use mosquito nets, or bars, as we called them; therefore, those balmy nights were comfortable. We sat around on beds, listening to the grown-ups talk. If we grew bored, we usually scuffled about like puppies on the side of the levee. We liked best the ghost stories and the funny incidents of past Simpson-McIlvoy history. When the Civil War was rehashed, we grew bored. It was still a raw thorn in the side to most Southerners. Grandpa, who was only eight or nine when it ended, claimed to be an authority on the war. He grew very vehement in his condemnation of Yankee soldiers. Most of his bitterness about the war probably stemmed from the fact that it left him orphaned at a very early age. His youthful father marched off to serve the CSA and was never heard from again. Deprivations caused by Federal troops, who confiscated food needed by Southerners to feed their undernourished families, no doubt caused the death of his young mother before 1870. I suppose I listened to this bitter talk more than I realized at the time. Abraham Lincoln was spoken of in the basest terms. I absorbed these hatreds felt by everyone in the area in the 1920s. (This was to later get me in hot water; for to the North, Abraham Lincoln was almost a god.)

Sometimes our families got into heated arguments; not about the Civil War, for they were all of one mind regarding that. Most times, they couldn't remember, the next day, what the disagreement had been about. But once in a while these quarrels led to a few blows being exchanged. They would be in heated argument one moment; the next, they were laughing and talking. They might squabble amongst themselves, but closed ranks at any outside threat to one of them. We children were like our parents in this respect.

Mama and Papa were in disagreement, and she kept it from Ermal and me as long as possible. But our clan respected no one's privacy. What affected one, affected all. Mama had talked to Edna, Aunt Vick, and Aunt Belle about her intention to go to Indiana to her parents, and soon everyone in camp was offering opinions. Although she was loved as a sister by all, the consensus was that she should go and one and all told Papa this. He was humble and pleading, then petulant and sulky, by turns. He also began drinking more than usual, even though I'm sure he knew that his drinking was a part of Mama's reason for leaving. She had devoted seventeen years to the task of helping him grow up, and, I suppose, she had decided it was a lost cause.

On May 18, Mama worked all day, putting the tent in order, washing and drying all clothes and bed linens. Then she washed her waist-length black hair. Orage bought her sewing machine; that was to pay our train fare. He had gone up the levee to make arrangements for Mr. Andrew Wargo to take us to Rosedale, Mississippi. Mama let Ermal and me play with our cousins until almost dark, then, after supper, we got the scrubbing of our lives and were told there would be no more rolling around on the levee for us.

That night everyone gathered at our tent. It was the quietest evening we spent on the levee. Long silences prevailed. Even used to giggling and acting silly as we children were, we now sat in silence, as if we were strangers. Once or twice, Aunt Vick and Aunt Belle started to say something and began crying; Uncle Lonnie, Uncle John, and Uncle Charlie did an extraordinary amount of clearing of throats and blowing of noses. Jewell and Eunice kept hugging me and crying a little, too. Papa, a little the worse for drinking, began singing "Red River Valley," looking soulfully at Mama. She tried not to look at him. I think she was relieved when everyone left and we could go to bed. I could still hear Papa murmuring to her as I fell asleep.

Mama was up very early the next morning, feeding us, then washing up the dishes. Also, very early, everyone was gathered around our tent. Mrs. Fehr brought a dress which belonged to her married daughter for me to wear on the trip. It was a pretty, light green plaid dress of soft cotton. It was much too big. It came well below my calves and I hated myself as I looked down at my bare brown feet below the long dress. I began griping about having no shoes to wear on the train and Mama told me that if I would just be quiet, she'd buy me shoes in Rosedale. I suppose that between my grumbling and Papa's pleading, she was half out of her mind.

I had mixed feelings about this move to Indiana. I didn't know how I'd survive without Cecil, Jewell, Eunice, and Lester, but on the other hand, the unknown was an adventure, a challenge, and this I looked forward to with gusto. Mama had warned me that her parents were very religious and the fighting and rather salty language I sometimes used would not be tolerated. Since she always took a switch to me when a curse word slipped out, I didn't see any worse punishment that my grandparents could dole out, short of killing me. Also, as Lester had pointed out, I would miss the typhoid shots which were due any day now. Mama had also said there was no malaria in Indiana; therefore, no more quinine or that nasty Groves chill tonic.

Soon we were bidding goodbye to our kinfolk and Mrs. Fehr and Lydia, and were boarding Orage's boat for the trip to Wargo's Landing. The water on the river side of the levee was calm as we held near the levee. When we had to swing out to go around a dike, it was very swift. I thought we would surely be swamped while going around those dikes.

Mr. Andrew Wargo, Sr., his wife, Victoria Bains Wargo, and three sons, Tim, Percy, and Andrew, Jr., were all standing on the levee as we came up alongside the large inboard with its high sides which would take us to Rosedale. Mr. Wargo and his grown son, Tim, got in the large boat and started it as Papa and Orage helped us to board it. Papa wiped tears and kissed all of us goodbye. Orage kissed Edna before helping her in the boat. I cast a swift look at Mama and was amazed to see her smiling at them.

I don't mind admitting that I was scared to death part of the time on that trip. When we reached the point where the Arkansas and White rivers entered the Mississippi, for some miles there was not a tree top to be seen. It was like an ocean. When I looked over the side, I saw huge whirlpools, some fifty to seventy-five feet across. The whirling, sucking water seemed a bottomless vortex. Mama's arm would tighten around my shoulder and she would smile reassuringly, but I knew she was scared. She was always afraid of water. To Mr. Wargo and Tim, this was just a trip. They expertly piloted the twenty-foot boat around the outer edges of those whirlpools and deposited us safely in Rosedale, Mississippi. There was no time to buy my shoes so I rode barefoot to Cleveland, Mississippi, griping all the way.

We had a lay-over in Cleveland and I got the ugliest pair of brown sandals in the store. The clerk was rather put out because she had to wipe my feet with a damp cloth before I tried them on. I heard her tell the manager we were refugees, a word I had never heard before. We received a discount because we were refugees, but as I marched out of that store, I looked quickly at Mama; she wasn't watching me, so I turned at the door and stuck my tongue out at the clerk.

As we climbed aboard the train in Cleveland, heading north, I squared my thin shoulders, unafraid of the future—after all, I was a big girl now; I would be nine years old tomorrow when we reached Indiana.

1980

Looking back after almost fifty-three years, I feel it is appropriate to tell of some changes time has wrought since May 19, 1927.

First, my mother divorced my father in 1928. Orage came to Indiana for Edna; they were married March 12, 1928, and returned to Kelso. They celebrated their Golden Wedding Anniversary in 1978. My mother lived only seven years after reaching Indiana. She died January 29, 1934, at the age of forty. Ermal and I returned to Kelso in May 1934 to make our home with Edna and Orage until we married.

Grandpa Simpson died in 1930; Papa died July 27, 1942; Aunt Vick died in December 1945; Uncle Charlie, Uncle John, Uncle Lonnie, and Aunt Cynthia are all dead. Uncle John's daughter, Nettie Mae, was killed in an automobile accident in 1967. Just before Christmas in 1979, Lester McIlvoy was killed by a truck in Port Gibson, Mississippi.

Of the older generation of the Simpson-McIlvoy clan, only two remain: Papa's oldest sister, Aunt Belle McIlvoy, aged eighty-two, and his youngest sister, Aunt Kate Burnett, aged about seventy-four.

Geary Hobson

Geary Hobson (Cherokee–Arkansas Quapaw) was born in Chicot County, Arkansas, on June 12, 1941. He enlisted in the U.S. Marines a day after his high-school graduation and served in the early part of the Vietnam War. He holds B.A. and M.A. degrees from Arizona State University and a Ph.D. from the University of New Mexico. Hobson is the editor of *The Remembered Earth*: *An Anthology of Contemporary Native American Literature* (1979) and the author of *Deer Hunting* & *Other Poems* (1990) and a novel, *The Last of the Ofos* (2000). He also has at present three more books in press, awaiting publication. He has been a professor of Native American literature at the University of Oklahoma since 1988. In 2003, Hobson received the Lifetime Achievement Award from the Native Writers' Circle of the Americas.

From *The Last of the Ofos*

In the Name of Science

One day, while I was skinning some coons by my back door, I heard my two dogs bark in that way they got to let me know a stranger is coming. I ducked around to the front of the house to see who it be, and it was this old white man dressed in a brown suit and toting a brown leather briefcase. He was tall and thin, with a full head of white-gray hair and he had a slight stoop to him. We nodded to each other and then he say, real gentlemanly and in a voice that showed right away he wudn't no Louisiana man, "Do I have the honor of addressing Thomas Darko?"

"Yes," I say. "I am Thomas Darko."

"Mr. Darko, I am Dr. William Allerton Payne, of the Smithsonian Institution in Washington, D.C.," he said. Then he added, with a sad but friendly smile, "We had the honor of meeting one another many years ago, but I expect you probably don't recall it."

"No, sir," I say. "I can't say as I do." And it was true. l couldn't recall ever seeing this feller before, much less meet him.

"Well, I'm not surprised. You were a very small boy then. I was here visiting your parents and grandfather—please pardon the possible rudeness in my mentioning of them—I was visiting them, as I say, as well as meeting numerous Biloxi and Tunica folks along with your Ofo relatives."

"Well, yes, sir," I say. "That mus' all been a long time ago. All my folks, sir, have all passed on."

"Yes, I know, Mr. Darko. That is why I'm here. And, please, will you accept my condolences on their behalf?"

I nodded my head for his respect.

He went on to tell me that he was representing the Smithsonian in a new program they was setting up having to do with Indian languages. He say they was recording languages with tape recorders, making records and dictionaries and such, and that was why he come to see me.

"You are, by all accounts, Mr. Darko," he said, "the last speaker of the Ofo language."

Now I knowed nobody else around Sherrillton talked Ofo, not since Mama and them all got killed in that truck wreck, but I knowed in a vague way of some other relatives living away from Sherrillton who I thought still might talk it.

"Well, now, sir," I said, "they's my Aunt Gustine, over at Shreveport, and all her kids. What about them?"

"I'm sorry to say, sir," Dr. Payne said, "your Aunt Augustine passed away ten years ago and apparently none of her four children grew up learning any of the Ofo language at all." He paused and then added, "I'm sorry, sir. I perceive you had not heard of your aunt's death?"

"No, I never," I said. "I appreciate you telling me."

"I certainly didn't intend to be simply the harbinger of sad tidings," he said. "I hope I haven't offended you by my intrusiveness."

"No, sir," I said. "I am not at all offended, and I be thankful for your words." Then I thought to add, "What about my cousin Rejean LeGarde over in Longview, Texas? I knowed he used to know some Ofo, but not a lot."

Dr. Payne ducked his head slightly and coughed, then he say "Again, I'm sorry to say, Mr. LeGarde passed on about five years ago."

I set there a minute, thinking.

"Then I am all alone."

"Yes, it would appear so, sir. You are the last of the Ofos."

Then he begged my pardon and ast to be excused while he went back to his car, he say, to git something he forgit to bring with him. Instead, I think he jist want to give me some time to myself. Cause when he come back in about five minutes, I never seen anything he bring back with him, and he left that brown leather briefcase on my front door step. Anyhow, I appreciated his thoughtfulness, and while he was gone I thought about all of them now gone—Mama, Papa, Rejean, Aunt Gustine, Grandpapa Arceneaux, and all my brothers and sisters—and I spect I felt more than ever before like a lonesome pine tree. But when Dr. Payne come back, I remember my manners and I invite him in for some coffee or ice tea. He say thanks much, he would like some ice tea, say he too old to drank coffee in the late part of the day, but he say he love ice tea. Me, too. Especially since I give up whiskey-drinking some time back, why, ice tea, with a lot of sugar in it, made up for it, I spect.

I got him to stay to supper. I put some fresh coon meat in a stew I had slow-cooking on my kitchen stove, made a pan of corn bread, and we had more ice tea. In the meantime, Dr. Payne told me about the purpose of his visit. Seem like he wanted me to come to Washington, D.C., for a while to help preserve the Ofo language on records and help them make a dictionary. I give it some thought, liked the idea of traveling again, but I wondered about the good of saving a language on records and in a dictionary when they wudn't nobody but me left to talk it. He say that In the Name of Science was the reason, almost like he was talking about a church or something. He say I would git paid good, have my hotel paid for, too, and would be contributing to Science. He say for me to mull it over and let him know in the morning. I invited him to stay the night, but he say he already have a hotel room in Alexandria and would come back in the morning. But before he left, he showed me a book he dug out of that brown leather briefcase, and in it they was a picture of my Mama and Papa and all of us younguns, and they was Grandpapa Arceneaux, too. Dr. Payne told me how he taken that picture when he visit in 1909 when he first come to our country as a young scholar of our ways. Now, I never had no pictures of any of my family at all, and seeing them all like this was a little too much for me. They was Papa, wearing a white shirt all buttoned up to the neck and wearing his little-bitty black dribbly moustache, and Mama, a lot taller than him, wearing a white blouse with long sleeves and all buttoned up to the neck, too, and her hair in a bun, Grandpapa in dark overalls and a ragged suit coat, my spindly brothers Leland and Andrew and Baptiste Junior, and my twin sisters Martha and Marie. Dr. Payne pointed out the two littlest kids in the picture, and they was me and my little sister Camille. In the picture I was a scrawny little duck-egg-looking thang, all eyes and a bowl-over-the-head hair-cut and dark-skinned as a dirt-dauber, and Camille was a fat little two-year-old holding onto a cornshuck doll. Before he left to go back to his hotel room, Dr. Payne give me the book with the picture in it, told me it was mine to keep, and that night I read some of it. It was about little groups of Indian people in places like Louisiana and Arkansas and Texas—where they wudn't sposed to be no Indian people left. They was even a picture of John Desriusseaux—or Old Man Jack Darrysaw, as people call him—and one of Jed Thompson, two of the

Quapaw people I meet years ago in Arkansas. Sesostre Youchicant, a long-time Tunica chief, was there, too, and Chief Volcine Chiki and Chief Eli Barbry, what was also Chiefs of the Tunicas, too. I already knowed what I would tell Dr. Payne in the morning.

The Folks Left Out of the Photographs

From the mid-1880s until her death in 1911, a remarkable Indian woman held together not only her own immediate family but several other closely bound relatives and their families on a 360-acre domain, all in disregard of and in obliviousness to Arkansas law, which at the time precluded women of any race from being property owners. Within a few years after this women's passing, the land was quickly lost through the drinking and gambling of her white widowed husband and her two Chicot sons, and the family, and all the assorted cousins, were all dispersed to other areas of the countryside in Lincoln and Desha counties.

It is now well more than eighty years since the woman's death, but her personality is still present in stories that are told by the daughters and sons of her children and of her former neighbors. "She was a strong woman," "a tall, hard-working woman who kept her family together," "she was the caretaker of her people"—these are some of the summarizing statements that are still made of her.

This woman was my great-grandmother, and I, of course, never met her since she died thirty years before I was born. However, because of the things I always heard about her while I was growing up, and my reflections of her over all the intervening years, I often feel as if I had had the privilege of being in her presence, of having known her.

Adding to her near-legendary status in our part of the country is the rather surprising elusiveness of her actual identity. In the written records—census reports from every decade of her life, county tax records, a marriage record—her name is virtually myriad. She is rendered variously as Marguerite Jardelas (and all its variant spellings: Jirdelas, Jardela, Gurdlain, Jurdlain, Judlow), Margaret Pauley, Eliza Pauley, Lizzy May, and Margaret E. Simpson (as it is today on her tombstone in the Dark Corner Cemetery in Lincoln County, Arkansas). The land she held together was both part of the former Quapaw Reservation, extant from 1817 to 1833, and two Spanish land-grants which Marguerite inherited from *her* great-grandparents, Pierre Jardelas and his wife, Marie Languedoc. Many of their descendants, and my relatives, yet retain small portions of that land, and other former tribal lands in the area, not as legally franchised Quapaws, but as everyday run-of-the-mill Arkansas residents.

In the text of *Letters and Notes on the Manners, Customs and Conditions of Native American Indians*, George Catlin presents an incredible fabrication of the famed Indian scout Pierre Beatte as vehemently protesting Washington Irving's labeling him with that horrible epithet, "half-breed," in *A Tour on the Prairies*. Beatte, or Alexis Pierre Billet, had been Irving's and Commissioner Henry L. Ellsworth's guide on the now-famous month-long sashay they made into the heart of Indian Territory (now eastern Oklahoma) in the fall of 1832. Beatte was also on the ill-fated Leavenworth Expedition through the same lands and over into western Oklahoma in 1834. Catlin doesn't say where or how Beatte learned of Irving's having stigmatized him as such—only that he was reportedly upset about it.

What continually intrigues me about the Beatte-Irving-Catlin exchange is the man Beatte himself. Irving describes him in *A Tour* as "cold and laconic . . . unprepossessing," and "like all halfbreeds," as "distrust(ful) . . . and of an uncertain and faithless race." Catlin, on the other hand, doesn't describe Beatte at all, only his state of disgruntlement. This, to me, is rather utterly amazing, given that Catlin was a painter. In another consideration, given Catlin's rationale, it isn't surprising. Catlin tells us he was seeking Indians to paint, and he, unlike Irving, had determined that Beatte wasn't an Indian; indeed, he even has Beatte vehemently insisting on his Frenchness while protesting Irving's labeling him an Indian, or even worse, a "half-breed."

Many other writers later erroneously call Beatte a "Frenchmen," "an Osage," an "Osage half-breed," etc., without exploring the background of the man himself. Born around 1796, of mixed-blood Quapaw and French parents, he was the nephew and namesake of Alexis Jardelas, a voyageur operating out of Arkansas Post and La Petite Roche, who in turn was the grandfather of Marguerite Jardelas (aka, Lizzy May, Margaret Simpson).

While Beatte may not have been a half-blood, speaking strictly in terms of blood quantum, he was in effect a Metis, a mixed-blood, a Chicot. While neither of his parents was, strictly speaking, completely French nor full-blood Indian, they were both members of a Chicot community that had existed for decades, and still does in certain families in the shadows of latecomer whites in their home country.

And, to me, this is the crux of the matter. Two people, of inestimable value and importance to their people and their times—one known rather extensively in written history, and the other in local legendry—are the undiminished repositories of their people's culture, today as well as in their own times. Yet there is not a single painting, charcoal or pencil sketch, daguerreotype, photograph—no likeness whatsoever of any known sort of either of them in existence. Both are, indeed, products of erasure. It is not only true for them, but for the entirety of the Quapaw people who remained in Arkansas after the tribal removal to Oklahoma in the 1830s and well into the nineteen-teens. For eighty years or so, these people were never photographed by the ethnologically curious, and it was not until the 1920s that any of them could afford to sit for a photographer or to even purchase the standard cheap Kodak cameras of the day.

I have written in another context, an autobiographical essay entitled "I Am From People Who Have Always Been Lied About," of how our folks have been erased from Arkansas, and American, history. I use the term "enwhitened" in the essay rather than "erasure," but no matter the term, the overall deadening effects of cultural genocide are the same. In the American South, Indian people, mixed-bloods as well as full-bloods, who elected to remain in their traditional homelands, no matter the reasons, were designated by American (i.e., white) census-takers and public officials as legally white—not so that such Indian remainees might have better access to the white world but rather to facilitate these people's further disenfranchisement and exploitation. This happened universally throughout the American South and also throughout other areas of the country where enclaves of Indian people persisted. When Indian people were not legally Indian, then they were not subject to treaty stipulations; it was therefore easier for whites to dispossess these "off-whites" of their holdings than it was to deal with people protected by the sovereignty of treaty agreements.

From the 1850s, with the advent of the daguerreotype, until the third decade of the twentieth century, photographs of Indian people outside the Plains, the Southwest, and the Northwest are relatively rare. Frank A. Rinehart, William S. Soule, and other photographers of the era not only had no interest in Indian people outside the Plains area, but also, as a rule, dismissed the Indian people of Indian Territory. These Indians, many citizens of the Five Civilized Tribes, were too "white man–looking" for the cameras.

According to many white people of the time, Indianness, in the late nineteenth century and well up into the twentieth century—the old Vanishing American era—was determined in large part by one's appearance. Therefore, the numerous daguerreotypes, tintypes, paintings, etchings, sketches, and photographs played a major role in fostering the public images of Indians that are still to this day exasperatedly adhered to by Hollywood and by most of the American populace.

The image of an Indian warrior mounted on horseback; concretized to eternal form by Edward S. Curtis, Frank A. Rinehart, William S. Prettyman, William H. Jackson, William S. Soule, and L. A. Huffman, is the enduring image of an Indian for most Americans. Prettyman, noted for his striking photographs of Plains Indians in the Cherokee Outlet and in Oklahoma Territory in the decade before Oklahoma statehood, was reportedly rather vocal in his lack of interest in photographing Indians in Indian Territory. Indians wearing homespun britches and dresses, Mother Hubbard bonnets, black broadcloth suits, beards and moustaches and spectacles, or standing behind plows and cash registers, were totally outside his view of who or what an Indian should be. What is remarkable is how many other photographers held the same view, as well as Americans in general, who were locked into such images. What is even more remarkable is how these views and attitudes persist even to this day.

The remnant Quapaws of Arkansas between 1833 and 1910 are by no means the only Indian people left out of the photographs of the day. Quite simply, off-whites in North Carolina and Alabama and South Carolina and Louisiana and Missouri and Kentucky contain little or no fascination for American whites looking for Sitting Bull staring straightforwardly at the camera, or Cheyenne men on horseback framed against a sepia-toned sunset, or warbonneted Crows preparing for the next treaty parley. Nor will one find very many photos of remnant New England Indians during the same era, and the same can be said for the Ohio Valley country—Ohio, West Virginia, Indiana, Illinois, Northern Kentucky—even though there were, by most accounts, thousands of people more Indian than anything else in their racial make-up but generally disguised to others, and often to themselves, as whites or blacks.

The juxtaposition of the public notion of the Plains Indians being the coinage by which all other Indians are judged and compared, and Indian folks who were enwhitened (and sometimes enblackened), can be seen quite strikingly when one examines the life and career of a very public Indian of the day—Buffalo Child Long Lance. Long Lance (1890–1932) claimed in a purported autobiography, entitled quite simply *Long Lance* (1928), that he was a traditional Kainai (or Blood) chief and tribal member from the Blood Reserve in Alberta. The "life story" recounts the early days of the reserve's establishment, many stories of former Blood warriors and chiefs of warfare and buffalo hunting, of traditional tribal folk legends and tales, and of Long Lance learning his place in this world as he grows up in it. Long Lance went on, in the 1920s, to make several Hollywood movies and lent his name and support to various Indian causes.

Following his suicide, it became known that he was not a traditional Blood Indian at all. Rather, he was in reality Sylvester J. Long, a mixed-blood (i.e., Lumbee-black-white) man from North Carolina, who had determined early in his life to pass for Indian. He invented an entirely new tribal and cultural background for himself. Ironically, considering the rather pedestrian and second-rate quality of *Long Lance*, reworked as it is from Long Lance/Long's readings of Frank Linderman and George Bird Grinnell, in light of the author's actual mixed-blood North Carolina origins, one can't help but think that had he instead written his *real* life story, recounting his *real* origins, how much more valuable to students of Indian culture it would have been than the rather redundant book he wrote.

And this is the heart of the matter, the curdle on top of the cream that is Plains artifice suffused by literature, movies, photographs, etc., that, considering the very real dearth of data on Lumbee and other mixed peoples in the Carolinas during the Vanishing American era, the reader was instead served merely another mishmash of popular pablum straight out of the mindframe established by the photographers of Curtis and Rinehart and company. Many of Long's people had been enblackened, as well as some enwhitened, but most nonetheless maintained a unique Indianness that is still too little documented and preserved in the written and visual record.

Aside from providing white book editors and publishers with new editions of glossy coffee-table texts and continual reprises of the standard Plains Indian stereotype, reissued and re-shown photographs of Rinehart and Curtis and all the others do serve an important purpose. Once, in a class I was teaching on the Indian in American Popular Culture, as I passed around books of Curtis and Soule photographs, a Cheyenne student discovered the photo of a Cheyenne war chief with the name of Red Moon or Red Nose (I can't recall the actual name after twenty years). The student said she had heard the name mentioned by some older relatives of hers. (Grandparents? aunts, uncles? again, my memory fails me on the actual details.) Then, over the next several months, she researched as much as she could about the war chief, circa 1868 (the time of the Medicine Lodge Treaty, which Soule attended and recorded with his camera), and eventually she discovered that the war chief was her great-great-grandfather, an ancestor of whom she was previously unaware. Similarly, my wife, Barbara, soon after we met, told me about her great-grandfather, the Penateka Comanche chief Asa-toyet, and directed me to his photograph in the same Soule collection (*Plains Indian Raiders*, edited by Wilbur Sturtevant Nye, 1968). Barbara said the Soule photograph was very important to her and to her numerous relatives, all of them descendants of Asa-toyet. Such photographs taken during the Vanishing American era provide, therefore, important visual and factual linkages from the days of the ones whom Curtis and Soule were seeing as vanishing, and their descendants who are anything but vanished.

Quite likely, and hopefully, the reissued Rinehart photographs will signal a similar *Roots-* like awakening and connectedness for many others, just as the Soule photographs have done for western Oklahoma Indians. Ten years ago, the Minnesota Chippewa historian, Paulette Fairbanks Molin, collaborated with Mary Lou Hultgren to write the history and publish approximately seventy photographs of Indians undergoing the white man's educational system and acculturation in *To Lead and To Serve: American Indian Education at Hampton Institute* 1878–1923, a remarkably impressive visual and astutely documented record of an important segment of American Indian history. In my opinion, *To Lead and To Serve* is a major document in American Indian history because it is, in part, an enduring source for Indians seeking to make connections with their heritage. The Rinehart photographs can, at best, lead viewers not so much into the familiar morass of stereotypes and set images, but into new ways of viewing the past, new ways of creating connections with our relatives, new ways of reaffirming cultural identity.

Notwithstanding, I still look forward to some enterprising student of the present day or of the future who will discover a whole trunk full of tintypes and turn-of-the-century photographs of Marguerite Jardelas Simpson, of Pierre Beatte, of Marguerite's numerous cousins and neighbors around Dark Corner and Judlow Lake and Bayou Bartholomew and Amos Bayou and Wrightsville and Kelso and Plum Bayou, our home communities in Southern Arkansas. May entire attics someday reveal the dust-collecting tintypes of Connecticut Mohegans and Delaware Nansemonds and Alabama Creeks and Missouri Shawnees and Virginia Pamunkeys. I have a strong, abiding feeling that the last chapter of the American Indian people of the Vanishing American era has yet to be written.

LaVergne, TN USA
18 February 2011
217137LV00001B/3/P